CRIME BY COMPUTER

D1011016

CRIME BY COMPUTER

DONN B. PARKER

CHARLES SCRIBNER'S SONS, *New York*

This book is based in part on research supported by the National Science Foundation grant Nos. GI 37226 and GJ 44313. Any opinions, findings, conclusions, or recommendations expressed in this book are those of the author and do not necessarily reflect the views of NSF.

Copyright © 1976 Donn B. Parker

Library of Congress Cataloging in Publication Data

Parker, Donn B
    Crime by computer.

    Bibliography: p. 298
    Includes index.
    1. Computer crimes. I. Title.
HV6773.P37   364.1'62   76-1836
ISBN 0-684-14574-X

This book published simultaneously in the United States of America and in Canada— Copyright under the Berne Convention

All rights reserved. No part of this book may be reproduced in any form without the permission of Charles Scribner's Sons.

1 3 5 7 9 11 13 15 17 19 c/c 20 18 16 14 12 10 8 6 4 2

Printed in the United States of America

CONTENTS

INTRODUCTION

Our society is fast becoming dependent on the correct, reliable, and near-continuous operation by electronic data processing (EDP) personnel of digital computers and data telecommunications. As the sensitive functions of computers and the people who run them proliferate in society, the potential grows for serious and even catastrophic losses involving failures in computer systems, caused, of course, by people. If sound decisions concerning the safe use of computers are to be made, more people must have a deeper understanding of the nature of EDP technologists, their computers, and data telecommunications and of how such technologies can be misused. This understanding must transcend the giant electronic brain image of computers as depicted in the media and must be founded, instead, on a solid knowledge of both the theory and the practice involved.

A view of how safe and unsafe these powerful tools in the hands of our technologists can be is presented in this book, based mostly on actual losses experienced from the aspect most difficult to deal with—intentionally perpetrated acts. This view is presented at an appropriate level for all those people who come in contact with computers, those who are affected by the use of computers, and those who think seriously about the current role of computers. The level of understanding of the technology involved is based on an awareness of the following basic concepts and technical jargon:

- "EDP" means electronic data processing (ADP as used in government means automatic data processing).
- "Hardware" is the collection of electronic and electromechanical devices that make up computer systems, such as central processors, printers, magnetic tape drives, and disk drives.
- "Software" is the collection of computer programs which consists of instructions that direct the actions of computers.
- "Firmware." The term is basically irrelevant to this book and is ignored here.

Everything else of a technical nature should come easily.

The presentation is organized into roughly three parts: a discussion about computers and computer abuse, case studies of intentional acts involving computers, and finally a discussion of what can be done and what may happen. I have attempted to entertain as well as to inform—all work and no play is dull, and I want you to read the whole book.

The subject of this book originally became apparent to me in the mid-1960s when I wrote the first set of guidelines for professional conduct for the Association for Computing Machinery. At that time I was frequently giving talks to computer technologists on the need for establishing ethical standards and how ethical and professional we must become in our rapidly advancing technology. I found this subject was great for putting an audience to sleep.

At about that same time while on a business trip to Minneapolis, I found an article on the front page of the *Minneapolis Tribune* for Tuesday, October 18, 1966, with the headline: "Computer Expert Accused of Fixing His Bank Balance." This was the first computer crime I discovered. Based on the news article and several telephone calls to the perpetrator, his employer, and Stanley Green, assistant U.S. attorney for Minnesota, I wrote a brief report of the incident for my professional society as an example of the need for establishing ethical standards.

My interest in his case led to discovery of other criminal activities involving computers. As a result, I changed the approach in my crusade among computer technologists and started giving talks on the need for ethics based on how bad we actually are and the terrible things that we are doing. I found this was the easiest way to keep an audience awake. The direction for my future research was established even though it was only carried on as an avocation, until finally in 1970 at Stanford Research Institute I had an opportunity to work full time on the problem.

The first proposal for my research was titled "Computer-Related Crime." Law researchers reviewed the proposal, saying, "Parker, you are a computer technologist. What are you doing, trying to decide what is a crime? After all, there are only six people in the whole world qualified to address that subject." I next changed the name of the research to "Anti-Social Use of Computers." Sociologists who reviewed the proposal came back to me and said, "Parker, you are a computer technologist. What are you doing, trying to decide what is social and antisocial? After all, there are only six people in the whole world qualified to address that subject." I thought to myself, "All right, you guys, I will play your game." I changed the title of the research to "Computer Abuse"—a term that had not been used or at least formalized before. I was then able to define the problem as I wished and had no further difficulty on that score.

The research upon which this book is based has been done over the past four years in my capacity as a senior information processing analyst at Stanford Research Institute (SRI). The work has been funded by the U.S. National Science Foundation, the U.S. Atomic Energy Commission, the SRI Long Range Planning Report Service, and various private organizations. This support is gratefully acknowledged.

However, the opinions and positions expressed in this book are my own and do not necessarily represent those of any of the organizations that have sponsored the research upon which the book is based.

All of the computer abuse cases are true and accurate to the degree of the recollection of the persons interviewed, the correctness of documents used, and my interpretive skills. I have either changed names or avoided them entirely in most cases to keep the participants out of the public eye. Exposure by the newspapers has made these people and organizations suffer enough; they deserve the privacy of the ordinary. Now, without further embarrassment to those involved, the publication of their cases will impart the value of their experiences to others.

I thank the victims, perpetrators, and prosecutors of the computer abuse cases who provided the information I needed. They have done a great service for all of us in revealing their roles. And I especially thank my wife, Lorna, for her many hours of transcribing my tape-cassette encapsulated voice onto paper using an old klunker of a typewriter.

1 | THE GIANT ELECTRONIC BRAIN SYNDROME

Any sufficiently advanced technology is indistinguishable from magic.
—CLARKE'S THIRD LAW.

What can we believe in the newspapers? When I read an article in a newspaper about changing patterns of weather and the possibilities of technological control of weather, I tend to accept it. Experts are quoted and a logical argument is presented. The article creates a definite impression for me of a state of technology in weather control, and I take the presented information for granted. However, when I read an article on computer technology and realize how the technology can sometimes be distorted, sensationalized, and incorrectly represented, based on what I know in this field, it creates a highly insecure feeling about other technology as depicted by newspaper articles. The problem is that we mistakenly accept news as fact while newspapers give us news that is a mixture of fact, opinion, impressions, and fiction. We are well advised to heed the advice to scientists from the famous mathematician Polya, "Believe nothing, but question only what is worth questioning." The usual depiction of computer technology is worth questioning.

2 | THE NATURE OF COMPUTERS

What is a number that a person may know it?
What is a person that he may know a number?
                    —WARREN MCCULLOCH.

In the past we would blame Mr. So-and-So at the bank for bank statement errors; then we shifted the blame to the bank; now we just blame the computer at the bank. Mr. So-and-So is delighted at this state of affairs, because even though he is responsible for the computer, he now can also blame the computer; and he often gets away with it. The actual culprit may be the system designer, the computer programmer, the computer operator, the data preparation clerk, or the maintenance engineer. The complexity of computers and computer programs makes it difficult and often impossible to know where to put the blame among the people involved. The computer becomes a near-perfect scapegoat for those providing its services and those receiving them.

3 | ASSETS IN COMPUTERS

If it's not on paper, it doesn't exist.
—MACKENZIE'S FIRST LAW.

If it's not in a computer, it doesn't exist.
—A LAW FOR THE FUTURE.

"Government-bond collateral is all kept at the Fed, and there is no need to move pieces of paper: the Fed simply makes a book entry in the computer, transferring the ownership of such-and-such a Treasury issue. . . ."

—MARTIN MAYER, *THE BANKERS.*

Negotiable assets as payment in exchange for goods and services have changed significantly through history. Today, thousands of people in several countries no longer receive paychecks. My employer sends my bank reels of magnetic tape containing the name, account number, and pay amount of me and others. At the bank a pattern of small magnetized areas on the tape is converted to electric pulses which then cause a change of state in electronic circuits. Another set of electrical pulses diverted by the electronic circuits in an equivalent pattern to the one on the tape is sent to a device that forms a magnetic pattern on the surface of a rotating disk. My employer no longer has my pay. The bank has it and is authorized to pay my bills, including those for gas and electric utility use. Therefore, seconds later a similar process plus a further change of pulses and transmission of another set of pulses takes place through a telephone, wires, microwave carrier, switching circuits, another telephone, and into another process storing the pattern on a rotating disk in the EDP center at the gas and electric company.

This complicated process can also be explained at a higher level. What occurred was the reduction of the company's assets, a transfer of assets among accounts within the bank, an increase of my assets, a subsequent small reduction in my assets, and a small increase in the assets of the gas and electric company. These asset changes are reported to me and the other participants in printed reports produced automatically by the three computers at the company, the bank, and the gas and electric company.

No checks, monetary currency, precious metal, food, handcrafted items, or other forms of negotiable assets changed hands or ownership. Yet, assets were exchanged. A new form of assets has been used. The pulses of electricity, patterns of magnetic areas on tape, and disks and states of electronic circuits are the assets. They don't just represent assets in other forms, they are the assets! The pulses can be converted to the form of checks by a computer printer or to monetary currency by computer-printed reports that authorize cashiers to transfer cash from boxes to people or to other boxes. The pulses can also be converted to printed reports or mechanical functions that cause actions either manually or automatically involving goods and services.

Historically, forms of negotiable assets started with goods and services. Precious or rare objects became forms of assets along with advancing civilization, followed by printed paper in the form of paper money, negotiable securities and certificates, warrants, and checks. Now we have negotiable assets stored as data in computers, saved on magnetic tape and disks, and sent through wires and microwave carriers in electrical, electronic, electromagnetic wave, and magnetic forms.

These data assets are as different from printed paper assets as printed paper assets are different from goods and services assets. They are processed, transported, and stored in far different ways and are subject to quite different forms of abuse and loss. In fact, businesses, governments, and institutions should consider the hazards associated with data assets and the degree of safety possible before rushing headlong into the cashless, checkless, and paperless society. We can't revert to previous methods; there is no pulling the plug on the machines.

Fortunately, we are experiencing an intermediate step in the negotiable asset revolution in many important areas of business transaction. Data assets are used but are backed up with paper. A number of bank clearinghouses where bankers come together to exchange canceled checks for issuing bank account debiting and distributing to customers are operating in this mode. When checks are first received at a bank, they are converted to data asset form on magnetic tape. The data assets are then sorted by bank of issue and placed on reels of tape, one for each bank. The tapes are exchanged through the clearinghouse, with the checks often taking a slower route to the issuing banks for return to customers. The tapes contain the assets for processing, but the canceled checks are still available to prove transactions. The securities exchange concept is another example of this transition. Securities held by Wall Street brokerages for their customers are deposited at a central point which keeps the securities in two forms—as data assets in computers and as large-denomination certificates stored in vaults. When a customer wants to hold his stocks in his own hands, the large-denomination certificates can be converted to smaller denominations and delivered. Otherwise, all transactions are handled in data assets form by computer with a minimum of certificate processing activity. This is easing—if not completely solving—the infamous back office paper problem that has led to fraud and theft in so many brokerages.

The next step now seen emerging is the transmission of data assets by telecommunications from computer to computer rather than the physical exchange of reels of tape. But, the paper still follows along behind for backup and reference purposes.

To see how this drastically changes forms of abuse and losses, consider the frequent *Wall Street Journal* news items that tell, for example, of two men who drive up alongside an elderly messenger carrying several million dollars' worth of negotiable securities from one firm to another on Wall Street. One man jumps out, hits the messenger over the head, grabs the securities, and escapes in the car.

If securities are to be transmitted only by telecommunications between computers and if, as a result, backup paper disappears, this crime cannot take place. It becomes obsolete, and the types of crooks who thrive on paper-based crimes such as this will be put out of work or will have to seek different forms of crime. Not only that, the victims, auditors, fences for stolen property, police, FBI, investigators, prosecutors, lawyers, and courts will no longer have to contend with such crime. Does that mean the crime disappears? Not necessarily; it changes form. If this type of crime is to continue, it must adapt to changing target environments just as it is doing in credit card activities. As computers and telecommunications are used to take over the storage, transporting, exchange, and accounting of assets, so crooks with new skills, knowledge, and access will replace the old-style criminals.

The crooks must now deal with data assets and data representations of assets in computer and telecommunications systems. This is a highly complex activity. Data assets are not directly visible to men. Visibility requires the use of computer programs which cause the printing or display of numbers and words that represent or transform the data stored in systems. But first the data must be found. If the desired data are stored on magnetic tape, the proper reels of tape must be located—in a large organization, from among thousands of them stored in a tape library. Reels are identified by codes printed on labels attached to them. The codes must be found in printed indexes or lists that connect content of tape with their reel codes. The identified tapes must then be mounted on tape drives to be read by the computer. Data on mounted tapes or in other storage devices on-line to the computer must then be located by computer programs which search for them. Data are stored in a variety of forms and order. The form may be encoded in several ways, or even in encrypted form requiring a secret key. In addition, the word or number lengths must be known along with record and file formats. In many cases the data must be assembled from storage in different locations within the system to form meaningful information. Once the crook knows the form of the data, he must locate them. The order or addressing may be sequential, indexed, linked in numerous ways, or content addressed. If an index is required, it must also be found in the system or possibly somewhere outside the system.

Data stored in computers are also highly volatile and time-sensitive. A slight change in a program or stray pulse of electricity could cause the data to be erased forever. A magnet placed close enough to the surface of magnetic tape or disk can erase data; or scratching, heating, or warping the surface can make them unobtainable. Data are moved within the system or through communication systems at electrical speeds. Timing is measured in milliseconds (1/1000s), microseconds (1/1,000,000s), and picoseconds (1/1,000,000,000s). There is no known human thought process or action that can function in this time frame.

A crook confronted with an unfamiliar computer or telecommunications system containing his target would have great difficulty achieving his goal without a great volume of printed information or working programs and instructions for use. Programs are also data, a special form of data. This is complicated by the facts that programs are needed to manipulate data; that programs can be made to treat other programs as data; that programs can sometimes be made to treat themselves as data; and that programs in some special cases can be used in place of stored data, generating the data as needed starting with a few initial parameters.

A hypothetical example will demonstrate how this latter function works. The president of a firm established a trust for his 2,000 employees, each to benefit after ten years of employment from the time of death of the president according to their total years of employment. Each employee is to be informed semi-annually of the growing value of his share. The president dies.

A systems analyst and programmer are assigned to design and write a program to process investment data from the master trust which must calculate its growth and current value, maintain each subtrust account, and produce summary reports and individual reports to each employee. The systems analyst develops the specifications and turns them over to the programmer. The specifications call for maintaining and updating 2,001 permanent records, one for each employee plus the master. The personnel file must be used to keep track of current employment status.

The programmer studies the specifications and concludes it is ridiculous to maintain 2,000 records and have the program change the accounts each month the master trust is updated. The only time the individual subtrust accounts are needed is for the semi-annual reports. Therefore, he develops the program to calculate each subtrust share of the master trust only when needed to produce the reports rather than accumulating increments and adding to 2,000 permanently kept records. The program is also designed to produce the current value of any one subtrust at any time. This is done by calculating it rather than retrieving one of 2,000 permanent records stored in the system.

Now the trustees, computer center personnel, and even the systems analyst think the 2,001 records are being kept because of the way the program responds to inquiries and produces reports. Only the programmer and anyone bothering to look at his program or the program description (hardly anybody ever does that) would know that the master trust record alone is maintained on a permanent basis. Thus the subtrust records, the data assets, are represented in the logic of the program and don't explicitly exist.

Suppose an auditor decides to confirm the correct balances in the subtrusts. He asks for the location and format of the 2,000 accounts. He finds to his amazement only one: the master trust account. Where are the others? He is ready to yell fraud when he encounters the programmer and learns the awful truth. In order to confirm the accounts he will have to study and test the program with no hope of using an independent method of confirmation short of writing his own program to duplicate the production program—a formidable task. So he concludes he will just have to trust the programmer, does a perfunctory test of the program, and says all is well.

4 | MAXIMUM TIME TO BELLY UP

A large savings and loan association has numerous branches all tied on-line by telephone to a new central computer in the main office building. They used to have a smaller computer identical to one across the street in a competitor's building. There was an agreement that if one computer failed, the two institutions would share the other until the failed computer was back in operation. The old computer was reliable, and depositors' accounts could be updated with data punched on cards at the branches and delivered to the central site. But no more.

In the name of technological progress and in order to provide quicker service to more customers, a new and larger computer was installed. Sophisticated equipment was developed to multiplex and automatically receive and send data between the computer and over 100 teller terminals. The system is programmed to function in real-time, data flowing and accounts updated simultaneously with transactions at the teller windows. No longer is there any way to update accounts with punch cards sent in from branches; it's all done with terminals over telephone lines.

After the system was up and running it was found that the newer, higher performance system experienced more down time during business hours. When the old system went down, the data input stacked up, and running the computer a little longer when it was fixed caught up on the workload. When the new system went down, the teller terminals stopped working. Deposits, withdrawals, and interest updates had to be done by hand, recording the transactions on paper until the system was again operational.

This is no serious problem for short periods of down time, but what if the system is unavailable for a whole day or for several days? There is no other system of the same configuration conveniently located to fall back on. After several days of down time, the manual records stack up at the teller windows. Nobody knows the level of any savings account without painstaking checking of all tellers in all branches. When the system finally does become available again, many hours of overtime are required to feed the collected transactions into teller terminals. Extra people must be hired temporarily to work at night when the terminals are available. The potential for fraud by customers and embezzlement by tellers during these periods increases greatly.

How many days of down time could the association tolerate and still recover? What are the implications of failure to recover? After a sufficiently large number of days, recovery would not be possible. The law requires the savings and loan association to complete transactions on demand. If the situation is not recoverable, the only course of action is to declare default. The association must then ask depositors and creditors how much is owed them, ask loan customers how much they owe the association, and settle with them. The computer files must be reconstructed from the results of this action. If there are any assets remaining, the association is still in business; if not, the association is bankrupt and must dissolve.

In a talk for a group of FDIC bank examiners I described this process and received long, sad, sober looks from my audience. After the talk one examiner came up to me and said he had seen just such a situation occur in a bank in a small town in his region. He went on to say, "You'd be amazed at how solicitous, honest, and helpful the customers and creditors were in helping the bank to recover." But could we rely on recovery based on the honesty and goodwill of people in our largest cities?

Back to the savings and loan association. When periods of down time during business hours started occurring, the data processing management realized the implications of their much-praised efforts in utilizing advanced technology. How and what do you tell the board of directors? That problem was solved when evidence began accumulating that periods of down time were being mysteriously reported to certain employees out in branches even before they occurred. Knowledge of a possible conspiracy could not be held back from top management. The suspicions raised such interest and concern among top management that a high-level committee was formed to determine just how safe the new computer system was. That committee had not yet reached final conclusions at the time of writing this book, but enough was known that they were counting the number of days to disaster.

This problem is formalized in the concept of Maximum Time to Belly Up (MTBU). More and more organizations that rely on computers in real-time in sensitive aspects of their businesses are faced with the issue of MTBU as they move farther out on the limb of advanced computer technology.

5 | COMPUTER ABUSE

Highly publicized incidents over the past ten years which have involved computers in fraud, embezzlement, terrorism, theft, larceny, extortion, malicious mischief, espionage, and sabotage clearly indicate that a social problem exists in the application of computer technology.*

"Computer abuse" is broadly defined to be any incident associated with computer technology in which a victim suffered or could have suffered loss and a perpetrator by intention made or could have made gain. Any incidents are identified as computer abuse if there is information to be gained by studying such incidents that will make computers safer in the future.

I attempt to avoid debate over whether a particular case is a computer abuse or not. This seems to serve little useful purpose.

* This is reported in a Stanford Research Institute document entitled *Computer Abuse* that Susan Nycum, Steven Oura, and I wrote in December 1973. This report documents 148 cases involving computers. It was funded by the National Science Foundation and is available as report Number PB 231-320/AS from the National Technical Information Service, Springfield, Virginia 22151.

Early in 1974 I discussed the Equity Funding Insurance fraud with Walter Wriston, chairman of the board and chief executive officer of Citicorp of New York City. The Equity Funding case is a white-collar crime that resulted in the largest known losses in American business; it is described in detail later in this book. Mr. Wriston advised me that this was clearly a case of massive fraud by top management and was not conceived, planned, or carried out directly involving the use of computers. Therefore, it should not be defined as a case of computer abuse. This was substantiated by the Equity Funding Trustee's Bankruptcy Report, which stated that it was not a brilliantly executed computer crime. That is true, but there is still much to learn from the role computers played in the case that is applicable to the study of making computers safer.

A recent check fraud in the City of Los Angeles Treasurer's Office was touted by the Los Angeles district attorney and the newspapers as a major new computer crime. Evidence to date indicates that it had nothing whatever to do with computers. Twelve blank warrant forms were stolen, and one was manually forged for $904,000. These forms are normally used for printing on high-speed computer printers. The case may be of interest as a computer abuse if it is found that the forms were stolen from the storage area in the computing facilities. Then a study of this case might help in developing better methods of storing computer printer forms safely.

Computer abuse is a multi-faceted problem. It looks quite different from different points of view. The victims, the perpetrators, the potential victims, law enforcement officers, prosecutors, computer technologists, criminologists, psychologists, and sociologists all have differing viewpoints and concepts of computer abuse. This reminds me of a recent incident when I was flying on a United Airlines jetliner on its way to land in Chicago. I was using a headset to listen to the channel that picks up conversation between the captain and the controllers on the ground. The captain asked the controller what time it was. The controller responded by asking what airline the captain was flying. He responded by saying, "What difference does the airline make? I just want to know what time it is." The controller indicated that it made a great deal of difference. "If you are United, it is 3:00 P.M. If you are Pan American, it is 1500 hours. If it's Ozark, the little hand is on three, and the big hand is on twelve; and if it's North Central Airlines, it is Tuesday." (My apologies to Ozark and North Central—they may be very good airlines. The reader may substitute the most recent two airlines that caused him travel delays.) So the problem of computer abuse as described below can look quite different from various points of view.

Documentation ranging in degree of detail and quantity has been collected for 374 reported cases of computer abuse. The number is increasing weekly. The information is catalogued, categorized, and collected in a growing data base that will soon have to be entered into a computer in order to manage it. The amount of documentation varies from several sentences in a newspaper article to other reported cases recorded in several inches of news articles, court documents, and field notes.

Intentional acts resulting in computer abuse are probably only the third most serious problem that faces organizations using computers. Errors and omissions represent the most common cause of losses. However, data processing organizations have been fighting errors and omissions throughout the past 25 years of computer history. Errors and omissions are well known, and methods of controlling them are routine and receive significant attention. Next come natural disasters caused by fire, water, wind, power outages, lightning, and earthquakes that could cause significant disruption (or even destruction) of computer facilities, or at least crucial parts of computer facilities. Again, this is a well-understood problem that is part of the overall industrial security problem. It is well known and has been controlled in a number of ways throughout the period of industrialization. The treatment of this problem in computer environments does not present any particularly new or unsolvable aspects. Relatively standard methods of detection and protection are available and quite effective.

Next comes computer abuse. Even though computer abuse probably ranks third in order of seriousness and concern, there are significant reasons why it should be receiving the most attention, and in some respects can have more impact. Computer abuse has not been well understood. Many organizations are not aware of the potential for losses or degree of their vulnerability to it, and sufficient and practical methods of deterrence, detection, prevention, and recovery have not yet been implemented or even found.

Also, if a data processing manager is found responsible by higher management for significant errors and omissions or losses resulting from natural disasters, he is often treated in a sympathetic and forgiving manner. Higher management can easily be made aware of adequate methods of detection and protection and knows there is a possibility of such loss occurring in spite of adequate protection. However, when an intentional act by a person results in losses in the data processing function, the data processing manager often is not treated with the same sympathy and understanding.

On the other hand, intentional acts result in more embarrassment to top management, who feel they have been duped. Top management is usually not aware of the existence of significant vulnerabilities to fraud in the data processing organization, nor of the lack of ability to prevent its occurrence. The more harsh reaction of management can therefore make computer abuse sometimes more important than errors and omissions. The sensationalism and publicity associated with computer abuse also makes it a more sensitive issue than the other two problems.

There is a wide spectrum of reaction regarding the seriousness of computer abuse. At one extreme it can be said that if only 374 cases have been discovered since 1958, considering that there are approximately 150,000 computers in use in the United States today in business applications, data processing people must be unusually honest and computers must be relatively harmless. Therefore, computer abuse is minimal and under control.

At the other end of the spectrum, the people who deal with computer abuse can become quite concerned. When I show the range of cases to certified public accountants, they are not particularly impressed because I have included none of the cases that they are aware of in their work. They say they know of dozens of cases that are not included. "We can't reveal them to you because they are confidential to our clients. You are only looking at a piece of the top of the iceberg of what must really be going on today in incidence and losses from computer abuse."

The truth lies some place between these two extremes. Research in criminology reveals that 85 percent of all known crime goes unreported. There is reason to believe that a higher percentage of computer-related crime goes unreported. Victims tend not to report computer-related incidents because of the great amount of publicity they generate, which often has an adverse effect on their business. Also, they often discover that they do not know how to correct a vulnerability. The same thing could happen to them again, and they don't know how to stop it; therefore, they want as few people as possible to be aware of it. This leads to the handling of some cases administratively rather than reporting them to the proper authorities. "Administrative handling" of an incident is a euphemism for letting the perpetrator go with little or no sanctions imposed upon him. In some cases, the victim merely transfers the perpetrator to another division of the organization and even rewards him with a salary increase if he won't tell anybody what he did.

Computer abuse victims often lose more in the adverse publicity of being victims than they do in losses directly as the result of the act. I myself advise clients who are potential victims of computer abuse to handle the matter as confidentially as possible within the constraints of the law. Unfortunately, this advice is in conflict with my desire to see computer abuse cases reported and prosecuted to establish precedents, administer justice, and advance my research.

There is a threefold purpose for performing computer abuse research. First, it forms an empirical or practical approach to computer security research. Threat models can be developed from practical experience to play against models of secure computer systems. This can result in well-tested, secure computer systems. Secondly, reporting the results of the research is an aid to potential victims of computer abuse, informing them of the nature of the problem, alerting them, and making them more sensitive to possibilities of losses through their data processing organizations. Finally, it is important that consultants, helping their clients make safer use of computers, have as much background and experience as possible with real victims and real perpetrators in order to gain the necessary insight.

The most serious problem in this research is the unknown degree to which reported cases are representative of actual experience. Conclusions can only be based on the universe of the sample of known, reported computer abuse, rather than on the universe of total experience. Applying the conclusions based on the existing information beyond those warranted by the sample size is purely conjectural.

Computer abuse as defined above represents a wide range of incidents. A number of the cases are clearly criminal, where the perpetrator has been caught, tried, and convicted of a specific crime. Other cases have resulted only in civil suits or in mere disputes between businessmen that are settled out of court. Others are more innocuous, where a perpetrator might be chastised by his superior or his peers—a chastisement that might result in losing his job or embarrassment.

Computer abuse includes white-collar crime, vandalism, and malicious mischief. A few cases are included where computers have been used as instruments in planning violent crimes such as robbery. Also several cases have involved international espionage that might not be called white-collar crime. "Crime" is not a well-defined term in criminology and law enforcement. Types of crimes and their names vary among legal jurisdictions. "White-collar crime," since the term was first used by Edwin Sutherland in the 1930s, has been defined in various ways. For our purposes, a definition taken from the science of criminalistics will suffice: Any endeavor or practice involving the stifling of free enterprise or the promoting of unfair competition; a breach of trust against an individual or an institution; a violation of occupational conduct; or the jeopardizing of consumers and clientele.

Insight into the nature of computer abuse can be gained by considering the four roles that computers play. Every known case of computer abuse can be identified with one or more of these roles. First, the computer can be the *object of the attack*. The computer can easily be damaged and valuable programs and data within the computer system can be destroyed. Acts resulting in these types of losses are commonly identified as vandalism, malicious mischief, or sabotage. For example, there are four cases reported where computers have been shot at with guns.

In 1968 the *San Francisco Chronicle* reported a case where an unknown perpetrator, probably a person out of a job, fired two shots from a pistol at an IBM 1401 computer at the State Unemployment Office in Olympia, Washington. No significant damage was done. The bullets merely dented the metal cabinet of the central processor. It went right on functioning. In 1972 a case was reported by Reuters News Agency. A tax-processing computer for the city of Johannesburg, South Africa, was shot four times by a person firing at the computer through a window from the public sidewalk. The computer was also dented but continued to function. It was believed that the person may have received an exorbitant tax bill and was just venting his frustration. A verified case is reported in 1973 in Melbourne, Australia, where antiwar demonstrators attacked a United States computer manufacturer and shot a computer with a shotgun that did terrible things to it. It was a total loss.

In 1974 a verified case was reported at a life insurance company in an eastern state. A computer operator ran the computer all by himself during a night shift. He had to obtain paper and supplies to run the computer by crossing a dark alley in a high crime area of the city. It was his practice to carry a pistol in a holster for protection. One night he got so frustrated with the computer that he performed a fast draw and shot the computer right between the bits! The computer was seriously damaged and was returned to the manufacturer.

The computer can also play the role of the object of computer abuse in cases where the computer or parts of it are stolen. This represents a growing problem as computers and parts of computers become miniaturized and more easily transportable than the monoliths of the past. Also a large market has developed for used computing equipment, providing a means for the perpetrator to fence his stolen goods. In Boston, a student stole a Digital Equipment Corporation PDP-8 minicomputer from a university. He was caught by the campus police patrol and convicted. In another case, an employee of a manufacturer of mini-computers stole a computer, piece by piece, from the manufacturing plant and assembled it at home. He was caught and fired from his job. In one case reported by Susan Nycum a student stole a terminal, but it was a straightforward job to catch him. The terminal had an automatic identification answering device installed on it. The telephone company was called in, and the computer operators waited until the thief used the terminal, which immediately identified itself. The telephone call was traced, and they caught the thief red-handed.

The second role played by computers in computer abuse is that of *creating a unique environment* in which unauthorized activities can occur, or where the computer creates unique forms of assets subject to abusive acts. The computer may not be directly involved in such incidents. Data stored magnetically or electronically are in an entirely new form—one subject to new methods of abuse—but use of computers has not led to new kinds of abusive acts, at least in name. The names of the acts are the same: fraud, theft, larceny, embezzlement, vandalism, malicious mischief, extortion, sabotage, and espionage. However, after the act is named using one of these traditional terms, everything else about it can be entirely unique: the positions of the perpetrators, the environments of the act, the methods used in the abuse, and the forms of assets. These are all new. Acts of financial gain can be accomplished by merely transferring credit among financial accounts within a computer and between computer systems. Processing and data sabotaged within computers used in real-time applications—such as monitoring patients in intensive care units or scheduling surface or air transportation—could cause bodily harm. Poorly designed computer billing systems have caused much mental anguish among people attempting to have errors corrected.

Computer programs represent entirely new assets subject to theft. A large number of cases involve computer programs where the computer was not involved at all. Large computer programs can be worth many millions of dollars. Owners of computer programs often feel they are perfectly safe from theft, because the programs are custom-developed and unique to the particular computer installation and organization. However, there are several instances where victims have been denied use of their programs for purposes of extortion. Whether the program is of value to anyone else or not, its continued use is often vital to the owner of the program.

In 1971 a small company was providing accounting services. A brilliant young programmer was hired to automate their processes. He did a beautiful job of developing a well-documented set of programs. The small company was totally dependent upon them. As soon as they were operational, he took all copies of the programs and the documentation, went off and hid in the mountains. He called his employer and told him he would not return the programs unless he was paid $100,000. The programmer was only an amateur extortioner; within three days he was caught and charged with grand theft. The programs and documentation were impounded in the sheriff's office for evidence. Unfortunately, the small company could not operate without the programs, but the sheriff's staff was uncooperative and confused about what a program was and refused to let anyone touch the stolen programs. The president of the small firm felt he had no alternative, so he broke into the sheriff's office late one night and took the programs. He made punch card copies of the programs in a data center and then, in a reverse burglary, returned the programs to the sheriff's office.

The charges against the extortioner were dropped at the preliminary hearing. The reasons, according to the president of the small firm, were that the prosecutor was confused about the nature of computer programs, and that he felt it would have been impossible to obtain a conviction because of a lack of precedent involving computer programs in extortion.

The third role of computers in computer abuse is *the computer as the instrument of the act,* i.e., when it is used as a tool to aid in perpetrating the abusive act. In some of these cases the computer may not be the object or the environment of the act. An example is the case study in this book where an accountant embezzled $1 million over six years. He did not embezzle through a computer system; however, he owned and operated his own computer service bureau and used his computer to model his company. He ran simulations using both correct data and changed data to regulate and plan his embezzlement. In an unverified case in 1973 reported by the *Chicago News*, negotiable securities worth more than $1 million were taken from burglarized homes. A raid on the suspect's residence produced a computer output listing of affluent targets of the burglaries. Apparently, a computer had been used to search various files of personal information looking for the right characteristics to guide the burglary activities.

The fourth role of computers is where the computer can be used *symbolically to intimidate, deceive, or defraud victims.* In one case reported in the *Computerworld* newspaper in 1971, a collection agency established a new business of sending new invoices to people who had paid the bills a year earlier. Many people who receive bills just assume they must owe the money and pay them. The agency had a very successful business going with a very low overhead. Fortunately, there are some people who refuse to pay bills when they don't owe the money. These people would often complain to the collection agency about receiving bills. The collection agency became quite bothered by all these complaints, but the problem was easily solved by sending the complainers a form letter that started out, "We are sorry we sent the referenced invoice to you by mistake. Our computer made an error." Today, anybody will believe almost anything if they are told it is the result of a computer error. This situation is perpetuated by the giant electronic brain image so sensationalized in our news media today.

A number of cases are reported where computer programming trade schools have falsely advertised that they provide the use of computers in their training programs, whereas the closest they ever got to a computer was the standard manufacturer's pictures of computers used in their advertising. Dating bureaus have been prosecuted for advertising that they effectively match people for dates by using sophisticated computer methods. Some of the firms had at most a simple punch card sorter in the back room. Cases involving this role of computers do not seem to be a particularly difficult problem from a legal point of view. There appear to be sufficient laws to prosecute these deceptions successfully even though they involve a new technology.

Intimidation can be particularly insidious. In the federal government, we often find the Department of Defense coming into the congressional hearings to present and support its budgets for the coming year. The Department of Defense staff walks into the hearing followed by several clerks carrying piles of computer output listings several feet high, who plop them down on the tables in front of the staff at the hearing. The congressmen walk into the hearing, each with his little manila folder of papers. The congressmen look at the little piles of paper sitting in front of them and the huge stacks of computer listings sitting in front of the Department of Defense staff and start to wonder if there isn't some inequality in the data available to both parties. There is a strong element of intimidation in proving one's point with the support of massive amounts of computerized data, further implying that they must be correct and important since they came from a computer.

In another case a well-known lawyer and law professor was defending a doctor accused of fraudulent Medicare billing. The prosecutor appeared at the trial with a large stack of computer outputs. He proceeded to explain that he had run a statistical analysis on the computer of the income of all doctors in the state received from the Medicare program. He showed how the accused doctor's income from Medicare was several standard deviations away from the norm of all the other doctors' Medicare income. He said computers don't lie, and this computer proves that the accused doctor was guilty. This highly incensed the defendant's attorney who, among other defenses, claimed his client was being convicted by an inanimate object—the computer. He argued that the use of a computer and piles of computer printouts to intimidate the jury was unfair. The use of the computer may have helped the prosecutor since the doctor was convicted by the jury.

6 | COUNTING THE ABUSES

Our knowledge about the incidence of crime is small, and the data available are inaccurate. Criminologists have stated that only 15 percent of known crimes are ever recorded. This is deduced by surveys of samples of the general public, counting the number of people who have been victims of crime. These statistics are then compared with police reports of crimes that are compiled by the FBI and published annually as the FBI Uniform Crime Report. Most of the crime reported in this manner is of the more violent type, such as robberies, auto theft, and rape; far less is known about white-collar crime.

The incidence of white-collar crime is not reported but losses are periodically estimated. Two recent estimates were done, one by the President's Commission on White Collar Crime in 1967, and the other by the U.S. Chamber of Commerce Study of 1974.

Even less is known about computer abuse. In the first place, computer abuse is not limited to criminal acts but includes all kinds of intentional acts where losses may have occurred. Sources of reports of 374 cases of computer abuse are presented in Table 1.

Table 1 | COMPUTER ABUSE CASE SOURCES | March 1975

	Verified	Not Verified	Total
Questionnaires	71	0	71
Computerworld	14	57	71
Newspapers	21	54	75
Private sources	46	16	62
Magazines, Journals	4	39	43
Books	3	19	22
Oral Presentations	0	13	13
Law enforcement agencies	13	0	13
Unpublished documents	2	2	4
Totals	174	200	374

Source: Stanford Research Institute.

Seventy-one cases were reported as the result of a question-naire survey. In March 1974, a 20-page questionnaire was enclosed in each copy of my report, *Computer Abuse*. These reports were sent to 3,000 people who had requested copies after announcements of the availability of the report were made in a number of trade journals. People requesting the reports included many officers of companies, auditors, congressmen, government officials, students, and educators. The list includes Ralph Nader, Wendell Willkie III, and a member of the staff of the Herpetology Department of the New York Museum of Natural History. Three hundred questionnaires were completed and returned, and among them were the descriptions of 71 new computer abuse cases.

Newspapers were the sources of 75 cases. *Computerworld*, a weekly trade newspaper, has a policy of publishing information about computer abuse based on extensive news clipping services. The news stories are then followed up by *Computerworld* reporters. Private sources such as unsolicited letters, telephone calls, and conversations have produced 62 cases. Twenty-two cases have been found in books such as *Databanks in a Free Society* and *Computer Crime* by Gerald McKnight, a London journalist and author of business books. I give many talks on the subject of computer abuse in various parts of the world, and another source of cases is the members of the audience who occasionally volunteer to report them to me.

The cases in Table 1 are identified as Verified and Not Verified. A case is verified if I have had some personal contact with an individual involved in it, or a reliable person can convince me that the incident actually occurred. I don't count any of the cases reported to me after my talks on computer abuse as verified because I don't know the people who reported them. I also accept a case as verified if a report on it is published by an official source such as a law enforcement agency, a court, or an attorney representing a client in the incident.

It can be seen that reports from the public media are the predominant source of computer abuse information. Newspaper accounts of computer abuse are treated with particular skepticism. My experience is that the most one can derive from a newspaper article about computer abuse is that something interesting may have happened. What is reported is not necessarily true and is not necessarily false. It is just news. However, I feel justified in presenting statistics on computer abuse to count all such reports, regardless of sources, since there seems to be a little bit of truth, at least, in each. Also I am interested in the nature of the reporting of computer abuse, whether the cases are real or fictitious. To be perfectly correct, the file should be called Known and Suspected Reported Computer Abuse. Part of the computer abuse research is to track various cases to their sources in order to determine whether they are true or not. Progress is slow, but the goal is to attempt to verify all reported cases and remove cases that don't meet the definitional requirements. Only five cases have been found to be totally fictitious. Several more are of dubious veracity, and a number of cases proved to be totally different than was originally reported, but still qualified as computer abuse, an admittedly broad definition.

The total number of cases per year (year of occurrence or discovery of loss, whichever is later) known at different times in the study are presented in Figure 1. Notice that the humped-shape curve continues to grow over the entire time span. It appears that there were fewer reported cases in the most recent

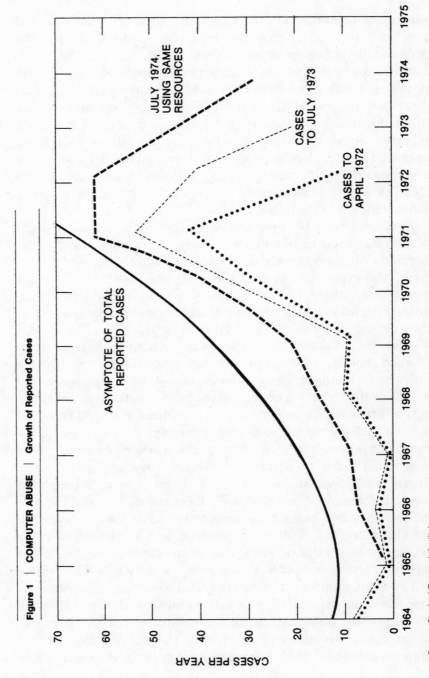

Figure 1 | COMPUTER ABUSE | Growth of Reported Cases

ASYMPTOTE OF TOTAL REPORTED CASES

JULY 1974, USING SAME RESOURCES

CASES TO JULY 1973

CASES TO APRIL 1972

CASES PER YEAR

Source: Stanford Research Institute.

years. The reason for this strange growth is that there is a lag between the time of occurrence of an incident and the time at which I receive the report. For example, the number of reported cases that occurred in 1972 has grown from 10 to 45 to 63 over a reporting period from April 1972 to July 1974.

Figure 2 | **COMPUTER ABUSE** | **Reported Cases per Year (to October 1975)**

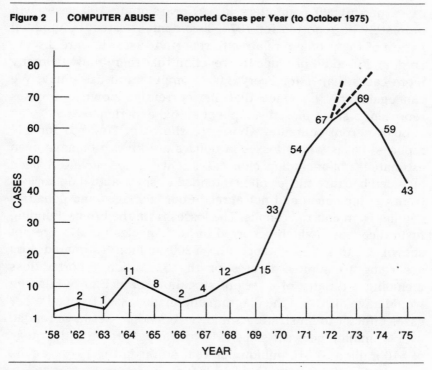

Source: Stanford Research Institute.

Figure 2 shows the incidence of reported cases up to October 1975. The dotted lines indicate the expected direction this curve will take in the next several years. The growth in this figure appears to be rapid and exponential. However, since the data are only a biased sample of the universe of computer abuse, the growth rate of all computer abuse cannot be accurately deduced from this sample. For example, the popularity of reporting computer abuse in newspapers may have been far greater in more recent years than in the early 1960s, or vice versa. This would have a significant effect on the shape of the growth curve. In any case, the curve represents, roughly at least, a lower bound of incidence of computer abuse.

The incidence of reported computer abuse relative to the number of computers (100,000 in 1965 and 200,000 in 1975, worldwide) is roughly 1 case per 10,000 computers in 1965 and 5 cases per 10,000 computers in 1975, assuming 100 cases will ultimately be reported for 1975. This demonstrates the minimal nature of the problem relative to reported cases that are discovered, and it could produce the reaction that there must be many more cases than 1 for every 2,000 computers in use today. We can again only conclude that the currently known 374 cases represent a small biased sample of actual experience.

Losses from computer abuse are shown in Figure 3 for 144 reported cases where losses in dollars are known or have been estimated, not including civil cases. Civil cases have not been included because the graph is intended to show actual dollar loss from the incidence and not agreed-upon damages and penalties coming from court decisions. The losses from the Equity Funding Insurance fraud which occurred in Los Angeles in 1973 are not shown in this figure since the $200 million estimated loss according to audited figures or the $2 billion reported loss including estimates of losses of stockholders of Equity Funding would have distorted the diagram and made losses from all other cases difficult to illustrate. As a lower bound, losses have totaled over $5 million per year since 1963 and appear to be in the range of $10 million to $15 million per year so far in the 1970s, again, not counting the Equity Funding Insurance fraud.

An attempt to determine the average loss per incident is more difficult. Simple arithmetic yields about $450,000 per loss. However, this average could not be applied to all computer abuse or even represent a rough estimate. The main reason for this is that the bias of the sample of reported cases can't even be guessed. It is not known whether more cases tend to be reported that involve large losses or whether more cases tend to be reported because of their unique aspects. It is also possible that computer abuse that has never been discovered or reported could significantly change this average.

An estimate of actual total losses from computer abuse could be calculated in the following way: Assume an average of 100 cases per year, with losses in the range depicted in Figure 3, will ultimately be reported for each of the first five years of the 1970s. Assume also that only 15 percent of known cases are reported. With an average loss of $450,000, a total annual loss, worldwide,

Figure 3 | **COMPUTER ABUSE** | **Losses in 144 Reported Cases (to September 1975)**

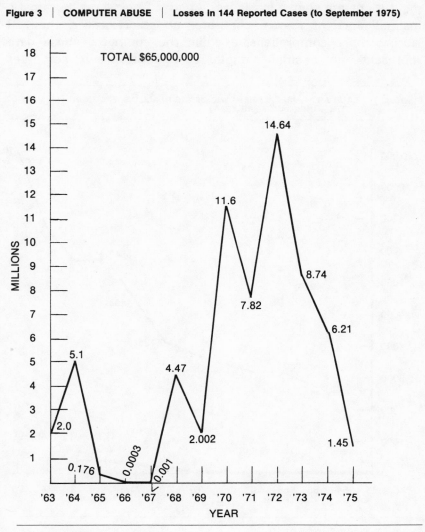

Source: Stanford Research Institute.

would be $300 million. This is three times the $100 million per year for the United States estimated by the U.S. Chamber of Commerce. It is also 150 percent the estimate of $200 million in America for the year 1974 made by Ted Linden of the National Bureau of Standards.

A comparison of computer abuse incidence and losses and the FBI statistics on fraud and embezzlement in all U.S. financial institutions are shown in Figures 4 and 5. They show a dramatic insignificance of known computer abuse. However, the FBI statistics are comprehensive while the computer abuse data represent only a small sample. The importance of computer

---

Figure 4 | **FRAUD AND EMBEZZLEMENT INCIDENCE IN ALL U.S. FINANCIAL INSTITUTIONS (CASES PER YEAR)**

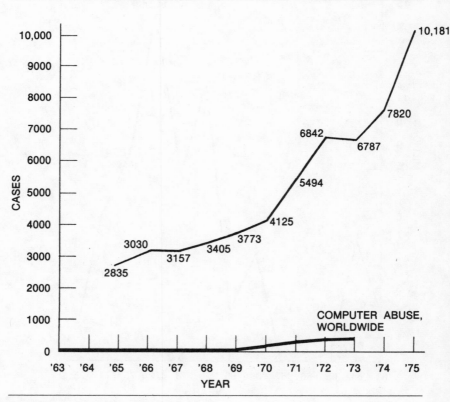

Sources: FBI, Stanford Research Institute.

abuse will emerge when most fraud and embezzlement in financial institutions can only be carried out in or with computers as computers take over the environments where this type of crime occurs.

Figure 5 | FRAUD AND EMBEZZLEMENT LOSS IN ALL U.S. FINANCIAL INSTITUTIONS

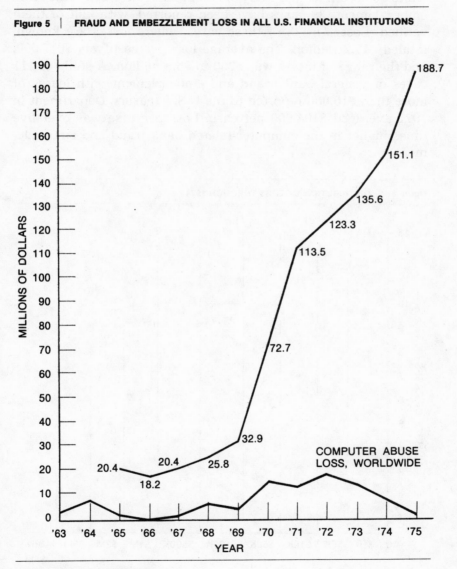

Sources: FBI, Stanford Research Institute.

Figure 6 shows the distribution of the amounts of losses for 90 cases through 1974. The losses per case are skewed to smaller amounts over the total range. A surprising number of cases have resulted in large losses compared to losses in other types of white-collar crime. In a study of computer-related bank fraud and embezzlement, 39 cases have been reported, with half of them verified. Losses in 28 of these cases, where losses are known, totaled $17.2 million. The average loss per case was $617,000, and the range of losses was $200 to $5.8 million. A study of 111 cases of general bank fraud and embezzlement with losses of more than $10,000 reported to the U.S. Treasury Department in 1971 averaged $104,000 per case. Loss per case was over five times higher in the computer-related bank fraud and embezzlement.

Figure 6 | **DISTRIBUTION OF LOSS THROUGH 1974**

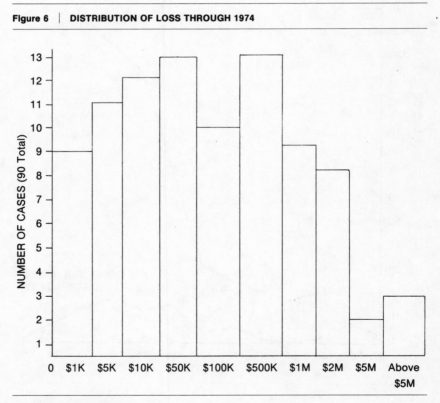

Source: Stanford Research Institute.

These are indications that losses per incident of computer crime are generally higher than for other kinds of white-collar crime, and it may be that losses in computer-related crime are higher than in equivalent crime in manual environments. There are some good arguments supporting this conjecture. Assets tend to be more highly concentrated in computer systems than in equivalent manual systems. The automation of crime required in automated systems means that it is just as easy to steal a million dollars as it is one dollar. Once a compromise of the system has been accomplished, more assets per unit time are available through the breach than in breaches of manual systems. A manual system could handle a payroll for 1,000 employees, but payrolls for 50,000 employees require computers, and the opportunity for theft of larger amounts of money is far greater with the same or smaller amount of effort by the perpetrator. It is also possible that the stakes are higher in terms of potential discovery of an act in a computer environment, forcing perpetrators to go after larger amounts of loot to make the risk worthwhile. In the future, the increasing use of mini-computers in smaller financial systems could lower the average loss.

Reported cases of computer abuse can be depicted in a number of other ways to gain further insight. Table 2 shows over 300 reported cases, divided according to the type of act and type of loss experienced by year since 1958. Financial fraud or theft predominates but surprisingly not by very much over the other types of acts. Newspaper reporting of crime probably emphasizes financial fraud or theft, vandalism, and property theft since those seem to be of more public interest than unauthorized use or sale of services. However, in reporting computer abuse the decision to publish information probably has more to do with the uniqueness of the case than the type of loss experienced; therefore, there may be a more equal distribution over types of acts and losses. Unauthorized use or sale of services is an important category because computer services are quite expensive in terms of time even though the services may be quite inexpensive in terms of cost per computation.

Vandalism has generally resulted in significant losses because of the great cost of computer systems, for instance in universities, where they represent tempting targets. Large computer

34 | CRIME BY COMPUTER

Table 2 | REPORTED CASES OF COMPUTER ABUSE, BY YEAR AND TYPE

Year	Vandalism	Information or Property Theft	Financial Fraud or Theft	Unauthorized Use or Sale of Services	Total
1958			1		1
1962	2				2
1963	1				1
1964	1	2	3		6
1965		1	4	3	8
1966	1		1		2
1967	2			2	4
1968	2	3	7	1	13
1969	4	6	3	2	15
1970	8	5	10	10	33
1971	6	19	23	6	54
1972	15	18	16	17	66
1973	11	20	26	11	68
1974	7	15	25	12	59
1975	6	7	26	4	43
Total	66	96	145	68	375

Source: Stanford Research Institute.

systems including all of the peripheral equipment can cost up to $15 million. Unknown to most people, the value of the software in such computer systems can be larger than the cost of the hardware.

Unknown bias in data samples is the enemy of the researcher. With computer abuse, skewed geographic distribution seemed to be a potential bias. A geographic distribution count was made in October 1974 with the results shown in Figure 7. The number of cases in each state are shown; numbers in parentheses denote the number of cases in certain large cities. The distribution correlates well with population centers, which in turn should correlate well with computer population. Fifty cases in California might seem a little high compared to 36 cases in the state of New York, 18 cases in Massachusetts, 13 in Michigan, and 11 in Illinois. The high count in California might be because of the location of the computer abuse research activities in Menlo Park close by San Francisco.

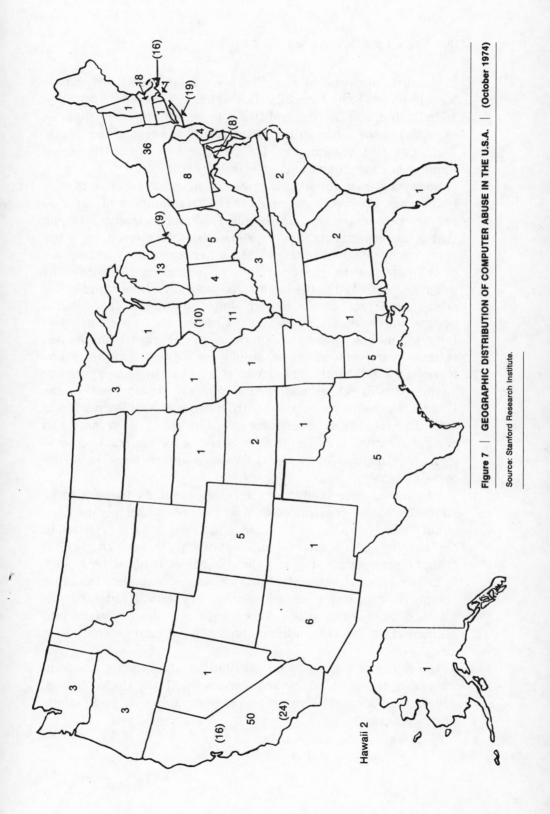

Figure 7 | GEOGRAPHIC DISTRIBUTION OF COMPUTER ABUSE IN THE U.S.A. | (October 1974)

Source: Stanford Research Institute.

Numbers of cases in large cities seem more evenly distributed, with 16 in San Francisco, 24 in Los Angeles, 19 in New York City, 16 in Boston, 9 in Detroit, and 10 in Chicago. More cases might be expected in the larger cities in Texas and the rest of the South. Eight cases in Washington, D.C., is consistent with the small number of cases found in the federal government.

So few cases in the federal government might be attributed to two causes. First, it is suspected that a large number of cases do not get prosecuted and are handled administratively, meaning that the perpetrators are reprimanded, transferred to other agencies, or quietly discharged. The other reason may be because of the paternalistic characteristics of federal civil service. This might be compared to the labor force in Japan where white-collar crime, until recently, has been almost unknown. In Japan, a person was normally employed for life by the same employer. Little job mobility has been experienced until recently. In the last several years, movement of employees among employers has increased significantly, and Japan is now starting to experience an increase in white-collar crime. Federal civil service in the United States is associated with long-term employment and attractive retirement benefits for long service. Civil servants also are apparently not as attracted to striving for financial achievement nor inspired by the profit motive as are workers in the private sector.

Of course, there is always the third possibility that far more computer abuse goes undetected in the federal sector and thus could exceed the amount of abuse in the private sector relative to the number of computers and opportunities for white-collar crime. Computer security in federal agencies is no better than it is in the private sector, based on a limited sample evaluating computer security for several computer centers in federal agencies and large corporations. This comparison does not take into account classified computing activities in national defense agencies.

The figures for geographic distribution of computer abuse in the rest of the world are shown here. As with the United States, distribution of cases seems to correlate roughly with populations of computers:

United Kingdom	17	Belgium	1
West Germany	13	Brazil	1
France	8	Denmark	1
Japan	5	Norway	1
The Netherlands	3	Sweden	1
Canada	3	Korea	1
Australia	2	Yugoslavia	1
South Africa	2		

Distribution of computer abuse cases by industry also produces no surprises among 372 cases, as of October 1975, shown in Figure 8. The cases occurring in government were mostly at the local and state level. The large number of cases in education involved students as perpetrators, and the acts were mostly vandalism or malicious mischief. The remaining industries seemed to be ordered by degree of financial activities and asset liquidity or the amount of computer usage.

There are many useful ways to analyze statistics from the file of computer abuse cases. One of these is particularly valuable for auditors who must perform financial audits involving computerized financial systems. Two kinds of computer abuse were identified, termed "inspec" and "nonspec." Inspec cases are those where computers were used within their correct specifications; there were no unauthorized acts directly against or in the computers. The acts involved manipulation of the data going into the computer systems or coming out of the systems. For example, an inspec case would be where a teller in a bank might be engaged in an embezzlement involving the transferring of money among bank accounts using an on-line teller terminal. The teller would use the terminal and computer exactly as they were supposed to be used, following all of the procedures carefully and correctly. The fraud would occur in the entering of false deposits, withdrawals, and no-book transfers of funds among the accounts.

Nonspec types of cases involve those where the computers have been used in unauthorized ways not according to the specifications or instructions for their use. Unauthorized changes have been made in computer programs, or utility programs have

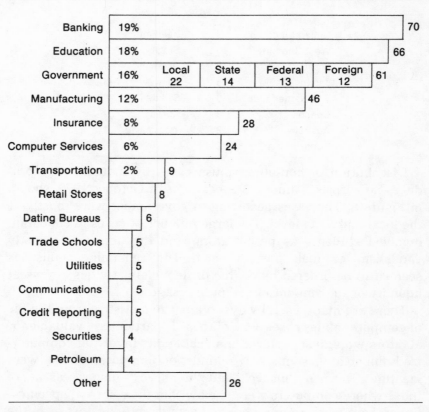

Industry	%					Count
Banking	19%					70
Education	18%					66
Government	16%	Local 22	State 14	Federal 13	Foreign 12	61
Manufacturing	12%					46
Insurance	8%					28
Computer Services	6%					24
Transportation	2%					9
Retail Stores						8
Dating Bureaus						6
Trade Schools						5
Utilities						5
Communications						5
Credit Reporting						5
Securities						4
Petroleum						4
Other						26

Source: Stanford Research Institute.

been used to modify the content of data files in computers in unauthorized ways. The nonspec type of cases are perpetrated by people with skills and knowledge in computer technology. In contrast, inspec cases tend to be perpetrated by people who have other skills and knowledge. A count of 334 computer abuse cases made in April 1975 produced 126 inspec cases and 171 nonspec cases. The remaining 37 cases were of an indirect nature, such as the theft or fraud associated with computer programs and various computer-related supplies but not directly involving the use of computers.

This typology of computer abuse is important to auditors in indicating the skills and knowledge they must possess and the types of controls and safeguards they must deal with. Dealing with inspec threats requires a minimum of technical knowledge of computers. The problem is primarily one of manual handling of data and of concern with the controls that are built into the application programs in order to detect deviations from normal activities and from normal ranges of values in input and output data. The integrity of the computer system and of its use can be assumed. On the other hand, auditors dealing with nonspec threats must have an in-depth technical understanding of computers because the integrity of the computer system has been threatened and attacked. The auditor must deal with the problem of correctness of computer programs and data files stored and used within the computer.

It is likely that fewer inspec computer abuse cases are reported than nonspec, because they are often not identified as being associated with the use of computers. For example, a survey was made of computer fraud within the federal government. A questionnaire was sent to a number of agencies asking them to report all computer frauds that have occurred in their organizations. One case was reported. The questionnaire instructions were changed to report all cases of fraud where data involved in the fraud may have entered a computer or come from a computer. This second attempt produced hundreds of cases from many of the agencies, and in one agency, literally thousands of cases.

Another effort produced the number of computer abuse cases found involving the various functions in EDP organizations among 263 reported cases. The results are as follows:

EDP Functions	Number of Cases
Application computer programs usage	109
Operating system activities	74
Operation of computers	43
Computer system development and maintenance	15
Computer facilities operational procedures	13
Programming office areas	4
Unknown	5

These statistics indicate that the largest number of computer abuse cases have to do with the software rather than the operation of computers.

A composite profile of a theoretically most vulnerable EDP operation, based on victims' weaknesses found in reported cases, has been compiled with the following results.

The most vulnerable EDP operation performs financial processing and produces negotiable instruments. Employee and management relations are poor, with a high degree of employee disgruntlement. There is a significant lack of separation of tasks requiring a great amount of trust and responsibility. In other words, employees are given wide-ranging responsibilities with minimal checking or observation of their activities. Employees are unsupervised when they are working in the EDP facilities outside normal hours. This weakness is supported by a number of cases that occurred at night or on weekends when employees, especially programmers, were given access to computers for program development work. The computer application programs lack controls to detect anomalous activities and events. The programs are difficult to test and provide few opportunities for the development of audit trails, the means by which transactions can be traced from the end product back to the source data. Finally, there is little or no accounting of use of the computer system. Programmers, computer operators, or any employees can use computer services without any direct accountability. Actual experience shows that any EDP organizations which have some significant combinations of these weaknesses are particularly vulnerable to computer abuse.

7 | THE ENEMY

O what a tangled web we weave,
When first we practise to deceive!
—SIR WALTER SCOTT, *MARMION*.

The profile of perpetrators of computer abuse, and their perceptions of themselves and their victims, are interesting and profitable subjects of study. The relationship of the potential perpetrator to the potential victim can be described metaphorically in the following story. A young man was drafted into the army in a South American country. Rifles had not yet been obtained, so he was issued a broom and told to practice with it. At the target practice range, he was told to pretend he was firing with his broom and say, "Bang, bang, bang!" In bayonet practice, he was instructed to use the broom as though it had a bayonet on it and say, "Stab, stab, stab!" The war came. He was put in the front lines with his trusty broom since the rifles had still not arrived. The enemy came at him. He did only what he was trained to do and said, "Bang, bang, bang!" as he aimed his broom. Several of the charging enemy soldiers fell, to his surprise, but more got so close he poked his broom at them and said, "Stab, stab, stab!" Several more charging soldiers fell. However, one of the enemy kept coming. "Bang, bang, bang!"; he wouldn't fall; he got closer; "Stab, stab, stab!"—still kept coming. In fact the enemy soldier ran right over him, broke his broom in half, and left him lying in the dust. But as the enemy soldier roared by, he was muttering under his breath, "Tank, tank, tank." The enemy often marches to the same drum as the potential victim but follows an unanticipated path. In order to discover these unanticipated paths—weaknesses in computer security—we must know and think like the enemy.

It would be a great achievement if the profile of the perpetrator of computer abuse could be accurately described as a person 6 feet, 6 inches tall, balding, wearing glasses, and with an evil glint in his eye. Unfortunately, we can't come quite that close to identifying potential perpetrators. However, after spending many hours interviewing 17 perpetrators, often in prison cells, and talking to many victims of computer abuse about the perpetrators, a profile seems to be emerging. It must be kept in mind that this profile is based on a relatively small sample of known computer abuse perpetrators. Improvement in the correctness, completeness, and comprehensiveness of this profile is achieved each time a new perpetrator is interviewed—if in fact a single profile emerges. The characteristics are common to the traditional white-collar criminal and to perpetrators of malicious mischief. However, some of these characteristics may be more prominent and universal among perpetrators of computer-related incidents.

Interviewing alleged and actual perpetrators is a tricky business. When an alleged perpetrator is interviewed before the completion of litigation against him, he has usually been advised by his attorney to avoid discussion of his case with anyone. This is frustrating for him, because he is eager to find a sympathetic ear to rationalize the reasons for his action. He is also often eager to tell about his achievement in perpetrating the act and in some cases do some boasting about it. His boasting one minute and showing contrition the next makes these interviews fascinating.

The perpetrator often puts more energy into rationalizing his action than he did in performing it. He also works very hard to reduce the element of criminality in his motives. He can often convincingly argue that what he did was reasonable under the circumstances, and that anyone would do the same thing. His actions caused the least amount of harm to the least number of people and successfully solved his problems or allowed him to reach his goals—if it weren't for the one thing he overlooked or circumstance not under his control that resulted in discovery of his actions.

Before and during litigation, perpetrators have only one goal, and that is to avoid or minimize the sanctions to be imposed on them. The evidence is usually so overwhelming against them that they generally will plead guilty. Therefore, their tactics are to reduce the seriousness and criminality of their acts and demonstrate appropriate remorse, sorrow, and repentance for what they have done. These people have usually never been in trouble with the law before, and they give the strong impression that after this sad experience, they will never be in trouble with the law again.

Perpetrators are presumed to be dishonest people, but all mortals are dishonest to some degree. Perpetrators tend to be very ordinary; they simply had a problem to solve or somehow developed a goal to achieve beyond ordinary means. They were in a position of trust where the violation of that trust could achieve their purposes. They almost always intend to restore or make up for the loss suffered by the victim and then often find that taking money from a victim is easier than trying to restore it to him in some undiscovered way.

I have developed a great sympathy and trust in several of these people which some of the experts advise me is misplaced and inappropriate. Detective Superintendent David Hind of New Scotland Yard, the London Metropolitan Police, assures me that few can ever be trusted again. Once they have put so much effort into the rational planning and executing of a crime, they are predisposed to follow the same pattern when the opportunity or situation arises again. He urged me not to consort with or befriend perpetrators.

When I lectured on computer abuse at the FBI Academy in Quantico, Virginia, to a group of agents-in-charge, I indicated confidence in the rehabilitation of a teller addicted to gambling who stole over $1 million from a bank. They assured me that according to their experience every white-collar criminal addicted to gambling will always be a repeater until the day he dies. They were convinced that some day this man will be back in prison.

Professor Donald R. Cressey of the University of California at Santa Barbara is one of the foremost criminologists and served briefly as a consultant to me in the study of computer abuse. He has probably interviewed more convicted embezzlers than anyone else in the world. He knows well all of the characteristics identified among computer abuse perpetrators. He states about the white-collar criminal: "By conceiving of himself as a borrower (not a thief) the violator cuts himself off from the influences of a social order which otherwise would deter him, and before he gets in too deep he is not fully cognizant of the social attitudes which later induce him to behave like a criminal. While he is able to look upon his behaviour as borrowing, his desire is to repay the money borrowed and not as may be the case later to avoid being caught and sent to prison . . . trust violators who take funds over a period of time by rationalizing that they are borrowing the money become criminals without intending to do so."

Perpetrators tend to be amateurs rather than emotional or professional criminals who take pride in their criminal activities. In one case, the amateur white-collar criminal with no criminal record was convicted and sent to a federal prison for three years. His accomplice, a professional criminal already convicted several times, was convicted also but fast-talked his way into probation and the same day the amateur was sent to prison, he was out on the streets, a free man. In another case involving computer abuse and credit card fraud, a professional criminal was caught and agreed to provide evidence to implicate his fellow Mafia brothers. He was gunned down in the streets of New York before he could accomplish this. In yet another case, a nineteen-year-old programmer convicted of embezzling had no more than a misdemeanor charge and conviction for possession of marijuana in his past. The other known computer abuse perpetrators have no criminal records.

Few women have been encountered among perpetrators in

computer abuse. When they are involved, they tend to be accomplices employed as key punch operators or clerks in EDP organizations. In one case a group of women key punch operators in a police department discovered that there was no audit trail of parking citations back to the forms that were filled out. The follow-up went back only as far as the computer records. They simply discarded the citations against them and their friends. In another case, a young woman convinced her boyfriend, a computer operator, to steal a valuable set of computer programs. She then tried to sell these programs to a competitor of her boyfriend's employer.

Most perpetrators are young, eighteen to thirty years old. A few of the embezzlers in management positions tend to be a little older. Jerry Schneider, a well-known ex-computer criminal, was nineteen years old when he conducted his fraud. The youthfulness of perpetrators is not surprising considering that most of them are in EDP occupations where the average age is quite low. Their youth relative to the great degree of trust that must be placed in EDP employees is a significant exposure in the misuse of computers. Fifty cases representing 19 percent of reported computer abuse up to the end of 1974 involved students. This accounts significantly for the youth of perpetrators. These perpetrators must have a combination of desperation and the type of courage and recklessness along with self-confidence that makes a person get into a ring with a bull or drive cars in races. Sometimes it is desperation alone that seems to generate the courage or recklessness needed.

The best way to identify the potential population of perpetrators is on the basis of the unique skills, knowledge, and access possessed by people engaged in computer technology. Professional criminals do not appear to have acquired the knowledge and skills yet. As computers penetrate into the environments in which the professional criminals work, more of them will be associated with computer abuse. Perpetrators are usually bright, eager, highly motivated, courageous, adventuresome, and qualified people willing to accept a technical challenge. They have exactly the characteristics that make them highly desirable employees in data processing. To design safeguards for computer systems on the assumption that perpetrators will not be aware of the technical intricacies is an exercise in futility. The principal threat against which protection is required is the penetrator who knows as much about the system as the designers do.

Studying and classifying motives is not a very helpful means of identifying potential perpetrators. Psychologists warn that attempting to identify motive patterns is not productive. However, several significant characteristics related to motives appear almost universal among computer abuse perpetrators. The Robin Hood syndrome identified among criminological studies is one of these. Actually it is a variation of the Robin Hood act, stealing from the rich and keeping it! Perpetrators tend to differentiate between doing harm to individual people, which they feel is immoral, and doing harm to organizations, which they believe is not immoral in certain circumstances. In fact, they often claim they are just getting even for the harm organizations do to society.

The perpetrators often take great care to avoid doing harm to people. The teller embezzler made sure that he took no more than $20,000 from any one savings account to avoid losses to his customers, on the basis that the insurance would cover the thefts. Where harm to people is intentionally done, there is always a great effort to identify them as bad and deserving punishment in the rationalization of the act. The accountant who embezzled from a family-owned company said that he disliked these people because of the abuse and the unfair treatment they showered upon him.

Rationalizing attacks on organizations has probably been supported to some extent because of the antiestablishment trend developed during the 1960s and early 1970s. In computer abuse not only is the act done against an organization, but it is often done to the computer, which is placed in the focus of the attack. It is not the organization the perpetrator is attacking, but the inanimate computer system. A computer is an ideal target for attack. It can't cry, have its feelings hurt, get mad, or strike back. Yet, it has certain personified characteristics that make it a highly attractive and satisfying target, and replaces the organization using it as the subject of the attack.

The differential association theory explains another characteristic according to criminological research. This theory states that perpetrators' acts often tend to deviate in only small ways from the accepted and common practices of their associates. A group of people working together can sometimes tend to reinforce one another in the minor unethical acts that grow to serious acts. This is the basis for employees taking pencils home today, pads of paper home tomorrow, and pocket calculators the next day. In the case of Fred Darm, who stole a computer program from the memory of his competitor's computer over a telephone line, civil trial testimony revealed that it was common practice for programmers in both of those competing firms to dip into one another's computers from remote terminals in unauthorized ways. Each programmer, it was said, reinforced the rationalization of the other in performing these acts to the extent that it became common and accepted practice. Darm was quite offended when he was arrested.

Other almost universal characteristics are the elements of challenge and game playing associated with computer abuse. These characteristics seem to be much stronger in computer-related acts than in general white-collar crime. Some people believe this is just the vending machine syndrome that is generally common today throughout society. How many of us would attempt to find the owner of 35 cents found in the coin return of a pay telephone? Dr. Stanley Winkler of IBM relates an experiment he conducted in his travels around the world. Whenever he had a few minutes waiting for transportation, he would go to the nearest pay telephone, call the operator, indicate that he had just found a small amount of change in the coin return, and ask what he should do with it. The telephone operators told him what he could do with it in no uncertain terms! In this respect and to this degree we are all criminals and certainly dishonest from time to time.

A general characteristic of computer programmers is their fascination with challenges and desire to accept them. In fact, they face the great challenge of making computer systems do their bidding day in and day out. Telling a programmer that a computer system is safe from penetration is like waving a red flag in front of a bull. The challenge of an unauthorized act often overshadows the question of morality.

The idea that an abusive act is merely playing an innocuous game with the computer is often accepted in EDP. Computer science students in universities, the so-called systems hackers, make a game out of attempting to compromise the campus computer system. Sophisticated compromises of campus computers abound. The idea of imparting to students the concept that the computer is an important, powerful tool upon which our livelihoods and the safety of society depends is almost nonexistent in universities. Although professional business ethics are passed from professor to student in university business schools, the same is not true of computer science departments. One exception is at the University of North Carolina, where Professor Fred Brooke teaches a course on professionalism to computer science students. Until students are taught that the computer is a sacrosanct, important tool not to be played with in unauthorized fashion, we will continue to have a flow of new graduates coming into our businesses, government, and institutions prepared to continue their game playing, but where the stakes are real. Only one perpetrator I have interviewed told me that playing the game was not a part of his rationalization. In his case, he had a serious personal financial problem and there was no game or challenge to it at all; he merely wanted to solve his problem.

It appears that perpetrators most strongly fear unanticipated detection and exposure. The importance of this characteristic makes detection as the means of protection at least as important as prevention. Perpetrators tend to be amateur white-collar types for whom the exposure of their activities would cause great embarrassment, loss of face and prestige among their peers and families. Exceptions are fatalists bent on self-destruction where the purpose of the act may be to be detected and exposed. At one point in his embezzlement, the teller in a bank said that he hoped he would get caught to put an end to the complexities of his embezzlement and solve his problem in an undesirable but at least conclusive way. This fear of detection is also in contrast to many professional criminals who want their peers to know of their accomplishments. Perpetrators are often highly frustrated until their discovery and exposure because they can't brag and tell other people of the tremendous accomplishments they performed in conducting their unauthorized acts. It is almost a relief for them, once caught, to have the opportunity of telling people what they did.

Some form of disgruntlement with their employers is almost always present among perpetrators of computer abuse. They must find good reasons for their acts. Discontent tends to be quite common in EDP because of rapidly advancing technology and the concomitant need to change practices and procedures. A lack of managerial skills among the new, young managers developing in the field and a lack of top management understanding of the technology and nature of data processing occupations is the major contributor. EDP people tend to identify with their technology to a far greater degree than with their employer or the business activity. Maintaining competence in this fast-growing technology occupies much of their time. The Peter Principle states that a person rises in an organization to his level of incompetence. In the computer field it isn't necessary to rise to reach a state of incompetence. If a person does not advance in competence, technology will pass him by.*

Programming can be such an overwhelming, intense, and challenging activity that it obscures many other values. In managing groups of programmers, I often had to chase programmers out of the computer rooms because of the many continuous hours without food, sleep, or visits to the rest rooms in their intense and all-encompassing efforts to debug their computer programs. There are also many mechanical and uninteresting tasks associated with data processing. This can often result in EDP employees being over-qualified for the jobs they perform. If active minds cannot be put to productive and authorized use, they will find antisocial and unauthorized exercise.

Dr. Joseph Weizenbaum, MIT Professor of Computer Science, described a dangerous type of programmer:† "Wherever com-

---

* This is a paraphrase of the Paul Principle expounded by Paul Armer, a noted author, philosopher, and activist in the computer field.

† From *Computer Power and Human Reason* by Joseph Weizenbaum. W. H. Freeman and Company. Copyright © 1976.

puter centers have become established . . . bright young men of disheveled appearance, often with sunken glowing eyes, can be seen sitting at computer consoles, their arms tensed and waiting to fire their fingers, already poised to strike, at the buttons and keys on which their attention seems to be as riveted as a gambler's on the rolling dice. When not so transfixed, they often sit at tables strewn with computer printouts over which they pore like possessed students of a cabalistic text. They work until they nearly drop, twenty, thirty hours at a time. Their food, if they arrange it, is brought to them: coffee, Cokes, sandwiches. If possible, they sleep on cots near the computer. But only for a few hours—then back to the console or the printouts. Their rumpled clothes, their unwashed and unshaven faces, and their uncombed hair all testify that they are oblivious to their bodies and to the world in which they move. . . . These are computer bums, compulsive programmers, . . . distinguished from a merely dedicated, hard-working professional programmer. . . .

"The compulsive programmer is usually a superb technician. . . . He is often tolerated around computer centers because . . . he can write small subsystem programs quickly, that is, in one or two sessions of, say, twenty hours each. . . . His position is rather like that of a bank employee who doesn't do much for the bank, but who is kept on because only he knows the combination to the safe. . . .

"The compulsive programmer is convinced that life is nothing but a program running on an enormous computer, and that therefore every aspect of life can ultimately be explained in programming terms. . . .

"Hence we can make out a continuum. At one of its extremes stand scientists and technologists who much resemble the compulsive programmer. At the other extreme are those scientists, humanists, philosophers, artists, and religionists who seek understanding as whole persons and from all possible perspectives. The affairs of the world appear to be in the hands of technicians whose psychic constitutions approximate those of the former to a dangerous degree."

Perpetrators are almost always involved in some form of trust violation in the acts they perform. Data processing occupations are rapidly becoming the most sensitive positions of unauditable trust in organizations that use computers. The most vital operations of organizations are rapidly being programmed for execution by computers, and the EDP people are often the only ones who are able to know whether these processes are being performed properly.

There is a high incidence of collusion in reported computer abuse. This might be the result of bias in the recorded cases because collusion may be more easily discovered and reported since it often makes more interesting stories for the news media. However, the more likely reason for a high incidence of collusion is that it takes more skills, knowledge, and access than may be possessed by any one individual to carry out a computer abuse in this highly complex technology. Collusion tends to involve a technical person who can perpetrate the act and another person who is in a position to translate the act into some form of gain. The differential association theory probably plays an important role in fostering collusion.

In ordinary white-collar crime, collusion has been found to be of low incidence. Among 111 cases of bank fraud and embezzlement involving losses over $10,000 reported in 1971, only 13 cases involved collusion. In computer-related bank fraud and embezzlement, almost half of the cases involved collusion. Among all computer-related cases, collusion represents about half of the cases. Collusion is often not limited to just two people; a number of cases have involved six or a dozen people. Twenty-two people were convicted in the Equity Funding Insurance fraud. Another case involved more than 30 people, and yet another showed 64 people all involved in collusion in a data processing activity. The fact of much collusion is important in the development of safeguards in EDP facilities.

Only 4 cases have been identified among 175 cases of collusion where programmers and computer operators were working together to commit the act. This might be the result of the mutual antagonism between programmers and computer operators, who function in almost adversary roles. Programmers are almost always demanding more performance from computer operators, and computer operators insist on more explicit instructions from programmers. It is more likely the case that programmers don't need computer operators and computer operators don't need programmers to carry out their unauthorized acts. What each needs is assistance in converting the acts to gain.

The occupations of perpetrators of computer abuse determined from the known cases provides further insight into the identity of the enemy. A comparative study of positions held by bank embezzlers in 111 general cases involving losses over $10,000 reported in 1971 by the U.S. Treasury and 39 computer-related cases produced the following results:

Perpetrators' positions in 111 general cases		Perpetrators' positions in 39 computer-related cases	
Position	Number	Position	Number
Operations vice president, manager, clerk	32	EDP clerk	11
Loan officer, manager	29	Customer	9
Teller	22	Programmer	7
President	14	EDP vice president	7
Cashier	8	EDP manager	3
Director, stockholder	5	Outsider	2
Bookkeeper	3	EDP operations manager	1
Trust officer	3	Teller	1
Auditor	1	Sales executive	1
Computer operator	1	Branch manager	1
Proof Department supervisor	1	Trust officer	1
Systems analyst	1		

A rough analysis indicates that perpetrators in general cases have centered in occupations directly involving negotiable instruments. Perpetrators in computer-related cases are people who have access to computer input, output, and stored data, and people who can convert manipulated data into financial gain— customers. This lends support to the proposition stated in this book that computer use is causing replacement of paper negotiable instruments by financial assets in the form of electronic pulses and magnetic patterns.

Occupations identified in 293 cases of computer abuse—all reported cases up to December 1974—are as follows:

EDP employees	Persons	Cases	Non-EDP People (cont.)	Persons	Cases
Computer maintenance engineers	99	5	County commissioner, supervisor	2	2
EDP employees, undesignated	87	60	Insurance agents	2	2
			Salesmen	2	2
Programmers	32	29	Physicians	2	1
Computer operators	24	18	Army officer	1	1
Key punch operators	17	3	Chief buyer	1	1
EDP managers	6	6	Controller	1	1
Systems analysts	3	3	Auditor	1	1
Tape librarian	1	1	Mayor	1	1
Non-EDP People			Messenger	1	1
Nonemployees	91	33	Order entry clerk	1	1
Students	49	31	Pharmacist	1	1
General managers and vice presidents	17	16	Public relations specialist	1	1
Accountants	8	8	Real estate broker	1	1
Clerks, assistants	6	5	Company secretary	1	1
Law enforcement officers	3	3	Head teller	1	1
Political rioters, nonstudents	3	3	Senior airline official	1	1
Auto driving school owners, employees	3	2	Senior analyst	1	1
Claims personnel	3	1	Non-EDP employees, undesignated	6	4
Presidents of firms	2	2	Undesignated		66

There is a growing concern and interest in professional responsibility and ethics, both within the computer occupations and within segments of the public affected by use of computers. However, such concepts are only in the formative stages in these occupations with their 25 years of existence compared to other occupations such as medicine, law, accounting, and engineering with hundreds of years of history and development. Computer abuse perpetrators have been notably lacking in a professional image of themselves and in ethics as a concept practiced in their work.

In 1973 attendees at a professional society dinner meeting completed questionnaires after being told to answer the questions assuming malicious intent in the acts described. Definitions of what constitutes unethical, dishonest, and illegal behavior were purposely left for each respondent to decide. Fifty-four attendees answered the questionnaire, including 18 managers of programmers and 36 programmers. The questions were also presented to 28 auditors who attended a talk on embezzlement at an EDP auditing conference sponsored by the Institute of Internal Auditors Chapter in Indianapolis on May 8, 1975. Several of the cases and their evaluations are presented below:

1. Request a listing of a program from a time-sharing computer through a terminal, discover a statement on the listing that the program is proprietary property, but use the program in another computer in spite of the proprietary statement:

	OKAY	UNETHICAL	DISHONEST	ILLEGAL	CAN'T DECIDE	HAVE DONE IT
Auditors	1	10	9	8	0	0
Managers	2	10	3	3	1	0
Programmers	7	13	8	10	1	0
Totals	10	33	20	21	2	0

2. Attempt to discover unpublished (secret) system commands by trial and error for the purpose of using them from a terminal attached to the computer system:

	OKAY	UNETHICAL	DISHONEST	ILLEGAL	CAN'T DECIDE	HAVE DONE IT
Auditors	6	8	12	1	1	0
Managers	12	4	2	1	0	7
Programmers	22	5	2	3	2	5
Totals	40	17	16	5	3	12

3. Attempt to gain access to a time-sharing computer service for which you are not an authorized user:

	OKAY	UNETHICAL	DISHONEST	ILLEGAL	CAN'T DECIDE	HAVE DONE IT
Auditors	0	8	7	13	0	0
Managers	4	7	4	5	0	4
Programmers	9	5	8	12	2	6
Totals	13	20	19	30	2	10

4. Offer the use of a program you have written at your employer's expense to an employee of a different employer without permission:

	OKAY	UNETHICAL	DISHONEST	ILLEGAL	CAN'T DECIDE	HAVE DONE IT
Auditors	0	14	8	5	1	0
Managers	3	10	3	6	0	4
Programmers	10	16	6	8	4	3
Totals	13	40	17	19	5	7

5. Accept and use a program given to you by a friend working for another company:

	OKAY	UNETHICAL	DISHONEST	ILLEGAL	CAN'T DECIDE	HAVE DONE IT
Auditors	5	11	4	5	2	1
Managers	11	6	2	0	0	4
Programmers	22	8	7	2	2	5
Totals	38	25	13	7	4	10

6. Exchange programs with others without written agreements:

	OKAY	UNETHICAL	DISHONEST	ILLEGAL	CAN'T DECIDE	HAVE DONE IT
Auditors	12	8	4	2	1	1
Managers	11	2	1	1	3	5
Programmers	19	6	5	4	4	5
Totals	42	16	10	7	8	11

7. For amusement, attempt to do things through a terminal not described in the user's manual:

	OKAY	UNETHICAL	DISHONEST	ILLEGAL	CAN'T DECIDE	HAVE DONE IT
Auditors	12	10	2	1	2	1
Managers	16	0	1	0	1	7
Programmers	31	1	0	0	0	7
Totals	59	11	3	1	3	15

8. Accept the challenge offered by a time-sharing service to penetrate the security of a computer system:

	OKAY	UNETHICAL	DISHONEST	ILLEGAL	CAN'T DECIDE	HAVE DONE IT
Auditors	15	6	2	4	1	0
Managers	13	2	1	1	2	3
Programmers	22	4	3	2	5	6
Totals	50	12	6	7	8	9

Examination of the above results uncovers a significant lack of agreement among all respondents over what constitutes accepted practices. Question 3 shows almost an even distribution of reaction to attempted unauthorized use of a time-sharing computer service, except for auditors who say this practice is unacceptable. Questions 4, 5, and 6 indicate that some programmers feel they have at least certain rights to programs they have written for their employers. Answers also indicate considerable support for the "Peninsula Ethic" (see chapter 11) that a computer program found in a time-shared computer system is in the public domain unless demonstrated otherwise by elaborate precautions (this ethic relates to a 1971 criminal case involving the theft of a trade secret program). Managers and especially auditors disagree with programmers to a significant degree, but they also disagree among themselves. It is easy for a computer abuse perpetrator to rationalize his acts in a field where there is little agreement or precedent over what constitutes unethical and illegal practices.

If the art of programming were taught to and limited only to those with high moral values and professional ethics, the criminal and unethical elements of society would still find a way to practice it while there is a dishonest dollar to be made. To what extent are we encouraging the criminal element in society to acquire this highly sensitive skill and knowledge? In prison criminals learn new skills that are highly adaptable to forgery, counterfeiting, lock picking, and safe cracking. Why not teach them programming as well?

William Perrin, a consultant, and former director of an EDP education program for the Department of Corrections, State of North Carolina, found way back in 1969 that 26 states were already offering EDP training in prisons. The U.S. Department of Agriculture had plans to hire inmates at Leavenworth Penitentiary to assist in the programming of a huge, national on-line time-sharing system to control the billions of dollars spent in farm subsidies. On-line terminals would be placed directly in the prison with access to the computer system in which the application was to be developed. The system was never implemented.

Malcolm Smith of Honeywell Information Systems in Waltham, just west of Boston, has developed an extensive EDP training program at nearby Walpole Prison, supported to a significant extent by Honeywell. This program at Walpole results in about 12 paroled graduates per year and has been running for about 8 years. One-third of the graduates are known to have entered the EDP field. The prisoners have their own small computers in the prison. The more advanced inmate students teach the beginners. Courses cover programming languages, business mathematics and administration, hardware maintenance, systems analysis, and advanced systems programming. The prisoners form companies to use their new skills while in prison to perform program development work for clients under contract.

Only prisoners with the highest probability of succeeding once out on parole are allowed into the courses, based on tests given to any of the prisoners in the prison who want to take them. While the general rate of recidivism among state prisons is 60 to 70 percent, recidivism among the EDP program graduates is less than 6 percent in Massachusetts and North Carolina. The convict students tend to be those convicted of violent crimes rather than white-collar crimes.

When graduates are paroled, they get jobs with the same government organizations that had sponsored the in-prison programming work. In one recent graduation class of 20 convicts in Walpole, Honeywell employed 3 of them, Digital Equipment Corporation has 1, the State Department of Education has 1, and the education staff of a local town has 1.

One alumnus is quite amazing, and Smith enjoys telling about him. He was over fifty years old when he graduated. He had spent most of his life in prison and never held a job for more than one day during the few days of freedom he had over the years. He was an old-timer convict who went by the nickname of "Ironballs"—won in his early prison life when he attempted to escape, and the guards caught him as he was straddling an electrified fence. He had become almost a living vegetable in prison but somehow got turned on to programming, which sparked him into a new life. Ironballs became one of the best programming instructors in the school; after a successful parole, he is now one of the leading programmers with a large computing firm.

The ex-convict graduates are normally hired into EDP jobs with the full background knowledge and cooperation of their employers. An employer with a strong management staff and adequate security, including separation of sensitive responsibilities, should have no qualms about hiring one of these ex-cons. His background will always be well known, probably far better known than that of programmers hired in the usual ways. The ex-con lives under strict personal performance rules while on parole, and a good paying job creates circumstances in which he is highly motivated to make good.

He also knows that if any unauthorized actions occur in his working facilities, he will be the first to be blamed. Two conflicting decisions may confront him in such a situation. Cooperation in apprehending the perpetrator keeps his reputation clean and improves his chances of success. However, the unwritten law among ex-cons that forbids ratting may be more influential in such situations. Ex-cons are also prime targets for extortion and influence by former criminal associates that may force them to perpetrate criminal acts. Nonetheless, the fact that they are known quantities and attempting to make good under adverse circumstances makes them attractive potential employees when hired in small numbers for rehabilitation purposes. Among 374 cases of reported computer abuse, only one is known to have been committed by an ex-convict. The few graduates who do get into trouble with the law again have perpetrated crimes not associated with their EDP employment.

It is easy to conclude that EDP training in prisons demonstrates that professional criminals have an opportunity to acquire the necessary computer technology, skills, knowledge, and access to perpetrate computer abuse. But this source of potential perpetrators is insignificant compared with the many more successful white-collar and professional criminals with opportunities for EDP education in high schools, trade schools, in-service training programs, colleges, and universities. EDP is an ideal technology for training in the confinement of prisons and is an absorbing, mind-consuming activity well suited for that kind of environment. The expansion of EDP training in prisons is well justified and probably results in far more good than harm. However, potential victims must be aware that professional criminals are rapidly gaining expertise in computer technology, whether it is in prison training programs or computer trade schools.

8 | JERRY SCHNEIDER: EX-COMPUTER CRIMINAL

Jerry Neal Schneider and I have continued to stay in touch ever since I interviewed him on October 16, 1972, not long after he had finished 6 weeks in the hospital and 40 days in the county jail. Jerry is a handsome young man of twenty-three years. He is 6 feet tall, weighs 160 pounds, has thick black hair ending in long sideburns and brown eyes. His looks and personality played an important part in his crime. He is also a very smart young man.

At age ten he was a child prodigy who had developed his own extensive telecommunication system. He lived with his mother and father as an only child in Cheviot Hills, a suburb of Los Angeles, California. His father is a successful shoe store owner in East Los Angeles.

Jerry was going to Hamilton High School in 1968, the same year in which he started his first company, called Creative Systems, to sell his electronic inventions. Every day on his way to and from high school he walked by a Pacific Telephone and Telegraph Company supply office. That's when his troubles started.

Bright, curious, and technically competent, he noticed that the trash cans outside the supply office were always filled with fascinating material, including damaged equipment which he salvaged for his own use. He also found documents: Bell System Policies and Practices, Bell System Guides to Ordering Parts, Plant Operating Instructions, Catalogues, Computer Program Listings, Management Training Instructions describing how Pacific Telephone and Telegraph Company orders supplies from Western Electric Company. Some of the documents were thrown out in unopened packages that had been sent from a Western Electric centralized district in San Francisco to Pacific Telephone in Los Angeles. The other documents were all in perfect shape except for a few coffee stain rings. Jerry meticulously sorted out all of the documents and put them in ring binders until he had a complete library of Pacific Telephone and Telegraph Company operating guides. He also found used bills of lading, invoices, company memos, and computer-produced budget listings.

By the time he had graduated from high school and started night classes at Santa Monica College and U.C.L.A. in electrical engineering, he was an expert in telephone company business. He spent the rest of the time expanding his Creative Systems Company into a wholesale electronic supplier. He associated with phone freaks who were ripping off telephone companies in those days by stealing long-distance telephone time, but that kind of thing was not really his bag. Jerry had bigger things in mind. He was selling refurbished Western Electric Company telephone equipment and his mouth watered at the thought of all the telephone equipment he saw passing through that telephone supply office.

Jerry was always looking for a new challenge and was eager to make his telephone supply business highly successful very rapidly without waiting until he was middle-aged. He decided that the telephone company could help him a great deal, although involuntarily. He looked at Pacific Telephone as a giant regulated industry that could afford to throw out slightly damaged equipment. They could certainly afford to supply him with just a small amount of good equipment. He only needed a little more information to pull it off. He claims that he posed as a free-lance magazine writer and told Western Electric and Pacific Telephone that he was going to write a magazine story on their computerized equipment-ordering system. They were highly flattered by this earnest and bright young man, so he was given special presentations on their systems, tours of their facilities, and all the documents he wanted. They introduced him to key management and computer operations people.

Jerry started his methodical planning late in 1970; seven months later, in June of 1971, he said he knew more about the operations of supplying telephone equipment within Western Electric and Pacific Telephone than anybody in either one of those companies. During this period it took several months of trial and error in completing his foolproof methods of obtaining equipment. In the meantime as his business grew, he moved Creative Systems Enterprises into a 6,000-square-foot warehouse and offices in a red brick building at 2050 Westgate Avenue in West Los Angeles. Next, he acquired a 1962 Ford van at a Pacific Telephone auction. The van still had the telephone company's emblems. Now he needed keys to open the gates to get him into the equipment delivery areas. He said he got his first key for $50 from a friend who had just left the telephone company and reported his key lost. That key opened a box containing other keys for other sites. Jerry used a micrometer and key codes to duplicate all the keys he found, including a master key for the particular site and a master/master key that allowed him access to supply delivery locations for the entire Los Angeles area.

According to Jerry, the telephone company operated a computerized ordering system using an IBM 360 computer. Orders for equipment came in from the supply sites and were keypunched onto punched cards. Each morning the punch cards were batched together at 10:30 A.M. and taken to the computer. By that evening all of the orders had been printed out by the computer and inventory levels adjusted. The orders were then sent to the transportation organization, which drop shipped all the supplies by 2:00 A.M. the following morning.

Jerry bought the last piece of equipment he needed—a Touch-tone telephone card dialer along with a set of cards similar to that used by each equipment site to submit their equipment orders.

He found a phone number written on an equipment guide for one of the equipment sites. Posing as another supply attendant, Jerry called the number and asked, "Do you know the new number for computer access?" He was immediately told the telephone number and the switched network number for ordering equipment. Each equipment site within a 10-mile radius has an identification number and an account code number that are punched into the card used for automatic dialing. As Jerry explained it, equipment sites also had quarterly budgets fixed to cover the maximum amount of equipment they are currently ordering. For example, it might be $60,000 for one site. This amount was automatically paid to Western Electric for equipment to be sent, but the total actual equipment ordered was usually less—say $45,000. As long as the cost of the equipment ordered was less than $60,000, little accounting of it was made. Jerry said he knew the telephone company made no special effort to keep track of what happened to the equipment as long as the cost stayed within the allotted budget. But Jerry had to know what these budgets were, what the inventory of equipment was, and the reorder levels for equipment. Among the documents he collected, he said he found the access codes to gain on-line terminal entry to a commercial time-sharing service used by the telephone company for inventory control and parts distribution analysis. During the period that Jerry was engaged in his fraud, he said the telephone company changed the time-sharing access code three times, but each time it was done a news notice was automatically sent out to all users through the terminals supplying the new number.

Now Jerry was ready to make his move. One morning in late June 1971 he entered his order for $30,000 worth of telephones and switchboards to be delivered to one of the sites he had chosen. By that evening the order had been filled, and the equipment was delivered by 2:00 A.M. the next morning. At about 5:00 A.M. Jerry drove to the site in his telephone company truck, opened the gate, drove up to the loading dock, filled his van with the equipment, and took the attached bill of lading. He moved the equipment to his warehouse, signed the bill of lading, and returned it to the central office in the mail. He repeated this activity almost every day for the next seven months.

Sixty percent of his business was legitimate. The other 40 percent came from his early morning supply activities. He had a total of 10 employees and 10 to 15 regular customers who were amazed at how quickly Jerry could deliver a broad range of telephone equipment. He advertised in various trade journals. His staff repackaged the equipment, stamping it with an official-looking rubber stamp, "Released for Resale," and used Western Electric labels and cartons, making the equipment look as though it had come refurbished from Western Electric. He only stole equipment after he had received special orders.

By this time he was getting pretty imaginative. He had some of the equipment delivered to large construction sites where there weren't even any locks to protect it. In one instance, Jerry claimed he had a $25,000 switchboard delivered to a manhole at 2:00 A.M. on a Los Angeles street where he easily picked it up for his eager customers. Jerry also claims that he kept track of reorder levels for various kinds of equipment. He would then order enough of that particular kind of equipment to reduce the inventory below the reorder level, knowing that the telephone company must acquire more equipment to bring the inventory up. Then he went to the telephone company indicating that he had a supply of that equipment and sold it back to them, knowing they were eager to restore their equipment inventory levels quickly. This allowed him to recycle the same equipment around and around, selling it back to the telephone company repeatedly.

After a while Jerry started to wear down. He was still going to night school, running his company during the day, and carrying out his early morning supply activities. This cut into his social life and was keeping him very busy. Finally he confided in one of his employees and told him what he was doing; the employee was recruited to do the early morning pickups. This worked well until one day his accomplice indicated that $300 a week pay was not enough. He wanted a $40 a week salary increase. Jerry refused, the employee started threatening him with disclosure, and Jerry fired him. Two months later the ex-employee went to Pacific Telephone and told them what Jerry had been doing.

This was in December 1971, seven months after Jerry started his theft. Telephone company officials couldn't believe their ears. They assigned two investigators, Bob Skibel and Herb Kinsel, to the case. After a month of observing Jerry's activities they were convinced and filed charges against him at the district attorney's office. On January 19, 1972, a group of district attorney investigators headed by Ronald Maus swooped down on the warehouse and offices. They found 400D line cards, Call Director Key Sets, and Cord Sets in the warehouse—all belonging to the telephone company. Jerry said they found equipment worth $5,000; the D.A.'s office said it was worth $8,000 and that Jerry had taken a total of $125,000 worth of equipment. In a later civil suit against him, the telephone company indicated they had identified $73,452 of stolen equipment, but he said the total was close to $800,000 or $900,000. A little arithmetic shows that if the theft went on for about 150 business days at up to $30,000 worth of equipment per day, it would have been possible to take equipment worth millions of dollars.

Jerry claims his computer fraud was so ingenious that there was absolutely no record of how much equipment he actually took. Headlines in newspapers across the country the day after his arrest announced one of the most famous computer crimes ever: "How to Steal a Million from a Computer"; "Computer-Wise Thief Turns Criminal Skills into Profit"; "A Computer Used Against Its Owner"; "Computer Accomplice in Theft"; "How He Folded, Spindled, and Mutilated."

Pacific Telephone kept quiet and would not give out any information except to downplay the role of the computer, implying that Jerry was just another ordinary thief. Victor Esposito, chief special agent for Pacific Telephone in Los Angeles, stated that Jerry did not gain access to a time-sharing system. Tom McNaghten, public relations official for Pacific Telephone, claimed that only $65,000 worth of equipment was lost.

After the game was up, Jerry went into hiding for a month to figure out what to do next. He finally turned himself in to the D.A. on February 8, 1972, and he was immediately released on $2,500 bail. After a preliminary hearing on February 17, he was indicted on two charges of grand theft, two charges of burglary, and one of receiving stolen goods. He initially pleaded not guilty but finally in a plea bargaining he agreed to plead guilty to one count of grand theft of $5,000 worth of equipment. On July 5, Superior Court Judge George M. Dell sentenced him to two months in the minimum security correctional institution at Malibu, followed by three years probation. Jerry served 40 days and paid a $500 fine. He had an expert lawyer paid for by his parents, who were dismayed at their son's use of his initiative and imagination.

Jerry claims the money made from the theft was poured back into his company. He said he didn't even receive a salary, and the only income he personally received was business expenses for entertainment.

In jail Jerry was put on a road-working gang with a pick and shovel until his electronic engineering and computer programming capabilities became known. He was then transferred into a job developing a part of the county computerized inventory system, an ideal job for such talents. It wasn't surprising to learn that two days after he got out of jail he had started a new business called Security Analysts with himself as the chief agent.

Soon afterward, Jerry was struck by a car while walking through a restaurant parking lot. In the hospital for six weeks he had time to reflect on his life, where he wanted to go and how he was going to get there. He decided rather than letting his criminal past inhibit him he would use it to best advantage in publicizing his new business. From then on, Jerry capitalized on his past criminal activities. By November 1972 he opened an office in the name of Security Analysts at 1888 Century Park, East, in Century City, Los Angeles—the same building where within a year another famous computer-related crime was to blossom in the Equity Funding Insurance Company of America.

He decided that it takes a thief to catch a thief. He offered his services to help businesses protect themselves from people like him. He went into business with two partners, a lock expert who handled physical security problems associated with computers and a business consultant. Their first client was an advertising agency. They had four clients in the first six months of operation.

Jerry had tried to sell his services to Pacific Telephone and Telegraph Company, indicating that he would tell them how to prevent anyone from doing the same things that he had done to them. Not surprisingly, they didn't get particularly excited about the possibility. Jerry then went to New York City to talk to the head of security for AT&T. He likewise did not indicate any particular interest in using Jerry's services. Jerry's company performed penetration studies and perpetrator analysis for clients. He was to be paid 50 percent of the first month's losses that he discovered. He did his work under a performance bond and his staff was bonded. He claimed at one point he had 13 people employed, including 9 programmers, 1 CPA, and 1 attorney.

The business side of his activities became more complicated. He soon changed the name of his company to EDP Security and took on a new partner who supplied financial backing. This high-pressure venture capitalist took over Jerry's business to make a fortune for him. He promoted Jerry like a prize fighter, taking him around and showing him off to prospective clients. Jerry was still very young and somewhat naïve concerning both the world of business and the world of computer technology. The promoter took Jerry to the Rand Corporation, but the Rand scientists were not particularly impressed, especially with the promotional tactics.

However, Jerry's talents and capabilities should not be sold short. Although in my opinion he did not have any great depth of expertise in modern computer systems and the technical aspects of computer security, he should be quite effective as a consultant. First of all, he can attract the attention of top-level management because of the publicity associated with his crimes, and he can be a great con artist. He is quite effective in showing how he can con his way into a data processing facility simply by using his charms and modest, friendly demeanor. He has shown organizations that their most significant weaknesses do not have to do with advanced computer security on a technical level but with the vulnerability of their data processing personnel. With the cooperation of his client, he would demonstrate how he could steal valuable information simply by convincing data processing people to cooperate with him. Data processing personnel have been highly vulnerable to this kind of activity since they have assumed that they work in a benign environment and not the hostile environment of today.

One particular incident indicates Jerry's methods. In early 1974 I was assisting Tom Alexander, a writer for *Fortune* magazine who was doing an article on computer-related crime that appeared in the June 1974 issue. I suggested that he go to Los Angeles and visit Jerry for a unique perspective on the problem, and one evening in his office at Century City Tom said, "Jerry, I understand that you claim you can get into any time-sharing system in the country. Is that true?" Jerry said, "Sure, I'll demonstrate it for you."

Jerry turned on his time-sharing terminal, dialed the telephone number for a service he was currently using, and then incorrectly typed his own password twice, intentionally attempting but failing to get into the system as a legitimate user. He then called the service by voice on the telephone. Because it was 11 P.M. the computer operator answered the telephone. Jerry told him that he had forgotten his password and asked the operator to please supply it to him. The operator refused, adding that he was not allowed to provide passwords over the telephone. Jerry persisted with all his power of persuasion. He told the operator he would not be able to continue the service unless he got his work accomplished that night.

The operator finally said, "Let me call you back." He then looked up Jerry's telephone number on his customer list and called Jerry's office, speaking to whoever answered the telephone. In this case it happened to be Jerry. The operator asked Jerry if a demonstration password might be sufficient for his needs. Jerry said, "No, I need my own password to get into my files stored in the system." The computer operator finally reluctantly agreed. He created a new password at the computer console and assigned it to Jerry's files. He then told Jerry the number. Jerry thanked the operator, turned to his terminal, typed in the new password, and obtained printouts of the contents of one of his files. He turned to Tom Alexander and said, "See, I can get into any system there is." Tom laughed and said, "Wait a minute. I thought you could technically compromise a computer system in some unauthorized fashion." It was Jerry's turn to laugh. "Why should I go to all the work of trying to technically penetrate a computer system when it is so easy to con my way in through the time-sharing service personnel?" Jerry made his point, that putting technical security controls into a computer system is like building steel doors in paper walls unless the staff is adequately instructed and alert to fend off hostile activities. This is what Jerry sells in his consulting service.

During 1974 and 1975 Jerry was assisting the training of security personnel in New York City and developing training seminars. In mid-1974 he requested that his probation period be terminated since he felt that it was interfering with his business. He decided he no longer needed the publicity and exposure associated with his past criminality. Jerry had matured significantly in the last two years and seemed from all indications to be a responsible and valuable member of society. However, Judge William Drake denied an early end to the probation period because Jerry was continuing to be uncooperative in settling the suit filed against him by Pacific Telephone and Telegraph Company. The telephone company was suing him for $250,000 and presumably attempting to have him reveal the names of his customers in order to recover the equipment that had been stolen. Jerry lost, and on November 26, 1974, Judge Ernest J. Zack decided that Jerry should pay Pacific Telephone almost $8,500 over five years in $141.50 monthly payments. This should not be too difficult since Jerry recently reported that he was close to making $100,000 a year in his consulting business.

What makes Jerry tick? Is he an honest, trustworthy man today? How do you differentiate between an honest man and a white-collar criminal? A psychiatrist who examined Jerry during his criminal trial testified that he is not a criminal type but a brilliant, young, immature person who used bad judgment and let his enthusiasm carry him into trouble.

Soon after Jerry got out of jail, he told me there were three reasons why he engaged in his crime. First of all, he was impatient and wanted to make a lot of money fast and make his company a great success. Secondly, he did it for the challenge. He was thrilled with his power and technical capabilities. The challenge of beating the system and being so clever that his victim was unaware of being ripped off was a great attraction to him. He said that he had planned to stop his theft within another six months after the time he was caught and then go tell the telephone company what he had done, confident that they would not be able to prove that he took anything. The third reason he gave at the time was that he had an intense hatred for regulated industry, and telephone companies in particular. He felt that they did great harm to society and that anything he could do in return was fair game. He said he strongly supported a strictly free enterprise system. In thinking back on his motives, however, he now claims that this was really not a significant one and in fact he never did feel that way about telephone companies.

Is Jerry an honest person? I asked him that question and was not surprised to get a positive response. I asked him if he found a wallet with money in it lying on the sidewalk, would he attempt to return the wallet and the money to its owner? He said of course he would. He would never steal money from another person. However, he went on to add that if he saw $10,000 sitting on a cash register in a store and knew he could take it without being observed, he would do so, he said, like any "normal" person faced with such a temptation.

It must be remembered that this conversation took place at a time when Jerry was still immersed in a value system acquired during his criminal activities. Today, evidence I have seen indicates that Jerry at age twenty-four is a valuable functioning member of society, working hard to make data processing safer to use. He now seems to be trying to live down his past reputation, but finding it quite difficult with such newspaper headlines still appearing as: "Teen-age Tycoon Settles His Debt After Tricking Company's Computer"; "Computer Bandit Ordered to Repay Telephone Firm"; "Computer Rip-Off Settled for $8,500." Jerry's association with his business promoter soon fell apart, and he has more recently been consulting under the company name Jerry Schneider and Company. Occasionally he can be seen on television demonstrating with a computer terminal how the bad guys are still ripping off computer systems.

A look at Jerry's crime from what might be the telephone company's point of view provides some valuable insight. Since this case was described from the perpetrator's point of view, it puts the telephone company in a bad light. Actually, they functioned in responsible and reasonable fashion under the circumstances, and their equipment-ordering system was run in a cost effective manner discounting a Jerry Schneider-type of threat. They did exactly the right thing by keeping quiet and riding out the storm. When asked, they admitted to being a victim, but only to an ordinary crime.

The telephone company was probably no more vulnerable than many other large organizations, and, after all, how many Jerry Schneiders are there? A large company must realistically evaluate the risk, how much money it is worth to reduce that risk, and how much they are willing to lose. Most companies are probably far more vulnerable to theft by their own employees. Doubtless it was not cost effective to increase safeguards just to protect against Jerry Schneider types. However, the potential for programming computer systems with controls so as to detect unusual activities for auditors' examinations is there, and it can be cost effective. This potential is something most companies have only recently started investigating.

Large organizations may prefer to write off big losses from criminal activities because the cost of prevention is often even higher than the loss. However, an organization must consider other factors. Their public image is worth a great deal and often suffers, as in the Schneider case. Even more important, an organization has the responsibility for reducing the temptation of wrongdoing by employees, customers, and the public at large. These factors must also be considered in risk analysis decisions.

9 | A TOOL OF EMBEZZLEMENT

The computer has been found to be a highly effective tool and instrument for carrying out embezzlements. The case of Val Smith* shows how this automated embezzlement can be done.

Today Smith lives quite comfortably with his wife and children. He is financially independent as a result of having probably almost a million dollars stashed away. But he worked very hard for that million dollars, including six years of meticulous effort at embezzlement while working as an accountant and subsequently serving five and a half years in prison. His story of his past 12 years seemed almost unbelievable as I sat listening to him in a restaurant. But I knew it was substantially true, based on my own extensive research over the past five years in reconstructing Mr. Smith's fantastic criminal schemes.

This case started for me several years ago when a newspaper article from UPI appeared with the headlines: "Embezzler of 1 Million Dollars Faces 10 Years in Jail." The article stated that "an

* Not his real name.

accountant who found a use for a computer not included in the manufacturer's instructions faced a 10-year prison term today for embezzling more than one million dollars. . . ." It was exciting after all these years to be face to face with the criminal who used a computer to embezzle a million dollars. Sitting across the table from me was a short man of slight stature with red hair and a moustache and freckles to match. He is now forty-four years old, an expert accountant, an expert in certain legal matters, a university lecturer, a prison reformer, and a teacher and salesman for motivational development courses. The capacity for his successful embezzlement became clear to me in recognizing the courage, intelligence, and intellectual capacity of this quick-witted and highly energetic man. Like most of the computer criminals I have interviewed, he is the kind of man that any manager would be most eager to hire.

Smith is a member of a prominent family, living in a small city. He went to work for a company in his home town after receiving a B.A. degree in economics at a major university. Before long he needed something more challenging and moved to the big city, where he became controller for a chemical firm. He returned to his home town to handle his family's estate. He still had great ambition but no definite goals in mind. He shifted around the area for some time and frequented a truck stop café overlooking the main highway where, over steaming coffee, he became acquainted with the truckers and local farmers. His previous employer heard that he was back in town, and one of the executives met him one morning in the café. He explained to Smith that the accounting for the company was in a terrible mess and said that he would pay him a handsome salary and a percentage of the profits to return to the company and straighten things out. Smith said he was reluctant because he was unhappy and felt abused in his previous experience with the company and was concerned that the abuse he might receive on the job was almost more than his intellectual and sensitive nature could take. But the tempting money offer and the challenge of putting the books in order was enough to make him accept the offer. Smith subsequently became unhappy with a simple accountant's life, and so, to satisfy his ego and find a use for his energies, he started a computer service bureau with a small Univac computer as a side business. The company management thought this was a great idea and encouraged him. He now was not only the head accountant but also provided the computing services for the company.

Once back at the company, however, he said that what he perceived as abusive harangues and fighting might be more than he could take. He claimed the company started cheating him on his share of the profits. He also believed that the lack of auditing and the complicated accounting and purchasing practices in the business made this environment perfect for taking the extra money that, in his mind, would compensate for the company cheating him and for having to put up with what he thought a miserable job.

It was easy. He set up several dummy vendor companies to provide imaginary services to his employer. He opened accounts for these companies in the local branch of a bank. He then proceeded to engage in an ordinary accounts receivable, accounts payable embezzlement. The price of raw materials might be 18 cents. He would show the company purchasing the materials at 23 cents. The differential would then be paid to the dummy companies for services presumably rendered. He said the other executives seemed preoccupied in bickering among themselves and with the trucking and shipping firms and suppliers, and they apparently never considered the possibility of Smith's extra-curricular activities. They appeared delighted with this young man's hardworking attitude and conscientious bookkeeping activities.

Unfortunately, as the embezzlement progressed, it became more complicated and very time-consuming hard work. The computer solved this problem. He developed a computer program that modeled the activities of the company. Each time he developed fictitious numbers, he would input these into his computer along with the correct numbers and run comparative simulations using the programmed model. In this fashion he was able to regulate and control his embezzlement so that he would not call attention to his activities by taking more money from any one account than was normal. Now he was ready to embezzle on a long-term, grand scale. In addition, he developed programs that would accept as input the bottom line totals of accounting data and then produce all of the detailed supporting data by working backwards from the total.

His embezzlement activities were almost completely automated, but they still required a great deal of attention and care. However, he had little difficulty in making his bosses believe the numbers he was giving them, because they were in the form of computer printouts, and any numbers coming from a computer must be right. He told them falsely that he sold the computer service bureau to avoid possibility of suspicion of his special use of the computer.

His biggest problem was dealing with the auditors. As the business became more complex, it was decided to have an annual certified audit. They tried it once and, appalled at the cost, decided that they would arrange for a cheaper, more limited form of auditing, but it was still enough to cause Smith some problems. He confided to me that he had handled the auditors successfully with his quick-witted conversation and his ready assistance. They became his friends socially and relied upon him to assist them. On one such social evening together they complimented him on the excellent accounting system he had developed and asked him if they might install the same system for another client of theirs. He was so struck by the irony of it all that while driving home that night he laughed so hard the tears were streaming down his face. Smith said he always knew what the auditors were going to do next and was always aware of the stages of their work. He never manipulated the net assets or cash on hand, but it was simple to show inflated expenses and artificially reduced profits.

Even in the increasingly complex financial activities of the company, with highly fluctuating freight and labor charges and various complicated financial activities in dealing with the suppliers, service vendors, and customers, the embezzlement went on successfully for six years. He was fearful of taking vacations but thrilled with his dangerous life. Smith said he was happy in the knowledge of his continuing rip-off, which compensated him for being cheated and for the abuse he felt and the difficult working relationships that he encountered. In the last two years he was getting $250,000 per year.

By 1969 he had accumulated a million dollars. He decided that he had enough money and concluded there was no longer any need to work in such an environment. The problem now was how to stop the embezzlement and go away with his money. He first decided that he would frame one of the executives and make it look as though each had been stealing from the other. However, he finally concluded that although he was dishonest enough to steal a million dollars, he could not bring himself to put the blame onto other people, even his bosses. He couldn't quit his job because whoever took over the accounting would easily discover what he had been doing for six years. I asked him why he didn't just stop his embezzlement and go on working for another year or two until the records faded into history. He replied that he could not stand working there without the compensating satisfaction of ripping them off. The increasing number of Internal Revenue Service audits bothered him, and if he left, he would always be fearful of later discovery of his acts.

In desperation, he said he went to a lawyer in a nearby town. He told the lawyer the whole story and asked him if he could get him off on a criminal indictment resulting in minimal penalties. The lawyer said he could, and it would cost only $50,000. Smith paid him $25,000 and they got down to the business of bringing the embezzlement to a successful conclusion. The lawyer indicated that the first thing that had to be done was to get Smith caught, but caught in such a way that the criminal penalties would be minimized. It was decided to let the bankers in the local branch of the bank where Smith's dummy companies had accounts discover the fraud and report it to the authorities.

Smith caused the accounts of the dummy companies to be overdrawn. However, this apparently failed to catch the attention of the bankers. He overdrew by larger amounts of money. They still said nothing to him. There didn't seem to be anything he could do to get caught. Finally he said he overdrew one account by $78,000. This led the bankers to discover this strange company and the unusual activities associated only with the one other company.

Smith quickly found himself in jail on criminal charges of grand theft and forgery. While sitting in jail awaiting bail, he idly picked up a copy of the local newspaper. In the society column he read an item announcing the marriage of the daughter of his lawyer. An exclusive wedding was held with only the closest friends in attendance, including his former boss. Smith immediately became suspicious and started thinking about his precarious situation. Everyone seemed to be against him. And why not? He had taken $1 million from a well-known and prestigious company in the area, and he had brought shame to his family. His attorney didn't seem to be making much progress in presenting an effective case. Therefore he gave up on him and went directly to the prosecutor and the judge. Smith concluded that if he pleaded nolo contendere, he might get no more than 18 months for his crime. A million dollars for 18 months in jail sounded like a pretty good deal. However, it didn't quite turn out that way.

Smith was convicted; then followed a hearing with the probation office. Smith knew he was not going to get probation, so he treated the hearing with a distinctly cavalier attitude. The probation officers found that he was unrepentant. He claimed the company owed him that money for being cheated and for what he put up with for six years. He would not tell them what he did with the million dollars. Anyone knowing how much money can be lost in running a computer service bureau might guess where part of the money went. Also, at the time of his arrest Smith owned several expensive homes and an airplane. When the judge was confronted with the worst probation report he had ever seen, he had no alternative. Smith was shocked to hear the judge say, "Ten years."

Prison doesn't stop a man like Smith. He became a model prisoner and received a college degree in humanities. Several years later he wrote a letter to a friend indicating that he had just completed an extensive COBOL computer programming course and could hardly wait to get out. At that time I thought that we could hardly wait to have a man like that out, especially with his kind of talents and experience, besides being an expert computer programmer. In prison he also taught motivational development to the other prisoners in training courses. He was well liked by the prison officials and became a personal friend of the warden. All this stood him in good stead in receiving parole after only five and one-half years.

He came out of prison ready to start a new life and with all the resources he needed to succeed. He had money, a good family, and extensive knowledge based on his years of further study of accounting, the humanities, and law; a great motivation to be active in prison reform; and a continuing interest in computers. He started working in marketing for a motivational development company and is now managing a bookkeeping company. He gives talks to Rotary clubs and other service organizations on prison reform and is lecturing in a course at a university on prison psychology. He apparently doesn't have to work for a living today, but there are just too many interesting things going on in the world for a man with his interests and energy.

Three years ago I gave a talk in which I described this case, but without using any names. A friend of mine came up to me after my talk and said, "I know that guy; he was our time-sharing salesman." From the time Smith was arrested until he was sent to prison he functioned as a computer time-sharing salesman. My friend said that he often wondered why Smith called him one day to tell him that he would no longer be his sales representative and that he had received another offer he just couldn't refuse. Next stop, prison!

In another instance, I was giving a talk to a group of members of Parliament from Australia in a conference room in a high-rise building at a university overlooking a wide area. As I described this case, I came to the point of saying that the perpetrator is now serving his sentence in ————. Then I hesitated because I was looking out of the window directly at the prison. I completed my sentence by saying, "He is now in that building right over there next to the water tower." This rather impressed my visitors from Australia.

Smith fits the profile of the computer criminal quite well, although he is a little older than most. He looked upon his act as a challenging game and a great adventure to see how far he could go and how smart he could be in carrying out his embezzlement using the computer as a tool. His disgruntlement with his employer was obviously very strong. He seemed to differentiate between doing harm to people generally and doing harm to get even with his employers who presumably cheated and treated him so badly, but it would be difficult to conclude that the pure

Robin Hood syndrome was demonstrated here. The differential association syndrome of group rationalization doesn't seem important in this case. However, in view of how sympathetic the other employees were with Smith after his arrest, it's possible that this syndrome was at work to a small degree. At one time Smith indicated that he had seriously considered bringing a confederate into the crime with him in order to spread the benefits of his activities around. He came close to collusion only in that one instance. Otherwise, he seems to be a loner.

In addition to confirming the perpetrator profile, this case clearly demonstrates how the computer can be used as a tool or instrument for computer abuse acts. How many other intelligent people who have access to computers are using or thinking about using the computer to aid in their criminal activities or plans?

These cases of white-collar crime go far deeper into people's lives than the newspaper articles reveal. The company executives, whether they are the scoundrels depicted by Smith or not, suffered embarrassment and possibly loss of business by having been ripped off by "that little pipsqueak." The incident certainly could not have enriched the lives of the other employees or improved their lot. What of the Smith family? Smith was a black sheep according to family friends, but the harm done to the family members in their businesses and community standing must also be great. And the bank officials and auditors must have been chagrined at being deceived and duped in the whole affair. The computing profession loses in these types of abuses. Smith's computer service bureau went bankrupt, Univac lost a customer, employees lost their jobs, the image of computers as safe and reliable tools is thrown into doubt, and the professional ethics of computer people are questioned.

A direct monetary loss was suffered by the people of the state amounting to over $30,000 to prosecute and incarcerate Smith. In addition, society was deprived of the useful services of an intelligent, hardworking man. However, it was not a total loss, since he apparently was helpful to the prison administration and his fellow prisoners during his five and one-half years in prison. There is also the value of justice being served and setting an example for potential white-collar criminals.

Thus, the social losses in what might seem to be another million-dollar rip-off could add up to far more significant amounts. This makes the violation-of-trust type of crime far more insidious than many other types of crime.

10 | A KIDNAPER'S COMPUTER RANSOM

The most dangerous part of a kidnaping for the culprit is collecting the ransom. All sorts of ingenious ways have been devised, but none more unique than the one that occurred in 1974 in Tokyo, Japan. On July 19, Masatoshi Tashiro opened a cash card bank account at the Shinjuku Branch of the Dai-ichi Kangyo Bank. He opened the account in the name of S. Kobayashi, using a false address. The cash card account provided him with a plastic magnetic stripe card that he could insert in any one of 348 computer-controlled automatic cash dispenser stations located throughout Japan. By inserting the card into the dispenser and entering a specified code number on a keyboard, he could withdraw amounts up to 300,000 yen ($1,000) as soon as the computer verified that there were sufficient funds in the account.

Tashiro opened the account with 15,000 yen (about $50). He made several small withdrawals amounting to 14,000 yen. Apparently by making telephone calls to the bank at several short intervals after making withdrawals, he was able to determine that it required 15 to 20 minutes for the bank to determine from which cash dispenser a withdrawal by a customer had been made.

Tashiro had discovered what he thought was the perfect solution to ransom collection problems. All he had to do was instruct that the ransom be placed in the account under the fictitious name. Over a period of time he could withdraw the ransom in small amounts with plenty of time to get away from each cash dispenser before being discovered. He was now ready to execute his plans.

This case was described in an article, "Computer Catches Kidnaper," by Sadatoshi Suzuki, director of the Criminal Investigation Division of the Tokyo Metropolitan Police Department. It was published in the *FBI Law Enforcement Bulletin* for June 1975. "At about 3:25 A.M. on August 15, 1974, a police officer on duty in a residential district of western Tokyo was startled to see a man clad only in his pajamas running toward him. The man was strained and nervous, and his words were hardly coherent, 'My baby . . . gone . . . someone took her,' he blurted out to the policeman." The victims turned out to be Masahiko Tsugawa, a well-known Japanese movie and television actor, and his actress-singer wife Yukigi Asaoka, the daughter of the late painter Shinsui Ito.

"Simultaneously with this incident the Tokyo Metropolitan Police Headquarters received a call on the police emergency number '110' from the maid at Tsugawa's residence who reported that at around 2:30 A.M. Mayukochan, the four-month-old daughter of Tsugawa, and his wife had disappeared from her nursery, apparently abducted by an unknown intruder. Detectives of the Tokyo Police Flying Squad responded immediately to the complaints.

"While they were interviewing the family the telephone rang. Instinctively, the maid handed the receiver to a detective—a sergeant of the Flying Squad, who pretended to be the father. A calm business-like voice stated from the other end of the line, 'We have your baby. We want 5,000,000 yen ($16,500). Deposit the money to account number 1326387 in the name of S. Kobayashi at the Shinjuku Branch of First Kangyo Bank. You have until noon tomorrow.' The caller then hung up . . . police officers stayed with the grief-stricken parents, but care was taken to reveal no unusual activity at the victim's home. . . . The team in the house waited for the next phone call from the suspect, but no call came. It was a sleepless night for both the family and the police."

The scheme that Tashiro had in mind soon became apparent to the police. They were discouraged to learn that it would take 15 to 20 minutes to identify which of the 348 dispensers had been triggered for the payoff. The victims had deposited 1.5 million yen ($5,000) in the cash card account. This was only part of the $16,500 ransom that had been demanded. This was done to provide an excuse for further contact and negotiation with Tashiro.

The bank cooperated with the police and called in the computer programmers to see what might be done. From the programmers' point of view, it was a straightforward job to insert a change in the on-line banking system computer program. This change would cause each cash dispenser transaction to be tested against the Kobayashi account number. The moment that account was accessed, the program would branch and cause an immediate printout at the console of the computer, indicating the cash dispenser that had just been used. Now the bank would know almost immediately which cash dispenser the kidnaper was using.

The Japanese do this kind of police work in a big way. The National Police Agency of Japan and the Tokyo Police used over 1,000 detectives to stake out all 348 dispensers, with 2 or 3 men at each dispenser throughout the country. Each team was equipped with a radio so they could be notified from the computer in Tokyo. The police put a detective at the console of the computer with a radio, and everyone sat back and waited.

"Anxiety was particularly present among the police assigned to the posts covering the south entrance of Tokyo Railway Station, the largest transportation center in Tokyo, as the cash dispenser there seemed to be the most nearly ideal one from which the criminal could best avoid detection and make a successful escape in the turmoil of passengers that surged through the terminal at all hours of the day. As a result, a decision was made beforehand to immediately arrest the suspect if he received the ransom at this location since there were slim possibilities, prior to his apprehension, of maintaining a discreet and successful police surveillance of him for the purpose of insuring the whereabouts and safety of the victim. It was a hard decision for the police to make but less risky, under these circumstances, than possibly never knowing who the suspect might be as well as where, and if the child was still alive. The police were haunted by the tragic fact that many, if not most, infant kidnaping victims have been killed or left to die by their abductors soon after commission of the crime.

"Peering intently past the surging tide of passengers entering and leaving the train terminal, the police, with radio transceivers held in anxious hands, snapped into action when, at 12:16 P.M., the signal came through: 'Urgent! We have a hit! Tokyo Station-South entrance! . . . Repeat. . . .'

"But before the message could be repeated, detectives had surrounded a young man wearing a yellow short-sleeved shirt who had just emerged from the automatic cash dispenser. In one hand he held the S. Kobayashi money card, and in the other hand, 290,000 yen in crisp bills that had just been dispensed by the computer. Never has any suspect been more surprised than Kobayashi.

"Under interrogation at police headquarters, the suspect at first denied implication in the kidnaping and refused to reveal his true identity or the location of the baby. However, a check of the suspect's fingerprints against National Police Agency fingerprint records revealed that he was a 24-year-old resident of Chiba Prefecture, about 10 miles from Tokyo. He had six previous arrests and was at the time on parole after conviction for theft. A Flying Squad team was dispatched immediately to stand by at his address. At 6:50 P.M., August 16, the suspect admitted that his wife was aware of the crime and was holding the baby at their apartment in Chiba. Radio instructions were sent out at once to the Flying Squad: 'Go in and rescue the baby!' By 9:30 P.M., the 49-hour ordeal ended, with the infant safely in the arms of her parents. The suspect was charged with kidnaping for ransom and was sentenced to 10 years' imprisonment. His wife was charged as an accessory.

"During a press conference the baby's mother commented: 'It

was a terrible experience. I could hardly eat and could not sleep. I probably could not have preserved my sanity if it had not been for the police superintendent stationed at my house, who spent two sleepless nights himself, but still was always kind and reassuring, bolstering our morale when we began to lose hope.'

"And in a dramatic television broadcast showing the baby's reunion with her parents, the father told the TV audience: 'I have never thought of police this way before, but after all they have done today to return Mayukochan to my arms, the police seem nothing less than an instrument of God.' "

In the same television broadcast the police who made the dramatic capture and the programmers who changed the program to catch the kidnaper were given awards.

Tashiro failed because he did not sufficiently understand computer technology and the flexibility in the programming of computers. This was one of Japan's first computer crimes. It is an important case in the study of computer abuse because it demonstrates two roles of computers. A computer was used as an instrument to perpetrate the crime, and the same computer was used as an instrument to detect and solve the crime.

11 | COMPUTER RAPED
BY TELEPHONE

Large-scale, on-line computer systems have time-of-day clocks in their central processors which allow programs being executed to receive the time of day in hours, minutes, seconds, and milliseconds. The computer operators running the large-scale computer for the ABC Company (not its real name) in a San Francisco East Bay city paid little attention to the on-line printer typing out the log of accesses being made to the computer by programmers at various terminals around the San Francisco Bay area over telephone circuits.

At 40 seconds past 6:15 P.M. on January 19, 1971, the printer typed out the message that a programmer at Bolts and Washers Corporation in Emeryville accessed the computer by logging in with a site code indicating the terminal's location and an account number used for charging Bolts and Washers with computer time used. Little did the operators know that the programmer was an imposter. Three seconds of computer time was then recorded for the Bolts account number by the operating system. The next line of the log was printed, indicating that the programmer had requested the punching of 515 punch cards. Simultaneously with the log entry, the card punch peripheral device noisily chewed holes in 515 virgin cards, neatly stacking them in the card hopper. The printer typed a new line, starting with the time, 6:17:20 P.M., followed by the code indicating that the programmer commanded 489 lines of data to be printed out at his terminal, approximately 11 pages of printed output. Again the operating system recorded these data under the Bolts and Washers account number. The printer typed the next line, 6:23:15 P.M., indicating the command to read 110 cards from the customer site terminal into the computer storage; but the operating system only recorded 1 second of computer time and the fact that 7 more lines of printing occurred at the terminal.

A few minutes later the printer typed the message on the log that the programmer's session at his terminal was aborted because of an unsuccessful attempt at performing an unauthorized activity. Seven minutes of connect time was charged to Bolts and Washers Company, and the session was completed. The account file in the computer indicated that Bolts and Washers was billed for 6 seconds of computer time, the punching of 515 cards, and printing 15 pages at a total cost of $2.54.

It was a routine session except for the fact that it was not a Bolts and Washers terminal nor a Bolts and Washers programmer. The computer access came from exactly the opposite direction, 30 miles south of the computer center diagonally across lower San Francisco Bay in a South Bay city where the XYZ Corporation (not its real name) had one of its computer centers.

The ABC and XYZ Computer Service Companies are in hot competition for the remote computing market in the San Francisco Bay area. They have almost identical computer systems and fight tooth and nail to lure the same potential population of customers to their services, including Bolts and Washers and Aerojet General Corporation in Folsom, California, near Sacramento. ABC had most of Aerojet's business. XYZ got only a small dribble of it. One of the reasons is that ABC offered a remote graphical plotting capability using a Calcomp Plotter and Controller located among the terminals at Aerojet. Although XYZ had remote plotting capabilities, they did not yet have the capability of providing plotting services directly from the computer to a Calcomp Plotter.

Fred Darm (not his real name), one of the best programmers at XYZ, had been spending the past several weeks attempting to develop this same capability in order to wrest the Aerojet account away from ABC. Late in the afternoon of January 19, Jerry York (not his real name), the marketing manager, was discussing the competitive aspects of the program that Darm was developing. He wanted to make sure that it had all the same bells and whistles the ABC program had. Darm assured him it was better than the ABC program, but York was not convinced and wanted to be certain that theirs was competitive. Darm said they already had a copy of the ABC program, but it was locked in another programmer's desk, and he was gone for the day. Darm concluded that the most convenient way to obtain a copy was the usual practice of using his on-line batch terminal and telephone to obtain a copy from the storage of the ABC computer.

Gaining such access should have been difficult, but for Darm it was a simple matter. He knew the unlisted telephone number allowing connection with the ABC computer from two years earlier when he had worked for a customer of ABC. And he knew the number was still good because on his last visit to Bolts and Washers he had seen it written on a piece of paper attached to the bulletin board above the Bolts and Washers terminal. Darm also knew the secret account number and two-digit site code number because, for convenience, Bolts and Washers had insisted that the two numbers should be the same for accessing both the ABC computer and the XYZ computer. Darm also knew the secret name of the computer program he was after, because he had often seen the name printed on various printer output listings at Aerojet where he had been working in his attempt to convert them to the XYZ service.

Darm simply made his terminal look like a Univac 1004 terminal, the same kind used by Bolts and Washers. He dialed the unlisted telephone number, typed in the two-digit site code number followed by the account number. The computer dutifully responded by asking what the Bolts user wanted. His first action was to command the printing of the Table of Contents of the files in the storage of the ABC computer. This was a legitimate operation that any customer could do. He identified the name of the file containing the program because he knew the secret name of the program. Next, he commanded that the program be punched on cards at his terminal. This was Darm's fatal mistake. He realized it when his card punch failed to respond, but it was too late. The cards were punched at the ABC computer center before he could stop them. He had forgotten that ABC did not provide remote card-punching capability as XYZ did. Desperate now to get a copy of the program, he commanded the computer to transmit the program to his terminal over the phone line and print it out at the terminal. This was readily done, and he completed his task, but finally he wanted to make sure that the cards punched at ABC would be thrown out. He attempted several commands to cause this to happen, and finally performed an unauthorized command to force his session on the computer to be aborted, assuming that would result in the operators discarding the punch cards. This was unsuccessful and later that evening an ABC courier picked up the punch card deck of 515 cards and delivered them to the customer whose name appeared on the last punch card of the deck, Bolts and Washers Corporation in Emeryville. Meanwhile, Darm assured himself and Jerry York that his program was competitive with the ABC program. He then went on with his development activities.

Two weeks later, on February 2, Ralph Fields, sales manager for ABC (not his real name), was passing the time of day with the Bolts and Washers Computer Service account manager in Emeryville. Fields glanced in the wastebasket next to his chair and idly reached down and picked up a deck of punch cards, too neatly wrapped with several rubber bands to be sitting in a wastebasket. He asked if they were really meant to be thrown away. The Bolts and Washers man said that was a funny thing, but a couple of weeks ago that deck had been delivered to them by mistake, and that no one had requested it. Fields tossed the deck back into the wastebasket with a loud clunk. He finished his conversation and was in the parking lot walking toward his car when the illogic of the situation hit him. Computers don't idly produce punch cards unless commanded to do so. What was punched in those cards?

Fields hurried back to the lobby where he had just signed out and signed in again as a visitor. He was escorted back to the same office where he again retrieved the mysterious deck of punch cards. This time, he looked at the printing across the tops of the last six cards showing what was punched into them. He immediately realized his return was probably worthwhile. The deck contained the source language version of ABC's highly proprietary and competitively valuable PLOT/TRANS Computer Program. The last six cards showed that the program had been requested by Bolts and Washers and contained the correct account number and site code. The Bolts man still insisted that they had not requested the program and would have no need for it since they had no remote plotting needs or capabilities.

A possible scenario of how the punch cards ended up at Bolts started to form in Fields's mind, producing in him a state of alarm and apprehension. He hurried out of the building without even bothering to sign out in the lobby, much to the consternation of the Bolts guard. Back at ABC Fields rushed into the storage room behind the computer center with the deck of cards still clutched in his hands. He rummaged through the ring binder logbooks looking for the January 19 log and the time, 40 seconds past 6:15 P.M., the date and time punched on one of the last six cards in the deck he carried. Sure enough, there it was—the log indicating Bolts and Washers access to the ABC computer. He also noticed that a computer printout had been requested, containing just the right number of lines to have been the PLOT/TRANS source program.

This time the Bolts man got mad when Fields called him and insisted that Bolts had obtained the program in printed form as well as on punch cards. Fields connected these results with other recent events and completed his scenario. He ran into the office of the president of ABC with his story—"Those guys at XYZ really did it to us this time. There can be no doubt that they stole our PLOT/TRANS Program." This was followed by extensive discussion over what to do next. If they confronted XYZ, they would merely destroy the evidence and plead innocent. More evidence was needed. A telephone call from XYZ is a toll call. The telephone company would have a record of the origin and destination of the call. It was quickly learned that the telephone company did have records of such toll calls, but these were not available except through an official police enquiry. Again, some agonizing discussion ensued. "Do we report it to the police and let our suspicions be known publicly? If we don't make an issue out of this, what will be stolen from our computer system next?"

Finally after another two weeks, on February 17, ABC met with the police in the Alameda County district attorney's office. It was a simple matter after a formal complaint had been charged for the police to obtain the toll call information and determine that the call had indeed originated from XYZ. It was also easy for ABC to conclude that the most likely programmer who could make use of PLOT/TRANS was Fred Darm, who had been spending considerable time at Aerojet, showing curiosity about the ABC remote plotting capabilities. This was enough to agree that further investigation would be justified. However, as concluded earlier, any suspicion by XYZ that an investigation was under way would most probably result in destruction of the evidence. Therefore, it was decided to conduct a surprise search for evidence to catch Darm and XYZ off-balance.

Sergeant Terence Green of the Police Fraud Detail was assigned as the search officer. He and Don Ingram, an investigator in the district attorney's office, and Keith Marcelius, a programmer from ABC, drove down Highway 17 to the Santa Clara County Courthouse to obtain a search warrant in the proper legal jurisdiction for XYZ. The reason for taking Keith Marcelius along was that he was the only one who would be able to recognize the materials being searched for and had the proper technical background to obtain them.

They arrived at the courthouse a little before 5:00 P.M. Judge Lloyd C. Doll of the municipal court, convinced of the need, signed the search warrant. This has since become a famous document since it is the first search warrant that has ever been issued to search the storage of a computer for evidence in a criminal case. Judge Doll also authorized that the search could take place day or night because of the lateness of the day and the

MUNICIPAL COURT FOR THE
SAN JOSE-MILPITAS JUDICIAL DISTRICT,
COUNTY OF SANTA CLARA, STATE OF CALIFORNIA.

SEARCH WARRANT

THE PEOPLE OF THE STATE OF CALIFORNIA

To any Sheriff, Constable, Marshal, Policeman or Peace Officer
in the County of Santa Clara:

Proof, by affidavit, having been made before me this day by
TERENCE GREEN   that there is just, probable
and reasonable cause for believing that: evidence of the commission
of a felony, to wit: Theft of Trade Secrets, described in Section
499c of the Calif. Penal Code, more particularly described below,
will be located where described below.

You are therefore commanded, in the daytime or nighttime, to make
immediate search of
                                            ,
                     ; the residences of
                                            ,
                                            ,
                     registered to said   ; and the
person of

located at   the addresses noted above   , County
of Santa Clara, State of California, for the personal property
described as follows: 1) Key punch computer cards, punched with the
                                    remote plotting programs; 2) Computer
printout sheets with printouts of   remote
plotting programs; and 3) Computer memory bank or other data storage
devices magnetically imprinted with
remote, plotting computer programs;
and if you find the same or any part thereof, to hold such property
in your possession under Calif. Penal Code Section 1536.

Given under my hand this 19th day of February, 1971.

LLOYD C. DOLL _____

_____
Judge of the Municipal Court

WPH:nas

intent of the search party to carry out their search immediately. There was no problem in doing this since XYZ, like most computer service companies, operated around the clock.

The most significant element in this search warrant is Item No. 3 among the personal property items to be looked for. Item 3 indicates "computer memory bank or other data storage devices magnetically imprinted with ABC's remote plotting computer programs." Keith Marcelius became the key man in the search since he was the only one in the search party who knew how to do this.

At approximately 6:00 P.M. the search team swooped down upon the XYZ computer center. A local police department detective was picked up to accompany the search officer. Fred Darm was working late that day and greeted Keith Marcelius warmly, even though he was surprised to see his key competitor's programmer walking into enemy territory. He was even more surprised to see Marcelius's companions. The second shift manager, when confronted with the search demand, immediately called the regional director, who in turn hurriedly called XYZ's local attorney. Everyone stood around for about another hour engaged in very awkward conversation, mostly about the weather. Finally all of the concerned parties gathered. The XYZ attorney assured the XYZ managers that the search warrant was valid and that the search party must be allowed to conduct the search.

Marcelius immediately took over the console of the giant computer. He was quite familiar with its operation since XYZ used the same computer operating system as ABC. He first had the computer print out a directory of the names of all data files stored in the computer. He then dumped the entire storage contents onto nine reels of magnetic tape so that he had a complete copy of the entire contents of the computer storage devices. These he stacked up in their plastic containers for Sergeant Green to watch over. Next, he went to the journal that listed the contents of the tape library consisting of several thousand reels of magnetic tape. He selected 19 of the tapes, all assigned by XYZ to Fred Darm and used for his programming activities.

Next, accompanied by quite a herd of people by this time, he searched the computer terminal area and the office of Fred Darm. In Darm's office he found a program listing of a computer run dated January 2; a white binder containing a number of computer listings of computer runs labeled "Aerojet General, F. Darm"; an olive desk folder containing six handwritten pages labeled "ABC Message Format, ABC Univac 1108 User's Guide, ABC Univac 1108 User's Guide, Revised"; a manila file folder labeled "Plot Packages," containing Calcomp plotting equipment manuals; another manila file folder labeled "Aerojet General," containing a number of reproduced pages and handwritten pages; a third manila file folder labeled "Aerojet Calcomp," containing five copied pages from ABC; and finally a mottled grey binder containing a number of listings of computer runs labeled "ABC."

By 3:30 A.M. everyone was pretty tired so they all decided to call it quits and go home. The search team drove back up to the East Bay and put all of the evidence into the main vault in the police department.

Sergeant Green's report stated that evidence was recovered in the office of Fred Darm that Keith Marcelius could say positively corresponded with the program taken without authorization or permission from ABC on January 19, 1971. In addition, evidence was recovered which would indicate that XYZ had been removing information from the ABC computer since at least April 1970. The tapes assigned to Fred Darm corresponded with the evidence taken from Darm's office indicating that this information had been processed through the company computer as part of the company's business and retained as company records. Among the materials found in Darm's office were a handwritten note on how to use the ABC computer, a copy of an ABC instruction sheet on how to use the remote plotting service, the ABC unlisted telephone number, and the printed listings of runs made on the ABC computer but printed on continuous form paper easily identified as belonging to XYZ from their standard paper stock. Six other handwritten pages were labeled with the ABC message format and contained information from ABC manuals. It seemed like Darm had more ABC material in his office than XYZ manuals.

Four days later, on February 23, Robert Haughner, deputy district attorney for Alameda County, filed a complaint and issued a warrant for the arrest of Fred Darm, stating that on or about January 19, 1971, "Fred Darm committed a felony to-wit: Grand Theft, in that said defendant did then and there take, fraudulently appropriate, and unlawfully make a copy of a trade secret as defined in Section 499C of the penal code of California to-wit: A remote plotting capability program from ABC Corporation of a value over $200." The complainant was the president of ABC, and the inspector was identified as Terence Green. Darm was informed by telephone of the warrant for his arrest. At 9:05 A.M. on February 25 in the company of the XYZ attorney, he surrendered to Sergeant Green at the police department. He was immediately released on his own recognizance.

It wasn't until March 2 that a newspaper reporter found the arrest record on the police blotter and realized that this was something more than an ordinary case of theft. The newspapers went wild. This case received more attention than any other reported cases of computer abuse; the publicity probably exceeded that received by the Equity Funding Insurance fraud, the largest known white-collar crime. On Tuesday, March 2, a local newspaper had a 4-inch headline: "Computer's Secrets Stolen by Telephone." Half the front page was taken up with a description of the crime, shoving into a corner of the page an article stating that the official U.S. assessment of the war in South Vietnam was that Hanoi was now on the defensive. Almost every newspaper in the United States carried the story with such headlines as "Univac's Brain Picked"; "Computer Expert Arrested"; "Computer Looter: Grand Theft Rap"; "Employee Charged in Program Theft." A friend of mine was in Paris on that day and reported that the Paris edition of the *Herald Tribune* had a front-page, 3-inch headline: "Computer Raped by Telephone."

On March 3 ABC, represented by Pilsbury, Madison and Sutro, one of the most prestigious law firms in San Francisco, filed a $6 million civil suit for "theft of trade secrets . . . intent to adversely affect business of a competitor . . . and exemplary damages." The suit was filed in Santa Clara County. XYZ immediately countered with a cross-complaint and was represented by Gibson, Dunn and Crutcher, one of the most prestigious law firms in Los Angeles. A tremendous battle could be anticipated and no one was disappointed. The civil suit and criminal case proceeded in parallel jumps and starts for the next 20 months.

Fred Darm pleaded not guilty on March 4, March 22, November 22, and right on throughout his preliminary hearing, which ended March 22, 1972. The preliminary hearing was held to determine if there was enough reason to believe that a crime had been committed in order to certify the case to the Superior Court. Darm was arraigned before Municipal Judge William R. Levins on two counts, one of grand theft under Code 487 and the other on the theft of a trade secret, Code 499C. Darm was the subject of such attention that XYZ finally had to suspend him with pay and send him on a skiing trip for a couple of months while awaiting the preliminary hearing.

XYZ retained the services of two top criminal lawyers, Stanley Golde and Spencer Strellis. Strellis, a young, dynamic attorney, handled most of the case with the advice and guidance of the more experienced Golde.

It was said that the district attorney chose a preliminary hearing rather than a grand jury indictment because he wanted a highly visible test of the theft of a trade secret law. This was a new law adopted in 1967 that had never been tested before, although it was a close copy of statutes that had been in effect in the states of New Jersey and New York for some time. The district attorney felt he had a better chance for conviction using the theft of a trade secret law rather than the straight grand theft law because it would have been difficult to identify the taking of a copy of a computer program over a telephone line as the taking of property defined under the state's grand theft law.

It is interesting to note the differences in law from jurisdiction to jurisdiction. In 1964, a programmer was convicted of grand theft in Texas for taking $5 million worth of copies of programs on printed listings from his employer and attempting to sell them to a customer of his employer. In Texas the grand theft law states that property subject to theft can include any writings to which value may be ascribed. California's grand theft law does not include so specific a description of property subject to theft that could easily apply to taking copies of computer programs. Therefore, the use of theft of a trade secret law seemed to be the more appropriate one with the highest probability of conviction.

Susan Nycum, my legal associate in computer abuse research, and I took Fred Darm up to the opening of his preliminary hearing. Fred was very talkative and a little nervous, not knowing what this new phase in his life had in store for him. However, he had little to say about the details of his act at that point. He felt highly abused and was convinced he was being set up as a victim for the district attorney intent on testing a new law. It seemed to me that he was trying to figure out what it was he did that was so terribly wrong to have caused all this attention. I got the impression that as far as he was concerned, there was nothing bad in dipping into his competitor's computer and taking a copy of the program that his associate at XYZ already had a copy of. There was only one aspect that he agreed might have been illegal, and that was the stealing of $2.54 worth of computer time from Bolts and Washers. He seemed perfectly willing to answer for that criminal offense.

The hearing started off in trying to get everyone in the court to understand the technological environment in which the alleged act occurred. Witnesses from ABC, the prosecutor, and defending attorneys, using flip chart diagrams and a blackboard, wrestled with the problem for several hours. Keith Marcelius as an expert witness contributed most to this part of the hearing.

At one point in Marcelius's testimony he was describing the procedure of using an on-line terminal. He went into so much detail that Judge Levins interrupted and stated that he had just completed taking a course in data processing so that the witness need not go into so much detail and be so elementary in describing the process. Marcelius then continued more rapidly, but when he got to the point of describing the terminal sign-on process, he was stopped by the court reporter who was confused by the term and asked Marcelius to spell it for him. After Marcelius spelled it, the judge interrupted again and admitted that he was having some technical problems. In his notes, he had spelled the term "synon." Haughner, the deputy district attorney, interjected that it sounded as though the judge had been hearing too many drug cases and confused the term with Synanon, the drug rehabilitation center.

The ABC hardware system was described in great detail, starting with the Univac 1108 computer with two Fastrand drums, each holding 132 million characters of data. The computer was connected to a multiplexer. Connected to the multiplexer was an expensive $7,000 per month communications terminal multiplexer controller (CTMC). This was connected to a set of telephone switches and in turn to a set of AT&T modems that convert the discrete digital electric pulses into a continuously varying analog voltage signal compatible with the telephone system. From there, the data passed through the public telephone circuits out to the customers where, for example, at Aerojet General a Univac 1004 remote batch terminal was located. It received the signals from a telephone handset and passed them through another modem, this time converting from the analog signal to digital signals and on into the terminal. A second telephone and modem fed into a Calcomp receiver connected to a Calcomp 663 Plotter.

Normally plotting data would have been recorded on magnetic tape at the computer center, and then the tape would be placed on a separate device converting the data for a Calcomp Sender. The data would be sent over telephone lines to the Calcomp Receiver and Plotter at the customer end. This equipment is supplied by the California Computer Products Company. It was the PLOT/TRANS program that replaced the Calcomp hardware at the computer end of the process to improve performance. It was explained that this program works only in the ABC computer configuration because of special hardware changes made to the CTMC.

Next, the evidence found in the search was presented to the court, and the prosecutor had Sergeant Green on the witness stand. Green stated that he was unable to identify any of the materials named in the search warrant that he was sent to XYZ to obtain. Therefore, he had to take an expert, Keith Marcelius, with him actually to identify and gather the evidence. Strellis came very close to getting the search and all of the evidence made inadmissible in the court because of this. However, Judge Levins stated that since this was a preliminary hearing, and the defendant was not on trial, the search and evidence was admissible.

The next major issue was to show that the program was protected to the degree that it could be identified as a trade secret. The program was stored in the computer in two forms. It was stored in source language form in the language in which the programmer wrote it, and it was stored in relocatable binary form, the code necessary for its execution by the computer. A compiler program was used to automatically translate the source language program to its relocatable binary form. At one point the officers of the court were confused in thinking that the source code was in human readable form, and the relocatable binary version was encrypted to the degree that it was not readable or comprehendible by humans. Through great effort on the part of witnesses it was finally made clear that the relocatable binary form was in fact readable by human beings but would be far more difficult to understand than the source code. In any case, the fact that it was stored in the computer in source code indicated that the program was readily available in a recognizable form to be read and understood.

It was pointed out that ABC has an encryption program available to all users of its services which would provide a high degree of protection for any programs or data stored in the system. However, none of ABC's customers had used the program. Ironically, several days before the theft occurred ABC had started a program of encrypting all of its proprietary data and computer programs, but had not completed the process far enough to have included PLOT/TRANS. Marcelius indicated that it had been an oversight to have kept the PLOT/TRANS program in the computer storage; normally, it was not supposed to be stored in source language form in the computer. The judge pointed out that errors in exposing trade secrets did not constitute precluding material from trade secret status. Therefore, this was not a valid argument that the program was not a trade secret.

The program was being kept secret in a number of ways. First, in advertising and offering the program ABC offered only the service of use of the program and did not offer copies of the program for sale or taking. There would be no sense in offering it for sale or taking because of the special equipment and the change in the computer-operating system needed to make it usable. In order to obtain a copy of the source program, a terminal user would need to have the unlisted telephone number for computer access, a secret site code number, a secret accounting number, and the name of the file in which the program was stored. The name of this file was kept on a confidential basis and used only by ABC employees. Actually, copies of the relocatable binary form of the program were included in larger programs developed at Aerojet General and stored in punch card form there. Fortunately this was not brought out in the hearing. It would have added a great deal more confusion and was not particularly material to the case.

I obtained an independent, expert witness for the district attorney who provided the most significant and interesting information in the hearing. The witness was Dr. Ned Chapin, an independent computer technology consultant in Menlo Park, California. It was Dr. Chapin's role to examine the copy of the program taken from Darm's office and compare it with a listing of the program from ABC to show that the program taken was in fact the ABC PLOT/TRANS program. Dr. Chapin indicated that it was possible for two programmers to write the same program functionally, but in detail the two programs would look quite different.

At this point, Strellis saw some possibilities in this prosecution witness and asked if he might have the witness go into more detail about computer programs stored in commercial computer service company computers. The prosecutor complained and said he was the one paying the witness, not Strellis. Strellis responded by saying that he would pay him. At this point Dr. Chapin became a witness for the defense rather than for the prosecution. The witness went on to say that any computer program stored in a commercially available time-sharing computer system was automatically in the public domain unless a significant number of steps were taken to protect it. In his opinion, not nearly enough steps were taken in this case, and he said that extracting an unprotected program is not taking a trade secret. The judge complained that Dr. Chapin had gone too far out of his area of expertise as an expert witness and questioned whether Dr. Chapin was actually stating an industry standard or his own opinion. The witness backed off and admitted that there is no industrial standard in this area and that this was his own personal opinion. (This concept that anyone through a terminal can fish around in a commercially available time-sharing computer and take whatever he can find, assuming it to be in the public domain, has become known as the Peninsula Ethic. Peninsula refers to the San Francisco Peninsula area where Ned Chapin works and where a considerable amount of time-sharing computer usage goes on.) Chapin went on to describe the many ways in which a program can be protected in a time-sharing computer system.

As the hearing drew to a close, the judge asked the prosecutor why Fred Darm was being prosecuted when apparently he was acting in his capacity as an employee for XYZ. The prosecutor stated that Darm acted of his own accord, and his employer did not explicitly tell him to perform the act. This issue will be covered in more detail in the discussion of the civil case.

Strellis gave a closing summary statement. He said that Darm's program, called WORDPLOT, was an attempt to duplicate the PLOT/TRANS capability. He admitted Darm took a copy of PLOT/TRANS but stated that there was no evidence that Darm used the program. It was analogous to a book in a library. Steps must be taken to protect the program. You can't just hope that it is safe. ABC is a public utility available to any person willing to purchase computer time. The contract that ABC had with Aerojet General placed no restrictions on the use of the PLOT/TRANS program. The advertising indicated no restrictions in the use of the program. There was no advantage for XYZ to take a copy of the program since special equipment would have been needed to use it. XYZ could have written and was in the process of writing a similar program for use by their own hardware. Therefore, the trade secret process was discoverable. He restated the Peninsula Ethic by saying that putting a program in a publicly available computer is a publishing of the work.

The judge pointed out that Marcelius had stated that putting the program in the computer had been a mistake. ABC had used an array of techniques to keep the program secret and was only selling the service of the program and not the program itself. The judge concluded that there was reasonable cause to believe that a crime may have been committed, and he certified the case to the Superior Court for trial.

The civil case trial then came stage center. The trial got under way at the Santa Clara County Courthouse late March 1972 in the courtroom of Judge Edward A. Panelli. The cast of characters was quite different from the criminal hearing. The litigants were ABC, the complainant, and XYZ, Fred Darm, and Jerry York, defendants. There were four teams of lawyers, each one representing the four litigants. Pilsbury, Madison and Sutro fielded Robert Westberg and the principal attorney, George Sears, to present the case for ABC. Wesley Howell from Gibson, Dunn and Crutcher in Los Angeles represented XYZ. Sears and Howell were the two principal lawyers during the trial. The jury panel included a number of computer technologists, but they were soon excused. The jury finally selected was composed of nontechnical people with a high proportion of housewives. The trial was an emotionally charged event. ABC and XYZ could lose millions of dollars.

Sears started it off, very formal in his conservative black suit and white shirt. His greying hair and imposing stature matched his radio announcer voice as he presented his case for ABC. He used an elaborate visual presentation of enlarged pictures, flip charts, and blackboard drawings. The trial was highly frustrating for a technical person to sit through. Although each attorney had several expert witnesses, they limited witnesses' responses to not much more than "yes" or "no." At the same time the attorneys did not seem to me to know enough of the technology to be able to ask questions answerable by "yes/no." At one break in the proceedings, I complained to Robert Westberg, indicating that if the court would give me one hour I could explain the technological basis for the case in a form easily understood by the jury. He looked at me rather blankly and said that he was not really interested in the use of my services. At that point I concluded that none of the attorneys wanted the jury to understand the technology but to understand only parts of the technology that were favorable to their case. It seemed to me that they wanted the jury to be confused and in some respects to have an incorrect knowledge about the technical aspects of the case that were not favorable to their positions. The trial went on endlessly, with the attorneys wrestling with the technical issues and apparently frustrating the witnesses in their attempts to explain the technology.

Sears described ABC as a small service company with annual sales of $1 million. This was compared with the giant XYZ with $125 million per year in sales and assets of $350 million. XYZ admitted the taking of the program, but their point was that this was a minor act that wasn't really wrong and didn't cause any harm. But they also played an aggressive role in the trial because of the cross-complaint they had against ABC, claiming the search and seizure was improper and designed to hurt and harass them. ABC, on the other hand, claimed that only XYZ is the culprit since only XYZ could have benefited from the act.

Howell, representing XYZ, was the opposite of the formal Mr. Sears. He was very loose, relaxed, and folksy. He leaned against the witness stand in his opening statements and started with: "I think you will find this an intriguing case." He attempted to show that PLOT/TRANS was not particularly valuable, and that it was not being kept as a trade secret. He said that any programmer with a year or two of experience could have developed it in about three weeks of effort. He also stated that it is common practice for programmers in both of these competing firms to dip into one another's computers over telephone lines to fish around to see what they can scavenge and to make comparisons of the speed and efficiency of their competitor's services. He stated that an ABC programmer had actually accessed the XYZ computer over the telephone 16 times within the last six months, without XYZ's consent and without any authority in order to gain a competitive advantage. He said he thought that was fair since it was standard practice for both firms to be doing this. It is just like in baseball, where one team tries to steal the other team's signals. He pointed out that the theft did not hurt ABC—they still had and still could use the program. It was only a copy that was taken, and XYZ never used the program and didn't make any money at all as the result of Darm having seen it. "This is a tempest in a teapot."

Darm's attorney added that accessing of computers goes on all the time. He stated that "we have accessed CDC's computers—they know it and don't care." He claimed that Darm used only about 40 lines of the 515 lines of code in the program. He simply used it as a shortcut and maybe saved one to two hours of his time. York's attorney then had to put his two cents' worth in. He stated that the whole case is a situation of giant overreaction. Sears then attempted to show that ABC actually lost business as a result of the incident, indicating that income from General Electric, one of their best customers, went from about $20,000 per month down to $7,000 per month after the publicity over the theft. So many lawyers in one court case can get confusing; to me they all sounded as though they were one-upping each other rather than just representing their clients.

Next, it was Howell's turn, representing XYZ, to refute Sears's arguments. He stated that Sears had mentioned he is a Methodist and against stealing. Howell thought that for a Methodist, Sears sure made some extravagant statements. Howell stated he is a Mormon. How's that for one-upsmanship? He pointed out that ABC's revenues were on a decline over a long period, showing that the specific incident had no effect in this declining trend.

After all of the lawyers had exhausted themselves, the judge gave his instructions to the jury. He defined a trade secret as an invention, formula, or process that gives one an advantage over a competitor. It must not be generally known. A computer program as a trade secret must differ materially from other methods revealed by the prior art. The plaintiff must show he had a significant investment, and that it was taken from him in a wrongful way and taken to gain a competitive advantage. He said if one of the individual people in the case is guilty of damages then his employer is also guilty.

The jury was finally asked to determine the following: Was any part of PLOT/TRANS a trade secret? Was any defendant guilty of unfair competition? Should compensatory damages be awarded to ABC? If so, how much punitive damages should be awarded? Should Fred Darm pay punitive damages? Should Jerry

York pay punitive damages? Was the cross-complaint filed by XYZ valid?

The trial started on August 15, 1972. Eleven days later on Friday, August 25, it ended. The jury decided in favor of the plaintiff, ABC. PLOT/TRANS was a trade secret. XYZ was guilty of unfair competition. ABC was awarded compensatory damages of $250,000. ABC was awarded $50,000 in punitive damages against XYZ. Punitive damages of $250 were awarded against Fred Darm and also against Jerry York. The cross-complaint filed by XYZ was ruled not valid. XYZ filed an appeal. At the time of this writing there had not yet been any resolution of the appeal.

The president of ABC was asked if he was pleased with the verdict. He said he felt the case was important and worth the effort. This was the first time a program had been identified as a trade secret. He said the jury, by its verdict, indicated a strong position against indiscriminate thieving of programs from another organization's computer.

On Friday, November 3, Fred Darm pleaded guilty to one count of theft of a trade secret. The prosecuting attorney claimed that he would do his best to get Fred Darm into a prison cell as an example that employees can be punished for illegal acts performed at the direction of their employers. He was only partially successful in this. With no need for a trial, Darm was sentenced on December 11, 1972, to three years probation and a $5,000 penalty. Unfortunately, the criminal case sets a very weak precedent since Darm pleaded guilty in a lower court and no contesting of the issues took place. Precedents established by the civil case remain to be determined, depending upon the results of the appeal.

Judge John P. Sparrow, who passed sentence in the criminal case, made some interesting statements in his memorandum of decision. He cited the pertinent parts of the theft of a trade secret Penal Code Section 499C: "Every person is guilty of theft who with intent to deprive or withhold from the owner, thereof, the control of a trade secret . . . does any of the following: (1) Steals, takes or carries away any article representing a trade secret. . . . (3) Having unlawfully obtained access to the article without authority makes or causes to be made a copy of any article representing a trade secret." He pointed out that an article must be something tangible even though the trade secret the article represents may itself be intangible. Darm did not carry any tangible thing representing ABC's PLOT/TRANS program from the ABC computer to the XYZ computer (*sic*—the judge confused terminal with computer) unless the impulses which the defendant allegedly caused to be transmitted over the telephone wire could be said to be tangible. It was the opinion of the court that such impulses are not tangible and hence do not constitute an article. Therefore, telephonic impulses would not constitute an article representing a trade secret. However, the preliminary transcript did establish that Darm made a copy of the PLOT/TRANS program without the authority of ABC and thereafter carried that copy from his terminal to his office at XYZ, thus providing the transportation required under the 499C law. In any event, a violation of Section 499C was established when the defendant made a copy of the PLOT/TRANS program irrespective of its transportation.

The judge went on to state that the program was still in a private library file within the ABC computer and not in a public library, and access was restricted to customers authorized by ABC. Access required the customer to have an unlisted telephone number, the site number, and the billing number. Anyone else gaining this access to the computer would be doing so unlawfully and without ABC's authorization. The fact that ABC was negligent in leaving the source code of PLOT/TRANS in the computer storage was not at issue. The judge pointed out: "To adopt the defendant's arguments, that what he did was not a crime, would mean that because from the standpoint of maximum security a person might place his jewelry in a safe, it could never be the subject of a theft if he places it in a less secure location."

The evidence at the preliminary hearing established probable cause to believe that: (1) the PLOT/TRANS program is secret in that ABC took measures to prevent it from becoming available to persons other than those selected by ABC to have access for the limited purpose of utilizing the service it provided (no one, not even a customer, was authorized by ABC to access and copy the program itself); (2) the PLOT/TRANS program was not generally available to the public; (3) use by ABC of the PLOT/TRANS program gave the latter an advantage over competitors, including XYZ, who did not know of or use the program (indeed the evidence establishes that no competitor of ABC at the time of the alleged theft on January 19, 1971, even had the capability of providing a remote plotting service because none had the special equipment that ABC had); (4) defendant Darm used the unlisted telephone number of the ABC computer together with the Bolts and Washers Company site and billing numbers to access the ABC computer from the XYZ office and made computer printout copies of the PLOT/TRANS program through the XYZ computer (sic); (5) that defendant carried the printout copy of the trade secret from the XYZ terminal to his office, thus providing the transportation required under the law.

At one point in the criminal proceedings Strellis filed a demurrer and motion to dismiss on the basis that Section 499C was not applicable in this case. The judge stated that a wrongful appropriation of any trade secret or article representing it can be properly charged, either as a theft of property under Section 487 of the Penal Code providing the requisite value and intent elements are established, or as a violation of Section 499C of the Penal Code which neither requires proof of value nor of an intent permanently to deprive. Accordingly, since the elements of the crime set forth under each of these codes are not identical, it is proper to charge both violations in a single case. The record establishes that ABC took measures to prevent the program from becoming available to other than those selected by the owner to have access for limited purposes. The program is therefore presumed to be secret under the definition of trade secrets contained in Section 499C. The fact that the owner might have taken additional measures to make the program more secure, such as by scrambling or adopting one of the number of other methods testified to by Dr. Chapin, is immaterial.

This case, weak precedent notwithstanding, represents an important event in the history of the development, use, and ownership of computer programs.

12 | TROJAN HORSES, TIME BOMBS, ROUND DOWNS, AND THE SYSTEM HACKER

The Trojans of ancient legend had nothing on our modern systems hackers. Every university has its systems hackers, students so entranced and challenged with the campus computer systems that they forgo food, sleep, shaving, and haircuts to poke about the complex innards of time-sharing systems. It's not that they work like Trojans; it's what they devised, without any idea that it had been thought of millennia before in the Trojan wars. Dan Edwards in the U.S. Department of Defense and a leading computer security expert shows again that there is nothing new under the sun by naming this type of attack.

It is important to understand some of the complexity of a computer-operating system to really appreciate a Trojan horse attack on a computer. A large computer system requires a set of resident programs in its storage devices that are enabled to execute all system functions on a privileged basis. They provide semi-automatic, efficient operation of the computer, with minimal human intervention for rapid input, scheduling, authorizing, signaling, trapping, connecting, disconnecting, journaling, accounting, and outputting. These programs, collectively called the operating system, consist of up to a million computer instructions requiring as many as 500 man-years of design and programming effort in some cases. A large operating system is the most complex set of human thought processes ever converted into an automated process. It is a man-made process close in complexity to the human body.

This is the environment that so delights the system hacker as he goes about his mischief of penetrating and compromising the computer in new, increasingly cunning and challenging ways. There is no known, practical way to stop him or prove that he hasn't already attacked the computer system. Existing large computer systems are not predictable, nor can they be proved correct. Because of their great complexity they cannot be fully tested; but more about this later.

A simplified example of how a Trojan horse works is presented below. Instructions to the computer and their locations in computer storage are listed on the left. On the right are explanations of what the computer does when directed to execute the instructions in sequence by location number. The process can be easily understood by playing the role of the computer and seeing what happens as each instruction is carried out. Think of the storage locations as mailbox addresses and the instructions as the contents of the mailboxes.

It can be seen that when the utility program (Trojan horse)—a basic program available for all computer users—is executed in the special privilege mode by a privileged user, it executes the instructions I previously secretly placed there when I created the program. Privileged mode allows access to all system commands and sections of storage. The result of this is that the legitimate privileged user has unknowingly authorized me—an unauthorized user of privileged instructions—to be a privileged user too because now, each time I log on to the computer at a terminal, the computer makes me—as identified by my password—a privileged user.

Do not be deceived by the simplicity of this example. The programs in the example would contain thousands or at least hundreds of instructions. Each line in the example would trans-

THE TROJAN HORSE TECHNIQUE
Objective: To obtain the special privilege level for my password.

Programs in Computer Storage	What the Computer Does
Utility Program for all users	Computer executes each instruction in sequence by location number.

Location in storage	Contents of Storage	
1248 1249 . . . 1631	(Normal instructions)	Computer executes utility function for any user, privileged or nonprivileged.
1632	Attempt privileged instruction.	Computer allows execution only if in privileged mode.
1633	If it was executed, go to 1634, otherwise go to 1637.	
1634	Insert the following instruction: "assign highest privilege level to my password," into system LOGON program at location 152	LOGON program instructions are moved down starting with contents of 152 and new instruction is inserted.
1635	Insert: "Go to 1637," at 1632	"Attempt privileged instruction" in location 1632 replaced with "Go to 1637."
1636	Erase contents of 1633 through 1636	Instructions replaced with blanks.
1637 1638 . . .	(Normal instructions)	Computer continues to execute normal utility instructions.

System LOGON Program (before Utility Program is executed)

Location in storage	Contents of Storage	
102 . . . 151	(Normal instructions)	Computer accepts new user at a terminal according to his password.
152	(Normal instruction)	Normal instruction is executed.
153 . . .	(Normal instructions)	Computer continues to execute normal LOGON instructions.

THE TROJAN HORSE TECHNIQUE (cont.)

Programs in Computer Storage   *What the Computer Does*
Utility Program (after privileged execution)

Location in storage   *Contents of Storage*

1248	
1249	
.	(Normal instructions)
.	
1631	
1632	Go to 1637
1633	
.	Blanks (no instructions)
1636	
1637	
1638	(Normal instructions)

1632 → Execute the instruction at location 1637 next.

System LOGON Program (after Utility Program is executed in privileged mode)

Location in storage   *Contents of Storage*

102	
.	(Normal instructions)
151	
152	Assign highest privilege level to my password
153	
.	(Normal instructions all moved down by one location)

late into an average of approximately five instructions in the form recognized for execution by the computer. The secret code buried in the Trojan horse utility program can be spread out among normal instructions to hide them. Finally, the total Trojan horse could consist of several or many chained programs, each transferring control to the next to perform each function.

One of the few attacks of this kind ever discovered happened at a university computer center. A time-sharing service is provided for hundreds of students, professors, and researchers through on-line terminals connected by telephone circuits. One day a systems programmer was tracking down a software bug after a system failure had occurred. He obtained a printed image of the contents of the part of storage containing the operating system programs. Some clues from the way the system failed led him to search several of the 400 pages. Buried in the middle of a program that just happened to be familiar to him was some strange code he did not recognize. Curiosity overtook his interest in bug chasing. He had never seen such a strange sequence of computer instructions in this part of the system. A closer look involving several hours of study—not an uncommon effort for system maintenance programmers—revealed its purpose. "He's at it again and this time succeeded," he thought as he headed for the office of the operations supervisor with his news.

The strange code revealed that the system would allow a terminal at one of the colleges served by the center to be the ultimate and unquestioned ruler of the system. Whatever instructions came from this terminal, it shall be done! A sufficiently knowledgeable expert at that terminal could have the complete content and resources of the system at his beck and call. The president's, vice president's, dean's, and other executives' salaries? Just type: "PRINT EXEC SLRY," and out they come. Credit for 100 hours of computer usage? That too can be arranged. Printing the most secret data, controlling any other users' terminals, or stopping the system at will could all be achieved through that marvelous bit of program, hidden until its accidental discovery.

How long had it been there? What had its owner been doing with it? How did it get there? Answers to these questions came as unexpectedly as the system penetration itself. Only one system hacker was known at the college, a graduate student there. All files of data stored in the system assigned to the student were printed. Among them was the text of a full confession and disclosure of the method used.

Reconstruction of this episode resulted in the discovery of a brilliant Trojan horse attack. About a year before its discovery the hacker wrote a useful utility program for manipulating data on magnetic tapes. Within this otherwise innocuous program he inserted some very special instructions. The first few were executed each time the program was run. They tested the privilege level at which the program was being run by requesting a function in the system to be used by only the highest privilege-level program in the system. If refused access to the function, the utility program went on about its business. If it was ever run at the highest privilege level, more of the secret instructions would be executed to do some strange and wonderful things.

First, a new, larger secret program was copied from the hacker's private data files into the system's primary storage. Next, control of the computer was passed from the utility program to the newly introduced program. When that program executed, it read the permanent program (the one discovered by the system programmer) from the hacker's file into its resident location in the operating system. Then it removed all evidence of the attack by erasing the special instructions in the utility program in storage and in its master copy on the program library tape. This was finished off by erasing itself and returning control to the utility program to continue its magnetic tape manipulation duties. The Trojan horse had been rolled into the fortified city and fully accepted. In the unsuspecting environment a trapdoor in its belly opened, and out popped the soldiers, who removed all evidence of their trapdoor arrival and hid among the populace ready at a moment's notice on signal from their leader to take over the city.

The system hacker got his utility program placed on the program library tape for all the time-sharing system customers to use, and the hacker was thanked for his generosity in offering it.

It took almost six months before a computer operator used it at the system's highest privilege level. From then on, the system hacker was in the driver's seat. It took another six months before the system maintenance programmer accidentally discovered him.

One of the frustrations a system hacker faces is that if he is to use his successful system compromise to advantage, he can't tell anyone about his stupendous feat because it would end his game. However, in this case apparently the hacker had that problem solved too. He was all ready to rig a time bomb when he was discovered. On some future date at a preselected time of day the system would be triggered to stop all routine activity, and simultaneously at all 100 terminals the startling announcement of the system compromise would start printing out. The complete description of the Trojan horse technique (found in the hacker's data file) would be printed 100 times in all its glory, followed by the name of its genius inventor, followed by the worst failure in the system's history. Of course, this would occur long after he had received his Ph.D. and left the university, out of reach of those who could cause him problems.

The university computing center did not want any more Trojan horses; but lots of customers, some as intrigued with system hacking as the graduate, knew the successful penetration method. The hole had to be plugged. The solution was to control the programs allowed to execute at the operating system privilege level. This was done by having the operating system check each program's identification number for a special imbedded code before passing control to it. Those programs allowed privileged execution are checked very carefully. Another hole plugged, but who will find the next one and when? Every large computer operating system is a Swiss cheese. We've got to design and build them without holes, but we are still only starting to learn how to do that.

A well-known method to perpetrate financial fraud in a computer has been described in numerous publications. One of the earliest reportings was on the front page of the *Wall Street Journal* in 1968. Several reported cases involving this method have been recorded, but none have been verified. Most of these cases probably lie in the realm of myth and apocryphal storytelling, but it is worth describing here to complete the reader's education, and besides, from myths great truths may grow.

The "round down fraud" requires a computer system application where large numbers of financial accounts are processed. The processing must involve the multiplication of dollar amounts by numbers—such as in interest rate calculations. This arithmetic results in products that contain fractions of the smallest denomination of currency, such as the cent in the United States.

For example, a savings account in a bank may have a balance of $15.86. The interest rate of 2.6 percent is to be applied, resulting in adding $0.41236 ($15.86 × .026) to the balance for a new balance of $16.27236. However, since the balance is to be retained only to the nearest cent, it is rounded down to $16.27, leaving $0.00236. What is to be done with this remainder? The interest calculation for the next account in sequence might be the following: $425.34 × .026 = $11.05884. This would result in a new balance of $436.39884 that must be rounded, this time up to $436.40, leaving a deficit or negative remainder of $0.00116, usually placed in parenthesis to show its negative value ($0.00116).

The net effect of rounding in both these accounts, rounding down to the calculated cent in the first and adding 1 cent in the second, leaves both accounts accurate to the nearest cent and a remainder of $0.0012 ($0.00236 − $0.00116) which is then carried to the next account calculation, and so on. As the calculations continue, if the running or accumulating remainder goes above 1 cent, positive or negative, the last account is adjusted to return the remainder to an amount less than 1 cent. This results in a few accounts receiving 1 cent more or less than the correct rounded values, but the totals for all accounts remain in balance.

This is where the creative computer programmer can engage in some trickery to accumulate for himself a fancy bit of change and still show a balanced set of accounts that defies discovery by the auditor. He merely changes the rules slightly in the program performing this operation by accumulating the round down remainders in his own account rather than distributing them to the other accounts as they build up.

An example using a larger number of accounts shows how this is done. First, if rounded down correctly, it would look like this:

Old Balance	New Balance	Rounded New Balance	Remainder	Accumulating Remainder
$ 15.86	$ 16.27236	$ 16.27	$ 0.00236	$ 0.00236
425.34	436.39884	436.40	(0.00116)	0.00120
221.75	227.51550	227.52	(0.00450)	(0.00330)
18.68	19.16568	19.17	(0.00432)	(0.00762)
* 564.44	579.11544	~~579.12~~	(0.00456)	(0.01218)
		579.11		(0.00218)
61.31	62.90406	62.90	0.00406	0.00188
101.32	103.95432	103.95	0.00432	0.00620
* 77.11	79.11486	~~79.11~~	0.00486	0.01106
		79.12		0.00106
457.12	469.00512	469.01	(0.00488)	(0.00382)
111.35	114.24510	114.25	(0.00490)	(0.00872)
* 446.36	457.96536	~~457.97~~	(0.00464)	(0.01336)
		457.96		(0.00336)
88.68	90.98568	90.99	(0.00432)	(0.00768)
* 14.44	14.81544	~~14.82~~	(0.00456)	(0.01224)
		14.81		(0.00224)
83.27	85.43502	85.44	(0.00498)	(0.00722)
127.49	130.80474	130.80	0.00474	(0.00248)
331.32	339.93432	339.93	0.00432	0.00184
37.11	38.07486	38.07	0.00486	0.00670
* 111.31	114.20406	~~114.20~~	0.00406	0.01076
		114.21		0.00076
$3,294.26	Total	$3,379.91		

The interest rate applied to the total of all accounts, $3,294.26, results in a new total balance of $3,379.91 ($3,294.26 × 1.026) and a remainder of $0.00076 when the new total balance is rounded. This is calculated by the program as verification that the arithmetic performed account by account is correct. However, note that several accounts have 1 cent more or less than they should (those marked with an asterisk).

Now suppose the programmer writes the program to accumulate the round down amounts into his own account, the last account in the list. The calculations will look like this:

Old Balance	New Balance	Rounded New Balance	Remainder	Accumulating Remainder	Programmer's Remainder
$ 15.86	$ 16.27236	$ 16.27	$ 0.00236	$ 0.00000	$0.00236
425.34	436.39884	436.40	(0.00116)	(0.00116)	0.00236
221.75	227.51550	227.52	(0.00450)	(0.00566)	0.00236
18.68	19.16568	19.17	(0.00432)	(0.00998)	0.00236
* 564.44	579.11544	579.12	(0.00456)	(0.01454)	0.00236
		579.11		(0.00454)	
61.31	62.90406	62.90	0.00406	(0.00454)	0.00642
101.32	103.95432	103.95	0.00432	(0.00454)	0.01074
77.11	79.11486	79.11	0.00486	(0.00454)	0.01560
457.12	469.00512	469.01	(0.00488)	(0.00942)	0.01560
* 111.35	114.24510	114.25	(0.00490)	(0.01432)	0.01560
		114.24		(0.00432)	
446.36	457.96536	457.97	(0.00464)	(0.00896)	0.01560
* 88.68	90.98568	90.99	(0.00432)	(0.01328)	0.01560
		90.98		(0.00328)	
14.44	14.81544	14.82	(0.00456)	(0.00784)	0.01560
* 83.27	85.43502	85.44	(0.00498)	(0.01282)	0.01560
		85.43		(0.00282)	
127.49	130.80474	130.80	0.00474	(0.00282)	0.02034
331.32	339.93432	339.93	0.00432	(0.00282)	0.02466
37.11	38.07486	38.07	0.00486	(0.00282)	0.02952
* 111.31	114.20406	114.20	0.00406	(0.00282)	0.03358
		114.23		0.00076	0.00000
$3,294.26	Total	$3,379.91			

The totals are the same as before and the verification shows no hanky-panky. However, now the new balances of some accounts are 1 cent less, but none are 1 cent more as in the previous example. Those extra cents have been accumulated and all added to the programmer's account (the last account in the list) rather than to the accounts where the adjusted remainder exceeded 1 cent.

It can be seen that if there were 180,000 accounts instead of the 18 accounts in this example the programmer could have made a tidy profit of $300 ($0.03 × 10,000). This could result in a significant fraud over several years.

There are only two ways that the auditor might discover this fraud. He could check the instructions in the program, or he could recalculate the interest for the programmer's account after the program had been executed by the computer. A clever programmer could easily disguise the instructions causing the fraudulent calculations in the program in a number of ways. However, this would probably not be necessary since an auditor or anybody else would probably not wade through a program step by step as long as use of the program showed no irregularities.

This program method would show no irregularities unless the programmer's account were audited. It is unlikely that his account would be audited, one account among 180,000. Besides, the programmer could have opened the account using a fictitious name or the name of an accomplice. He could also occasionally change to other accounts to reduce further the possibility of detection.

Experienced accountants and auditors indicate that the round down fraud technique has been known for many years, even before the use of computers. They say that a good auditor will look for this type of fraud by checking for deviations from the standard accounting method for rounding calculations. But to what extent is this done in the complex environment of computer technology? How many auditors know how to read complex programs or take the great amount of time needed to do it? How many round down frauds are currently under way in the tens of thousands of computer systems? How many programmers have retired to a life of leisure as their programs, long trusted and forgotten, continue to pump the pennies into their accounts at nearly the speed of light?

13 | EQUITY FUNDING— A COMPUTER FRAUD?

The Equity Funding Corporation of America (EFCA) fraud is the largest single company fraud that is known. The significance of this $2 billion fraud that was discovered in 1973 in Los Angeles, California, is overwhelming. *Fortune* magazine for August 1973 stated that the Equity Funding case resulted in the second largest bankruptcy under the United States Bankruptcy Code, Chapter X, in history. (The Associated Gas and Electric bankruptcy in the 1940s was larger.) The fraud was so large and complex that two books, a three-volume Trustee's Bankruptcy Report, and hundreds of magazine and newspaper articles have failed to encompass all of the issues and aspects. Twenty-two people have been convicted of federal charges. Over 50 major suits are in the courts, and litigation is expected to continue for another 10 years. We can learn a great deal regarding the safe use of computers by studying this case. Many of the same conditions found continue to exist in numerous other companies. Our purpose in studying this case is to determine how to avoid use of computers in future frauds.

For one thing, we must know the nature of the fraud and put to bed the dispute as to whether it constitutes a computer fraud. In the Bankruptcy Report Robert M. Loeffler, the Trustee, stated: "Much of the literature seems to characterize the fraud as the brilliant brain-child of 'with it' business and computer wizards . . . the impression given is that it was carefully planned and executed with a high level precision and sophistication which baffled the world until it was finally discovered in April 1973. Nothing could be farther from the truth than this misconception. None of the top management had any business experience outside of sales before they started the company. With a few exceptions top executives tended to be either lower level accountants or lawyers, none of whom had significant business experience prior to the time they were put in charge of EFCA.

"Least of all was this a modern 'computer' fraud. The computer did not even contain complete records for EFCA's legitimate business—let alone the fraud. For example, the critical records for the Company's legitimate funding business were kept on microfiche, and were dealt with entirely by hand. The only record for funding business kept on the computer was an inventory of funding accounts. Entries to book fictitious income were made by manual additions to the books and records in total disregard of the Company's computer printouts. . . . Hence, while the computer may have generated a paper 'screen' for some aspects of the fraud, in fact the role it played was no bigger and more complicated than that played by the Company's adding machines."

Gleeson Payne, the California state insurance commissioner, stated: "This massive fraud was peculiarly a crime of the computer. The computer was the key to the fraud. I would certainly call it a computer fraud. Under the old, hard copy methods of keeping insurance records, you sure as hell couldn't build up bogus policies in this kind of volume or in this kind of time. The insurance industry assumed computers were always accurate; computer fraud wasn't expected. Equity was the most advanced in use of computers. Few file cabinets or physical records were found. The computer was the key to the fraud. Auditors have computer programs, but Equity had a secret code which made the computer reveal only real insurance policies. We had a situation in which technology surprised and surpassed our examination system. We do not have a program to audit computers, nor do departments in other states. It is something that must be developed. Our examiners are not equipped to check out a computer run and find out if it is authentic."

Payne's position was supported by the media, including *Newsweek* magazine for April 23, 1973: "The Equity Funding affair will have a greater impact on the business world than the fraud itself. Equity Funding executives used company computers as a key tool in the fraud—probably on a grander scale than ever before—and neither standard auditing practices nor Wall Street analysis was sophisticated enough to detect it."

Mr. Loeffler states that it was not a brilliantly conceived computer fraud. Mr. Payne and the media say that it was. Who is right? A summary of the case with emphasis on the computer's role may shed some light on this issue. This summary is based primarily on the official Trustee's Bankruptcy Report; on my personal interviews with people who were involved in the fraud; on a book titled *The Impossible Dream. The Equity Funding Story: The Fraud of the Century*, by Ronald L. Soble and Robert E. Dallos, the most comprehensive study that has been written on this case; on *The Great Wall Street Scandal* by Raymond L. Dirks and Leonard Gross; and finally on the media, including newspapers and trade and general magazines.

The EFCA funding business consisted of four basic activities: the sale of programs to the general public, the financing of the operations, the purchase of mutual fund shares, and the issuing of insurance. These activities were conducted in three principal entities: Equity Funding Corporation CAL, Equity Funding Securities Corporation, and Equity Funding Life Insurance Company.

The fraud started in 1964 with EFCA's first public stock offering; it lasted for approximately 10 years until it was brought to the public's attention in April 1973. With the development of a public market for the stock, the company's earnings became a subject of intense concern to the handful of executives who until 1964 were its only shareholders. A good earnings record would increase the value of the stock and thereby enrich the conspirators, who held large amounts of stock and who received more through the years as bonuses. Furthermore, inflated reported earnings and assets made it possible for EFCA to acquire other companies in exchange for its stock and to borrow money with which to make other acquisitions and finance the company's operations which were losing huge amounts each year. Based upon the available evidence, it appears that these factors motivated the fraud. EFCA was eventually composed of over 100 subsidiary organizations.

EFCA grew from the temporary amalgam of two small securities and insurance marketing organizations. In the late 1950s, Gordon C. McCormick was developing and selling his own funding program. Stanley Goldblum, to become the president of EFCA, was running a small insurance agency. In 1959, they combined their organizations and began to make plans for an expansion of funding program sales. Eventually, four men each owned one-fourth of the company: Goldblum, Raymond Platt, Eugene Cuthbertson, and Michael Riordan. Platt and Cuthbertson later left the company, selling most of their stock. Riordan, as executive vice president and chairman of the board, concentrated his efforts on establishing the sales force and developing new sales programs and products. Riordan was often described as the outside man, Goldblum the inside man.

Riordan was killed by a mudslide in his home in January 1969. Stanley Goldblum then became the sole chief executive of EFCA. He installed a management team that was to govern EFCA until disclosure of the fraud. The two executives under Goldblum who were closest to him and who together with Goldblum dominated most activities of the company were Samuel Lowell, who joined EFCA as controller in May 1969, and Fred Levin, who came to EFCA in 1967 from a position in a life insurance company acquired by EFCA. Lowell became executive vice president, Corporate Operations and Finance, and was responsible for all accounting and financial functions. Levin was the executive vice president, Insurance Operations and Marketing. Both were directors of EFCA as well.

The monstrous fraud these young men (average age thirty-three) perpetrated was essentially a securities fraud. Their purpose was to make EFCA the largest, fastest growing, most successful financial institution in the world and in the process thereby to gain fame and fortune for themselves. Personal theft and embezzlement seem to have played a minor part in the fraud. ". . . The fraud was relatively unsophisticated in both design and execution . . . the fraud was not the brainchild of computer age financial wizards; it was [initially] to a great extent simply a pencil fraud, perpetrated by means of bogus manual accounting entries, with virtually no support for those entries in many cases. That the fraud persisted undetected for so long is attributable to the audacity and luck of the perpetrators and, just as importantly, to the glaring failure," according to Robert Loeffler, "of the Company's auditors to perform properly the obligations which they had undertaken."

It was carried out principally by inflating the company's reported earnings. Most of the real income during the early period of the company's history derived from commissions earned on sales of Equity Funding Programs, a combination of mutual fund shares and life insurance policies. The Equity Funding Program was based on a British Life Funding concept. This concept involves customers borrowing on mutual fund shares to purchase life insurance, in the hope that the income on and appreciation of the mutual fund shares will exceed the interest cost of the borrowing and pay for at least a portion of the insurance premiums.

The participant entered the Equity Funding Program over a 10-year period. He paid cash for the mutual fund shares. EFCA paid his life insurance premiums, recording the payment as a loan to the participant and retaining the mutual fund shares as collateral to secure the loan. In essence, the equity in the participant's mutual fund investment was used to finance his purchase of an insurance policy; hence the package was an Equity Funding Program, and the loan itself was called a funded loan. Upon termination of the program, the participant repaid his loan by direct cash payment or by application of the proceeds from the sale of a sufficient number of his mutual funds shares. If the participant's mutual funds shares had increased as hoped, the appreciation would have ideally paid for the policy entirely. The long-term success of the concept depended on steady increases in the value of the mutual funds shares, which in turn required a generally rising stock market. Therein lies the rub! The stock market didn't rise.

The funded life insurance program was not new; it was a refinement of a financial practice known as leverage which is used by most financial institutions and many major investors. This uses an asset to borrow money to purchase additional assets in the expectation that the earnings and growth of the assets will be greater than the interest cost. A participant who purchased $250 worth of mutual funds could get a $100 loan from EFCA to pay a $100 premium on a life insurance policy. The following year, when his premium fell due again, he would purchase another $250 worth of mutual funds and get another $100 loan for the insurance premium. This would go on for 10 years, at which point the policy holder would sell off enough of his mutual fund holdings to liquidate his debt, including interest to the company. By this time he hopefully would have a tidy amount left in fund shares and cash value in his policy as well. The loans mutual fund shareholders took to pay for these policies funded by EFCA—the funded loans receivable—amounted to a $117 million asset as of December 31, 1972.

EFCA sold other companies' insurance and other companies' mutual funds and received commissions for this sales effort. After 1969, most of the programs sold utilized EFCA's proprietary products, principally EFLIC insurance policies and mutual fund shares issued by Equity Growth Fund, Inc. The program was a unique sales tool to induce the combined sale of insurance and mutual funds. The amount of commission earned in connection with these sales was inflated in the companies' financial statements. Moreover, the sales of the programs provided EFCA with larger commissions in proportion to the participants' cash investment. EFCA received a commission not only on the cash the participant paid for his mutual fund share but also on the sum he borrowed to pay life insurance premiums. If, for example, the participant paid $1,000 for mutual fund shares and borrowed $400 against them to pay the life insurance premium, EFCA would receive a commission of one kind or another on the entire

$1,400. EFCA's top management had been extremely sales-oriented. The funding programs were designed with an overemphasis on sales appeal to the detriment of their profitability. Too little attention was given to all of the administrative details and the procedures necessary to efficiently service products and services added to the line.

This was the first phase of the fraud, identified as the "inflated earnings phase," and it exceeded $85 million over the years. It required only manual entries in the company's books; no effort was made to provide underlying documentation to back up the entries. This worked well until 1967. However, each dollar of bogus commission income resulted in a dollar increase in the funded loans receivable, representing the amounts supposedly borrowed by customers in the funded program and ultimately due for repayment to the company after the 10-year period. It became more and more difficult to support the excessive assets that were not to be realized for some time from this activity. Therefore, the funding fraud made EFCA appear to be more profitable than it really was and made it appear to hold larger assets than it really held, but it did not supply any cash to the company. After 1967 the cash needs became severe, mostly because of continued operating losses.

The fraud could have been exposed in 1967. According to an Equity Funding prospectus of May 1967, the company sold $226.3 million face amount of life insurance, the greater part written by Pennsylvania Life Insurance Company. Pennsylvania Life's prospectus, one month later, stated that it had underwritten only $58.6 million of policies for Equity Funding.

The next phase of the fraud is known as the "foreign phase," lasting from 1968 to 1970. This period involved several frauds, including borrowing funds without recording the amounts borrowed as liabilities on the company's books. This was done simply by not recording the sources of the funds at all, and also by incredibly complicated bogus transactions which went through many foreign subsidiaries. The conspirators referred to funds brought into the company in this manner as free credits that were applied to reduce the funded loans asset as though Equity Funding Program participants had retired their loans by cash payments.

During this phase EFCA formed Equity Funding Capital Corporation NV, a Netherlands Antilles Corporation. It also acquired Bishop's Bank and Trust Company, Ltd., a Bahamian merchant bank; an unsuccessful offshore mutual fund; the operation of a spaghetti factory in Italy; and a joint venture to develop a convention center in Senegal. EFCA was involved in overseas oil concessions in Ethiopia, Israel, and Ecuador.

In the United States acquisition was keeping pace. Presidential Life Insurance Company of America was acquired and became Equity Funding Life Insurance Company. Crown Savings and Loan Association and Liberty Savings and Loan Association were acquired and combined. An investment adviser and distributor of Republic Technology Fund, Inc., became Equity Progress Fund. Investors Planning Corporation of America was acquired. Ankony Farms, a cattle-breeding operation, was acquired. Bundy Development Corporation became Equity Funding Development Corporation, a real estate firm. Independent Securities Corporation, a sales organization, was acquired, and three more insurance companies: Bankers National Life, Palisades Life (a subsidiary of Bankers National Life), and Northern Life Insurance Company. Many of the subsidiaries were audited by different public accounting firms. This made it simple to transfer assets and liabilities from one subsidiary to another, with each transfer enhancing the total assets; but even these schemes proved insufficient.

This resulted in a third phase of the fraud, called the "insurance phase" in the Bankruptcy Report. The overstatements of growth had inflated EFCA's stock. As a result, EFCA was transformed from a simple marketing organization into a life insurance-based conglomerate. The center for this phase of the fraud was the Equity Funding Life Insurance Company (EFLIC), and it was the phase in which computers came into use. This insurance business involved the resale of insurance policies to other insurance companies.

The insurance fraud evolved in stages. To produce more insurance policies for resale, the company issued what it termed a special class of insurance, consisting of policies issued to its agents and employees on which it paid all or part of the first-year premium. The production of purely bogus policies followed soon after. These policies were reinsured with Pennsylvania Life Insurance Company (PLC), but the nature of the business was not disclosed to PLC. Insurance companies legitimately raised cash by selling blocks of new insurance to other companies—the reinsurers or coinsurers which have enough cash but want more insurance in force. The practice of coinsurance constitutes in effect the sale of a life insurance policy by the issuing company to another company called the coinsurer. The issuing company continues to service the policy and to collect premiums and transmit the appropriate portions of them to the coinsurer. Insurance companies operate among themselves on a high degree of trust. A reinsurance sale did not involve physically transferring policies. Often just merely a letter was sent to the reinsurance company identifying the blocks of policies sold by serial number.

EFLIC quickly sold its policies to the coinsurer in the year in which they were issued. Upon the sale, the coinsurer would pay to EFLIC a sum equal to 180 to 190 percent of the first-year premiums. Since EFLIC was required to pass the first-year premiums on to the coinsurer, it netted the remaining 80 to 90 percent. This high resale price took into account heavy first-year commissions which EFLIC paid its salesmen and, of course, gave EFLIC a nice first-year profit. In subsequent years EFLIC was required to pay to the coinsurer 90 percent of the renewal premiums, the remainder being retained to compensate EFLIC for servicing the policy. This payment of renewal premiums was to become a total loss to EFLIC in the case of bogus policies, since no premiums were received by it from policyholders.

In most cases EFLIC sold only 90 percent of the policies to the coinsurers, so the price that it received from the coinsurers in the first year and the premiums payable to the coinsurers in subsequent years were correspondingly reduced. Coinsurance results in the recognition by the issuing company—in this case, EFLIC—of all future underwriting profits on a discounted basis in the year of coinsurance. A company which regularly coinsures a substantial portion of its business must sell increasing total amounts of insurance each year in order to show continued growth in reported earnings because it cannot build on any significant revenues attributable to policies it has sold in past years.

In the next stage, in 1969, to help meet its reinsurance commitments and production goals, EFLIC posted insurance policies on the company's books which was only pending business, that is, insurance which had been applied for but not yet approved by the underwriting department. The company then ran into difficulty with PLC because of the high lapse rates on the special class business. To avoid this, the company had to pay renewal premiums on that part of the pending business which never became effective.

In the third stage, the conspirators created wholly fictitious insurance, starting in 1970 in order to generate a growing need for cash to cover the fraudulent policies already in existence; but the insurance phase of the fraud created new cash flow problems. Although significant cash payments were received from the reinsurers at the time of the sale of the policies or the reinsurance of the policies, EFLIC was required to forward to the reinsurers the renewal premiums. The conspirators tried to meet this cash need by reinsuring more bogus policies, but this only made next year's cash flow problem worse. In 1972 EFLIC had a negative cash flow of $1.7 million in connection with its bogus reinsurance operation.

Therefore, although EFLIC inflated its profits by creating and coinsuring bogus insurance, it had to increase vastly its real sales of new policies, which it did not do, or create even more bogus policies with every passing year in order to record increasing earnings. Furthermore, although it profited from the coinsurance of bogus policies in the year in which they were sold, the required payments to the coinsurer on account of renewal premiums in subsequent years were total losses, yet persistency guarantees in the coinsurance treaties left EFLIC no alternative but to pay them. EFLIC guaranteed its reinsurers that no more than 15 percent of its policies would lapse in their second year. To generate the cash needed to pay these amounts, even more bogus policies had to be created and sold. Thus, as a pyramid scheme, once EFLIC began to create and coinsure bogus insurance policies, the size of the manipulations had to increase geometrically to show continued growth.

Again, the purpose and effect of these various devices was to inflate EFCA's earnings and assets so as to support EFCA's borrowings, maintain its image as a growth company, and sustain the price of its stock—the key to its expansion plans and compensation structure. The fraud fed on itself, requiring ever greater exaggerations in order to cover prior fraudulent transactions.

EFCA continued to move assets and liabilities back and forth among the subsidiaries to deceive the auditors. The EFCA books showed money owed to it by a subsidiary, but the subsidiary didn't show corresponding debt, and vice versa. EFCA owed EFLIC $16 million in premiums supposedly paid on phony policies. EFCA paid it from a December 1971 public stock offering, but EFCA's books recorded the transfer as an investment in commercial paper in the form of falsified bank documents to show the purchase. When the maturity date of February 1972 fell on the commercial paper, the cash was moved back to the subsidiary, recording it there as an advance to EFCA. The situation was made more difficult because no original records were available. Premiums earned on commissions paid were held by a separate insurance agency subsidiary. In the end, two-thirds of the 97,000 insurance policies—at least 64,000 of them—were bogus.

It was Equity's practice to keep very little information on paper. A huge microfilm file was used to store copies of all documents. The paper was then thrown away. Types of policies were identified by a two-digit code such as 65 for policies belonging to EFLIC employees and 35 for a union group contract. Code number 99 was used for the mass marketing business. Since these policies were not billed to individual policy holders, it was the ideal classification for all of the bogus insurance policies.

At one point at the end of 1972, Equity Funding had 20,000 valid funding programs but was reporting 50,000 in its annual report. Seidman and Seidman, the auditors for Equity Funding, were given a printout of 50,000 programs, but in the listing the first two digits of the five-digit numbers which identified the individual programs had been left off. The computer had been programmed to repeat randomly the funding programs until they added up to 50,000. Seidman and Seidman decided to confirm 2,000 of these programs with holders. The sample that they chose, identified by number, was entered into the computer to retrieve the names and addresses. The programs within the 2,000 that were repeated required unique names and addresses. These were supplied by Equity Funding staff and included names and addresses of friends and co-conspirators who were willing to send back the confirmations.

There was only one way 64,000 bogus policies could have been created, and that is by the use of a computer. We go back in history to pick up the story in terms of the computer's role in the fraud. EFCA started with a Univac 1005 back in the mid-1960s. This was upgraded to an IBM 360/30, then a 360/40, and finally in the last few months of the fraud in late 1972 and early 1973 an IBM 370/145 was in use with the IBM Disk Operating System (DOS). In addition a subsidiary in Seattle, Washington, had an IBM 360/30, and a small computer was used in a subsidiary in New Jersey. The actuarial department of EFLIC in Los Angeles had a small IBM System 3 which played a significant role in the fraud.

In 1972 EFCA had over 100 programmers, computer operators, and other support personnel in the data processing organization called Management Informations Systems (MIS).

The operating cost in 1972 for MIS was $2 million. MIS was headed by William Mercado from February 1970 until June 1971, when operations became so complex that he needed assistance. He brought in William Gootnick, who was MIS director from June 1971 until June 1973. Over the years there were continual suggestions and proposals to make more efficient, better controlled and auditable use of the computer systems, but for reasons unknown at the time, top management always resisted this. In August 1970 Brian Tickler, a systems analyst, developed a reinsurance system to keep more accurate auditable records of the reinsurance program, but this was rejected. During this period the MIS staff at Equity Funding was treated extremely well. Liberal amounts of money were available for members of the staff to attend conventions and schools. Morale was high, and dedication to EFCA very strong. EFCA was going to become the greatest financial conglomerate in the world. The dynamic leaders of Equity Funding were looked upon by the MIS staff as geniuses.

The MIS organization was operated in the most dangerous way

possible, providing maximum exposure to errors, omissions, and fraud. An open shop EDP service was provided to over 100 companies within the Equity family. This means that anyone throughout the company could run their own programs on the computer; the computer was not restricted to use only by MIS programming staff. In addition, the master files for the entire company were also available to any programmers throughout the 100 companies using the system. Magnetic tapes containing the vital master files were kept in a library apart from the computer and were entirely uncontrolled, a setup allowing anyone to wander in, pick up a tape, and return it at a later time without any difficulty. It is easy to see how the fraud could have been carried out without direct involvement of the MIS staff.

The master files were available to the actuarial department of EFLIC. In March 1970, an auditor requested that a particular report be duplicated by running a second copy; but the original was not produced in the MIS system and did not agree with the new one. The original report came from the System 3 in the actuarial department. The actuaries did their own programming on their IBM System 3 computer. The computer aspects of the fraud were concentrated in this department.

All the programs used to create fictitious policies were written in the actuarial department, an outside user of the open shop computing facility. The MIS staff was misled until near the end of the fraud because it was explained to them that these special computer runs were merely creating policies to be used for insurance sales simulation studies. The MIS staff was asked to create lists of policy numbers that looked real to assist in these simulation studies. However, the MIS staff insists that the IBM System 3 in the actuarial department was the only computer actively used in the fraud. A corporation executive officer programmed it to fabricate the appropriate levels of cancellations, deaths, and lapses that would be experienced with real policies. The data processing department and the main computer were used to lend an air of authenticity to the otherwise bogus data.

In mid-1972, MIS started using the Consolidated Insurance Management Information System from a software house in

Chicago. This system records policy status, starting with proposals, then going on into force, and finally to billing status. It was proposed by MIS that this application should be interfaced to other applications in current use, so allowing an audit trail, but this would have exposed the fraud and made it impossible to continue. As far as is known, an auditor never entered the Equity Funding computer operation facilities, and no requests were ever made by an auditor to make copies of the master files.

One report indicates that the controls in the system were inadequate and in most cases nonexistent. Another source indicated that MIS had normal EDP controls, including project controls, file retention, and report balancing. It functioned as a service bureau. Robert McGindley, manager of Financial Systems in MIS, stated that the general ledger application had 10,000 to 20,000 entries. He said, "My only responsibility is that it balances. Entries got there from other sources like the commission system." It was clear that MIS did not have primary responsibility for the authenticity of the input data. Data processing organizations don't normally have this responsibility. They are only responsible for maintaining the correctness and accuracy of the data once submitted to them.

Frank Hyman, manager of MIS Systems, who has extensive accounting background and was a controller of a small company before coming to EFCA, told me that in the last several months of the fraud he suspected that excessive "aggressive accounting" practices were going on, but he was loyal to EFCA, hoping from week to week that the mess would all get straightened out as top management promised. Even after the fraud was discovered, he remained loyal to EFCA and was optimistic that the company would get back on its feet, especially to serve the thousands of valid insurance policies still in active status. After the fraud was revealed, he finally understood why his many attempts to establish an internal audit and EDP audit function reporting to the president of the corporation had always met with failure. He said the State Insurance Commission did only perfunctory audits, had a few martinis with top management and left the offices after several hours of spot checking, and that the external auditors readily accepted computer printout listings as documents of record. He feels that this was the basic reason for the success in deceiving the auditors. Hyman believes his staff in MIS was innocent and could not have known of the fraud that was carried out among the volumes of regular input and output data passing through the system. He personally felt that it would be ridiculous for him to question the validity of the new policies in this continual flow of data. He often saw up to 600 new policies entering the system in one day, and all specially coded because he was told they were sold as a group to members of a carpenters' union or some other organization and had to be separately identified. Hyman said he was not privy to the management activities in the company. He rationalized his company's aggressive accounting activities by pointing out that many companies engaged in similar activities.

A federal grand jury report of the fraud reported by Dirks and Gross in their book, *The Great Wall Street Scandal*, indicates a chronology of alleged data processing activities:

• December 15, 1969: William Mercado, then head of Equity Funding's Computer Operations, supervises the preparation of a computer printout of funded loan receivable accounts that are intentionally inflated.

• November 2, 1970: Computer specialist Mike Keller writes a computer program for the creation of fictitious insurance policies with a face value of $430 million and a total yearly premium of $5.5 million.

• December 16, 1970: Samuel Lowell discusses with William Mercado, the head of Computer Operations, the preparation of a computer printout of funded loan receivable accounts that would contain an intentionally inflated total.

• December 23, 1971: Art Lewis and Alan Green, a computer specialist (Actuary Department), discuss creating a computer printout listing which would contain fictitious funded loan accounts.

• January 14, 1972: Bill Symonds begins to manipulate computer records so as to falsely show 5,000 lapsed policies to be in force.

• January 5, 1973: Lowell confers with the management of Computer Operations, William Gootnick, concerning the company's fictitious life insurance business.

• February 27, 1973: Mike Keller and Al Green instruct unindicted co-conspirator Aaron Venuziou on writing computer programs for fictitious insurance business.

• March 22, 1973: Bill Gootnick supervises the writing of computer programs designed to conceal the existence of EFLIC's fictitious insurance business from auditors and state examiners.

It should be noted that only Mercado and Gootnick were MIS employees and that both were directors of MIS. The criminal indictment stated that computers were used to create data relating to fictitious insurance policies so they could be reinsured with other insurance companies. Equity collected commissions on the sales of these policies and collected death claims made on fictitious policies.

There is still no indication that the EDP staff was aware of the fraud. Harold Weiss, publisher of *Edpacs*, an EDP Audit Control and Security newsletter, stated in the October 1974 issue: "There is a broader question about the Equity Funding data processing staff in terms of professionalism and culpability. There were many suspicious symptoms that should have caused an honest computer staff to ask some questions. Special reruns of jobs and large, abrupt changes in the size of master files are two examples. Obviously, senior management of Equity did not want strong controls or any audit trails in certain systems. An experienced and prudent data processing management should have recognized that their requests were not kosher. There should have been a refusal to deliberately design poorer systems. This, of course, might have led to retribution and loss of jobs." Another private source believes that most of the MIS staff were aware of the fictitious insurance business during the last few months of the fraud.

Most of the computer programming to create the fake policies was done by Alan Green, the aspiring computer programmer in the Actuary Department. Soble and Dallos in their book, *The Impossible Dream*, quoted Green as he described this process: "Constructing the computer programs is just the first step in the process. After the main set of programs was completed, which took only a few months, the procedure became almost automatic. EFLIC could produce as many phony policies as were needed for any period of time. In other words, the phony program skeleton had been created and was ready to be fleshed out. I was instructed to inject certain basic phony data into the computers such as the dates and face amounts of the policies. The amount was just a rotating thing. I'd start with maybe $10,000. Just to confuse the issue, I would multiply it by 1.2 and the next phony policy by 1.3 and so on so that it would look authentic. A policy premium was computed in a similar random manner."

According to Soble and Dallos, Green would also feed in the type of life insurance policy and the name of the policy holder. Only the names of policy holders were duplicated. All of the other data was fabricated, with the names initially taken from policies held by Pennsylvania Life Insurance Company of Los Angeles and later from policies of other insurance companies. When a fraudulent computer tape of fake policies was completed, it was returned to EFLIC's data processing library for safekeeping.

Green said that a cash receipt, check and balance system was also created through the manipulation of the computer program. "With every policy that I created there had to also be a cash receipt generated and then merged in all of the real cash receipts. The phony cash receipts flow took into account, for example, premiums taken in by EFLIC on the policies and the phony commissions paid out to the salesmen, and in the final analysis," said Green, "you could look at the end of the year at all of the premiums coming into the company, and all of the real and phony cash receipts would be mixed up, and everything would look real. The auditors were apparently not prepared to double check the computer records. Part of the reason was that the actual computer printout would produce reams and reams of paper and might take months to check out. The personnel of the auditing firms, therefore, only random check the policies."

When the backup documentation for a policy was requested by an auditor, the paper had to be reproduced and microfilmed quickly. This was done by setting up a separate office several blocks away from the Century City offices of EFLIC. This office hired people for the sole purpose of creating the paper to support the fictitious policies. When the auditors asked for a policy file that was fake, they were told the file was in use and would be ready the next morning. The staff in the special office would then create the backup documentation needed for the next morning. The details of this operation are fascinating and are described at length in the Soble and Dallos book.

A number of personal frauds and embezzlements went on within the company. When these were discovered, the perpetrators were usually given additional compensation to pay back the money stolen, and the technique that they used was then incorporated into the overall company fraud. According to the Trustee's Bankruptcy Report, a computer-related ". . . embezzlement scheme was executed in 1972 by three EFLIC employees working in the Commissions Department: Robert Gibson, Otis Poole and Ronald Gordon, younger brother of Stanley Goldblum, the president of EFCA.

"These three individuals devised a means of causing the EFCA computer to issue unauthorized commission checks to them each month. The idea originated with Gordon, a registered representative, who approached Gibson, the Manager of EFLIC's Commission Department and convinced him to issue phony checks from the Commission Department, which the two men would split. The plan worked so well that Gibson then approached Poole, another registered representative and asked if he would like to join in the practice. The scheme was uncovered in February, 1973 during a routine comparison of actual commission earnings with checks made payable to agents.

"The matter was reported to Stanley Goldblum and Fred Levin who decided to keep the three on the payroll. Each man signed a promissory note to pay back the amount that was taken: For Poole that amount was $2,472.05, for Gordon $5,778.75 and for Gibson $8,250.60. Poole paid the full amount of his note to the company on May 11, 1973. Gibson paid only $125 against his note, and Gordon has as yet made no payment.

"In another scheme William Symonds, an EFLIC employee involved in the larger fraud, changed computer records to indicate that all premiums were paid up to date for certain policies which had actually lapsed. Symonds attempted to siphon off for himself the apparent cash surrender value of these policies. He did this by filing forged requests to surrender cash value of the policy in the insurer's name. Symonds then intercepted the EFLIC checks for the cash value before they were mailed. Although a number of lapsed policy records were changed, only two cash surrender checks totaling $11,568.39 actually went to Symonds. The monies thus embezzled were deposited in savings accounts opened by Symonds in the names of the insured, a common trick in embezzlement. In late March, 1973 as discovery of the larger EFCA fraud was imminent, evidence of Symonds's embezzlements came to the attention of Banks and Smith, other executives in the firm. Symonds was forced to return to EFLIC all of the funds he had taken, which he did on March 29th. . . .

"In retrospect the factors which motivated the increasing personal fraud and thievery at Equity Funding are reasonably clear. As the scope of the corporate fraud widened and the number of participants increased, there was a growing likelihood of discovery by the authorities. This steadily increasing risk seems to have prompted the escalation of demand on the corporate treasury made by certain of the fraud conspirators, particularly those on the middle management level who were not as well compensated as Goldblum, Levin and Lowell.

"Thus as the fraud grew, so too did the climate of personal moral decay. . . . The fraud does not appear to have been motivated by a desire on the part of the conspirators to provide a cover for large scale embezzlement. The primary purpose of the fraud, rather, was to cause EFCA to appear to flourish and thereby to inflate the value of its stock. At the same time, however, a closely associated object of the conspiracy was the personal enrichment of its members. This goal was furthered in various ways.

"At the very top, of course, Goldblum and Riordan, who had obtained many thousands of shares of stock at very little cost prior to 1964, realized huge profits through subsequent dividends and from stock sales. It is believed that Goldblum gained more than $5 million from trading in EFCA stock over the years. Similarly, Riordan is believed to have obtained well over $1 million from sales of EFCA stock prior to his death in 1969. . . . Executive compensation at EFCA was generous. In 1971 and 1972 Goldblum's annual salary alone was $100,000, and in 1973 he raised it to $125,000. Ironically, this raise occurred about the same time Goldblum was telling all department heads that a twenty percent cost reduction had to be effected within the company for 1973. Lowell and Levin each received annual salaries of $70,000 in 1971 and $80,000 in 1972.

"In the final years, however, salaries came to reflect less than half of the total compensation to top officers. This was due primarily to the company's stock bonus plan." According to a table in the Trustee's Report, in 1972 Goldblum received a total compensation of $304,063, Fred Levin received $243,250, and Samuel Lowell the same. Middle management received $36,000 to $62,000 in 1972 and were to receive $66,000 to $118,000 compensation in 1973. A number of fringe benefits were added, including an entertainment allowance. ". . . These allowances appeared to have nothing to do with company entertainment expenses but were simply Goldblum's response to a demand by Lowell and Levin for a raise as extra reward for the risk they were incurring by furthering the fraud. Goldblum determined that Lowell and Levin should each receive $1,000 per month and that $3,000 per month would be an appropriate amount for himself. Other fraud participants increased their fringe benefits by charging their medical bills to EFLIC. . . ." Stock option grants were also increased by changing the records and then changing them again to avoid income tax payments.

". . . A number of petty defalcations relating to expense vouchers used to reimburse employees for money spent while purportedly on business trips accounted for part of the abuse. One executive made a practice of charging the company twice for his travel expenses . . . once on a company credit card and again upon returning from a trip by submitting an expense voucher." Automobiles, gasoline, and mileage were all paid for. "One vice president loaned his gasoline credit card to his girlfriend, also a company employee. She charged her gasoline on his credit card, signed his name and later submitted the invoices on his expense report. . . .

"A myriad of personal expenses were charged to the company by officers including first class vacations to Hawaii, Mexico, South America and Tahiti, rented Rolls-Royce limousines for social occasions and substantial quantities of stereo equipment and television sets. One executive had a girlfriend in New York whose apartment was furnished for $2,000 at EFCA's expense. Another officer had the company pay the bill for his divorce.

"During EFCA's last days some of the fraud conspirators made a final grasp at company funds. In late March, 1973 Goldblum,

Lowell and Levin drew advances on their salaries and entertainment allowances before their employment was terminated. . . .

"Finally, in the realm of ego gratification it is worth noting that EFCA's executives conducted business in fabulously plush surroundings. In October, 1969 the company moved its head office to five leased floors at 1900 Avenue of the Stars, Century City. The offices of the president and other high executives were situated on the top floor and had a miles-wide view of Beverly Hills and Los Angeles. No expense was spared in furnishings or decor for these quarters. Goldblum's office, for instance, was an opulently furnished suite complete with fireplace, reception area, kitchen and bathroom. Loeffler's comment was, 'Mr. Goldblum's office is a splendid place for conferring sainthood, but I don't think I could work there.' There were other lavish touches on the top floor. For example, company practice was for the president and all of the executive vice presidents to meet daily in the richly appointed EFCA boardroom for luncheon prepared by Goldblum's personal cook. . . .

"After Goldblum was fired by the Board much controversy ensued between him and the company over the ownership of a number of items of furniture in his office including an old-fashioned telescope valued at more than $1200 which he said was a gift from his wife and a painting over the mantel for which he said he personally had paid $10,000. Invoices from the Equity Funding accounting department showed that, in fact, the company had paid for each of these items, and Goldblum's demands were rejected. The benefits flowing to the fraud conspirators had finally stopped."

The last days of the fraud—the gathering storm and collapse—are most vividly and surely most accurately described in the Trustee's Bankruptcy Report, which is used here to tell the end of the story.

"In early 1973, only months before the collapse of the Company, EFCA's management believed it had reasons for optimism about the future. For one, the conspirators had come through another year-end audit unscathed. They had anticipated many of the questions which the auditors asked and, as before, the explanations which they concocted were accepted. Second, the transformation of the Company from a funding program sales organization into a proprietary insurance conglomerate had been successfully completed. EFCA now referred to itself as 'a life insurance-based financial services company.' Third, the Company was preparing to issue its 1972 Annual Report reflecting its best year ever. A glowing press release on March 12th would chronicle EFCA's supposed recent accomplishments, with Goldblum announcing a 17% increase in earnings over the previous year and record sales of life insurance by the Company's subsidiaries.

"Despite such optimistic notes, however, a serious and dangerous situation remained: The very nature of the insurance fraud meant that it was growing in almost geometric proportions; more and more cash was required to pay renewal premiums on reinsured false policies; and the imbalance in the inter-company accounts was increasing. In short, the Company was like a time bomb.

"Without warning, on March 12th the Illinois Insurance Commission sent examiners into EFLIC for an intensive audit. The time bomb was triggered. There had been no time for the conspirators to prepare, and the events now moved too fast to be managed. By the end of the month, the explosion had occurred and the Company was being purged of the fraud and its perpetrators. This [part of the report] chronicles those last dramatic days . . .

"Beginning in mid-1972, some of the conspirators met on an irregular basis to attempt to deal with problems caused by the fraud. . . . At the meetings, the younger members of the conspiracy, pragmatically concerned about the magnitude of the fraud, pressed for what they saw as a way out. According to records these conspirators were keeping, operating losses had actually *increased* in 1971 and 1972, despite expansion and acquisitions by the Company. They argued that the only way to eliminate the phony insurance and bogus assets was to stop the artificial increases in corporate growth by reporting 'flat earnings' for a while. Earnings would have to be reported at the same level as for the prior year and no additional phony assets could be booked, while at the same time real sales would have to be dramatically increased but not reported. This action was to be coupled with the institution of a new cost control system and drastic cost reductions, hopefully to create real profits. However, Goldblum flatly rejected such proposals. A leveling of reported earnings would adversely affect the market price of EFCA's common stock, a prospect he would not entertain.

"[They] therefore came ultimately to focus on two less sweeping ideas which it was thought would help alleviate some of the pressure building up as a result of the fraud. First, a cost-cutting program was inaugurated by notifying department heads that a 20% reduction would have to be made in all departmental budgets. Every department was reviewed with respect to personnel and overhead expenses. At the same time, an effort was supposedly instituted to reduce expense accounts and eliminate the use of first-class air travel and limousines.

"The second idea involved a new fraudulent device conceived by Levin and Goldblum—the unrecorded annuities scheme. The Company would sell several large annuities, take in the cash but not record its receipt and use the proceeds to reduce the imbalance in the intercompany account with EFLIC. Together with the burgeoning 'false death claim scheme,' the annuities scheme was supposed to provide cash to help divert some of the increasing fraud burden from the funding and insurance areas.

"Neither of these programs progressed very far. Executives who were not involved in the fraud resisted the proposed cost-cuts in their departments, and the annuities scheme proved to be a flop. In retrospect, it seems clear that Project Z was a futile effort, for there was no 'way out' for the conspirators. There were no steps which could have been taken to eliminate or significantly reduce the cumulative effects of a decade of deceit.

THE GATHERING STORM

"On March 8, 1973, the last regular EFCA board meeting was held in New York City. All nine directors were present, plus general counsel Rodney Loeb. Spirits were high and the outlook for the Company was excellent. It is indicative of the upbeat mood that the directors considered raising the dividend on the Company's common stock, but finally settled on staying at the 10 cents per share declared the prior year. Four days after the meeting, EFCA issued a glowing press release to report 'record earnings from operations at $2.81 per share, up from $2.45 per share for 1971.' According to the release, Goldblum said consolidated net income rose to $22,617,000 in 1972, a 17% increase over 1971 earnings of $19,332,000. This enthusiastic statement painted the rosiest of corporate pictures only three weeks before the Company filed a petition in bankruptcy.

"The debacle was triggered the same day the press release was issued. Examiners from the Illinois Insurance Department arrived unexpectedly at EFLIC to audit the subsidiary's books. This audit was the result of growing rumors of fraud at EFCA which originated with Ronald Secrist, a former employee of EFLIC. . . . (Secrist went to work for EFLIC in 1970 as Assistant Vice President. Personnel records show that Secrist was terminated effective March 15, 1973 'due to overstaffing.') On March 6, Secrist had telephoned the Deputy Superintendent of the New York State Insurance Department and said that he had certain information that might be of interest to the Department. He requested an appointment the following day. On March 7, Secrist arrived at the Department offices and told an almost unbelievable story. He alleged that for several years Equity Funding Life Insurance Company had been padding its in-force life insurance with fictitious policies, and that this bogus business had been reinsured with other companies.

"Upon hearing Secrist's story, the New York officials relayed the allegations to the Chief Examiner of the California Department of Insurance, Christy Armstrong. The California officials, in turn, notified the Los Angeles office of the SEC, and then the Illinois Insurance Department, which shared regulatory responsibilities for EFLIC with California. By March 9, officials from the two states had concluded that a special examination of the insurance company should be conducted, disguised as a routine triennial audit by the Illinois Insurance Department so as not to unduly alarm the conspirators. The Illinois examiners were to arrive at the Company the following Monday, March 12, and the

California examiners would follow a few days later as would be normal for such an examination.

"The appearance of the Illinois examiners, however, greatly upset the conspirators. Goldblum called Levin, who had remained in New York after the EFCA board meeting, to tell him that the examiners were on the premises. Levin knew from his earlier experience working for the Illinois Department of Insurance that among the procedures employed in this examination would be a physical examination of EFLIC's assets. Thus, Levin feared the examiners would discover that $24 million of EFLIC's reported assets were non-existent bonds. Before returning to Los Angeles, he called up friends in the Illinois Insurance Department to ask them to postpone the examination, but to no avail.

"EFCA's management then engaged John Bolton, a former deputy insurance commissioner in Illinois, to try to postpone the Illinois examination, ostensibly because EFCA was in the midst of a pending acquisition of another insurance company. Bolton contacted Richards Barger, a Los Angeles attorney and former Commissioner of the California Department of Insurance, to ask him to undertake similar efforts with the California Department. When Barger contacted the Los Angeles office of the Department to request postponement, he was told that Maury Rouble was supervising the California examination and that it could not be postponed. Barger did not press further. To him, the fact that Rouble had been assigned to the case meant that something serious was involved, and that the audit was not routine.

"When the Illinois examiners arrived at EFCA's headquarters, they were given a room on the 28th floor. To find out what the examiners were looking for and what they were finding, a plan was developed by Goldblum and Banks to equip the room with electronic surveillance devices. On the evening of March 14, Collins and Banks, with the help of two experts, made the first of a series of installations of eavesdropping equipment. Partly as a result of information which the conspirators received through these listening devices, they took countermoves to attempt to hide the fraud from the examiners. The first problem they attempted to deal with was EFLIC's non-existent reported assets.

"The $24 million in bonds purportedly held in the EFLIC

custodian account at the American National Bank & Trust Company in Chicago presented the most pressing problem. When the Illinois examiners first sought to confirm the existence of these bonds, they were supplied with the bogus confirmation which Seidman & Seidman had accepted. Since Illinois examiners would be aware that branch banking was not permitted in Illinois, the confirmation had been altered to reflect the proper bank address rather than the address of the bogus branch in Highland Park. As expected, however, the examiners announced their intention to go beyond this confirmation and send one of their people to count the bonds personally. To solve this problem, Goldblum apparently wanted to utilize the counterfeit bonds which had been printed, but others persuaded him that they were not of sufficient quality to stand scrutiny. A new explanation had to be quickly devised to explain why the bonds were no longer in the bank.

"The new story to be given to the Illinois examiners was that at some time after December 31, 1972, the $24 million in bonds had been used in three different transactions. The conspirators planned to tell the examiners that part of the bonds had been transferred to EFCA, which held all of EFLIC's stock, as payment of a $3.4 million dividend to the parent; that $5.5 million had been used to purchase certificates of deposit; and that EFLIC had used the remainder to purchase 80% of the stock of Northern Life Insurance Company from EFCA for approximately $15.7 million.

"The purported Northern stock transaction required the most effort to document. Levin and Smith arranged to make appropriate alterations in company records. On March 16, Smith directed Bill Raff, an EFCA attorney, to prepare drafts of two back-dated agreements, as well as new Northern stock certificates, to document the purported purchase by EFLIC of 80% of Northern's stock in a two-step transaction: 40% on February 5 and 40% on March 5. Raff was told that First National City Bank of New York ('FNCB'), which held a certificate representing 100% of the stock of Northern as collateral under a 1972 Revolving Credit Agreement, had agreed to the transfer. The two certificates created to represent the 80% of Northern stock were then placed in an EFLIC safe deposit box. Levin next retrieved the already outstanding 100% certificate on March 23 by persuading his friend at FNCB, Hugh Brewer, to exchange it for a 20% certificate. Levin explained to Brewer that EFLIC could save $700,000 in taxes if it acquired 80% of Northern.

"In order to convince the Illinois examiners that the $5.5 million certificates of deposit had been purchased before their arrival, the conspirators determined that it would be necessary to go into the secondary market and purchase certificates issued before March 12. At either Sultan's or Goldblum's request, Dishy Easton [a New York brokerage firm] purchased the needed certificates in bearer form. It appears that Dishy Easton was also asked to supply an undated confirmation of this purchase, which the conspirators planned to fill in with a false date. The certificates were delivered to Goldblum's office on March 19. On March 21, they were placed for safe-keeping at Wells Fargo Bank in Century City, where they were found by the California and Illinois Insurance Departments on March 30.

"The conspirators also took steps to make it difficult for the examiners to discover the bogus insurance policies. The week the examiners arrived, Arthur Lewis, Smith, Edens, Banks and Collins met to plot their course of action. They instructed William Gootnick, a Company Vice President in charge of computer operations, to run the Company's master computer tape through the computer and scramble all of the code numbers which identified the bogus business, and then to replace the hard copy records of insurance business with a completely new set showing the scrambled code numbers. Gootnick had his staff perform the task. Gootnick was also instructed to destroy any evidence of the bogus business in the Company's computer tape library, but later the conspirators decided merely to change the tape log (the listing of information in EFCA's computer tape library). A member of Gootnick's staff carried out this instruction as well. . . . A couple of days later, Gootnick apparently had second thoughts about his actions and had his staff restore the tape log to its original form.

"All these efforts proved unavailing, however, because of the accelerating pace of events outside the Company. Between March 19 and March 27, rumors on Wall Street of fraud at EFCA began to significantly affect trading in the Company's stock. These rumors were based on information Secrist had given to Raymond Dirks, an insurance analyst with the New York brokerage firm of Delafield Childs Inc. Secrist had called Dirks the same day he met with New York officials and, by the end of the week, had told him the story of the fraud at EFLIC. Dirks proceeded to investigate the allegations. During the week of March 19, he came to Los Angeles and met with former EFLIC employees who confirmed many of Secrist's charges. Then on March 21, Dirks met with Goldblum and Levin and questioned them about the fraud allegations. Both flatly denied that there was any truth to the stories of phony insurance at EFLIC, and they arranged for other Company officers—Smith, Lewis and Edens—to join in the denials.

"In the interim, Dirks evidently told some of his institutional clients about the Secrist allegations, because while Dirks was in Los Angeles investigating, rumors in New York circulated wildly. The same day that Dirks interrogated Goldblum and Levin, EFCA's general counsel, Rodney Loeb received a call from Yura Arkus-Duntov [an EFCA officer and director] and Lawrence Williams (of EFCA's legal staff) in New York. They told Loeb of rumors circulating there that the Company had issued large quantities of nonexistent life insurance. Loeb conveyed this information to Goldblum and told him that an inter-office memo concerning the rumors was being typed. Goldblum scoffed at the story and told Loeb to destroy all copies of his memo. Loeb did not do so.

"While the rumors gathered steam, EFCA's stock became a volume leader on the New York Stock Exchange and its price declined steadily. On Thursday, March 22, Goldblum and Levin flew to New York City. Goldblum delivered an address the next day at the Institutional Investors Conference, and then met with New York Stock Exchange officials to try to squelch the rumors and reassure the market. But when trading opened the following Monday, EFCA was the volume leader with 768,400 shares traded. The price had dropped from $28 per share on March 6 to $16 per share on March 26.

"Goldblum was back in Los Angeles at the start of the next

week trying to grasp control of the rapidly deteriorating situation. This was to be the last week that he and the other conspirators would run the Company, and they were coming to realize that the game was nearly up. On Monday, March 26, representatives of Seidman & Seidman, which had just completed its annual audit of EFCA, met with Goldblum and Loeb. Goldblum claimed he was unaware of any irregularities in the insurance operations, but at Loeb's insistence Seidman & Seidman was directed to reopen an extended audit of EFLIC to determine if the Dirks rumors were true. Coupled with the Illinois and California Insurance Departments' examinations and inquiries from the New York Stock Exchange and the SEC, the Seidman & Seidman audit made it a hectic period at Company headquarters.

"On March 27, the rumors of phony insurance business on EFCA's books grew stronger. The Company issued a press release denying the allegations and announcing its intention to purchase one million shares of EFCA stock on the open market 'to take advantage of the currently depressed price of the company's stock.' But frenzied trading and rapid price deterioration continued. At 12:45 EST, the New York Stock Exchange halted all trading in EFCA stock.

"The stock exchange action shook the Company and its employees. Their suspicions aroused by the halt in trading, attorney Bill Raff and two other EFLIC employees began their own secret investigation of the rumors of bogus policies. Bill Gootnick, the Vice President who had helped to conceal some of the computer tape evidence, came to Goldblum and told him that he wanted no more of the fraud and planned to quit. Goldblum asked Gootnick to stay on as a favor to him until Friday because 'something magic' was going to happen on that day, and maybe everything would be okay. Gootnick agreed to stay.

"An Executive Planning Committee meeting was called for the same afternoon to discuss the situation. . . . No one at the meeting seemed to comprehend what was happening to the Company. One theory was that the stock was being manipulated downward so that someone could accumulate shares and gain control. Whenever the suggestion was made that the rumors could be true, it was rejected. The prevailing theory was that there might always exist some minor larceny in the Company of which these officers were unaware, but that it would be impossible to have false life insurance policies. After all, the premiums would have to be paid and reserves kept for false policies, so it made no sense.

"Finally, Glaser [an officer and director of EFCA] directly asked Goldblum, Levin and Lowell whether there was any substance to the Dirks rumors. Lowell denied knowing anything about the fraud. Levin characterized the allegations made by Dirks as 'bizarre' and denied the charges vehemently. According to him, the Company's problems were all a result of charges being made by a disgruntled employee who only had particles of knowledge. Goldblum's response, however, was not as reassuring. He simply said that anything was possible and that certain events could have occurred without his knowledge. Consequently, it was agreed that the legal department, under the supervision of [EFCA associate council] Williams, would conduct an internal investigation and work in conjunction with the Seidman & Seidman audit team.

"Although the conspirators kept a cool facade, their actions behind the scenes indicated that they knew discovery of the fraud was imminent. A number of meetings were held to consider what was going to happen to the Company and to the fraud participants, whether to hire attorneys, and who would pay the legal fees. In addition, plans were developed for several of the conspirators to flee the country. Levin, Lowell and Goldblum discussed leaving, and Levin suggested that they take the recently purchased $5.5 million certificates of deposit to finance their exile. Lowell agreed with Levin's plan, but Goldblum declined because he feared that his wife would refuse to leave with him.

"Having decided to run, Levin went to the Wells Fargo Bank on March 28, and removed the certificates from the EFLIC safe deposit box. He gave Lowell half, and Lowell began making phone calls to contacts in Argentina, Europe and the Bahamas to determine the marketability of the certificates abroad. A day later, however, Levin had a change of heart and abandoned his plan. He persuaded Lowell to give back the certificates by claiming that he would attempt to negotiate them. On March 30, Levin returned the certificates to the manager at Wells Fargo Bank, who placed them in an EFLIC safekeeping account.

"While the conspirators considered running away, the pace of events quickened. On March 27, Larry Baker, Chief Deputy Commissioner of the California Insurance Department, got a call from SEC officials relaying information received from an informer at Equity Funding. The informer revealed that alterations had been made on computer tapes the prior weekend, and that many tapes were being erased at that moment. The information was relayed to the examiners at the Company offices who moved to stop further erasures.

"The following day, Wednesday, March 28, the SEC suspended trading of all EFCA securities on all public markets and demanded that Goldblum, Levin, Lowell . . . [and other executives] give testimony at the Los Angeles office of the SEC and also sign affidavits swearing there was no phony insurance on the Company's books. The end was at hand.

COLLAPSE

"The final chapter of the EFCA fraud began on Thursday, March 29. At the Company, the day started with an impromptu meeting in Levin's office at which Goldblum, Levin, Loeb and Milton Kroll, an attorney from the Washington, D.C. law firm which handled EFCA's SEC work, were present. Goldblum wondered aloud whether he should have his own legal counsel. Kroll advised against it at this stage, since he felt it would imply that Goldblum had something to hide. The subject of the affidavits requested by the SEC also came up, and Goldblum indicated a reluctance to sign one. There was some discussion of the inflexibility of the written word in an affidavit, and Kroll explained that each man would have an opportunity to give testimony at the SEC the next day in addition to his affidavit.

"A little before noon, Loeb was notified that Frank Rothman, a Los Angeles attorney, was on his way to see him. Kroll was present in Loeb's office when Rothman entered. Rothman announced that he had been with Goldblum for the previous two hours, and had been engaged to represent him. He said he had heard a story from Goldblum, Levin and Lowell that he could only describe as 'incredible.' Rothman had recommended that Levin and Lowell immediately hire their own legal counsel and had advised Goldblum not to sign any affidavit for the SEC. Further, Rothman announced that Goldblum would not go to the SEC the next day to give any testimony. Loeb said he thought that if Goldblum did not appear voluntarily, the SEC would simply issue a subpoena. Rothman's response was that if his client was subpoenaed to testify, he would invoke his Fifth Amendment privilege. Kroll and Loeb then pointed out what such a move would mean for the Company. They felt the SEC would certainly ask that a receiver be appointed and the investigation of the Company would continue. Rothman said he had discussed such ramifications with his client.

"Loeb was now firmly convinced that the rumors of fraud were true and that Goldblum was involved. As Secretary of EFCA, Loeb arranged to call a special meeting of the Board of Directors for the week-end.

"Goldblum and Glaser then joined Kroll, Rothman and Loeb in Loeb's office. Loeb recited to Glaser the announcements that Rothman had just made about his client's refusal to testify and about the decisions of Lowell and Levin to retain their own counsel. Glaser excitedly told Goldblum that his refusal to sign an affidavit would ruin the employees and the shareholders of the Company and bring incredible hardship to everyone involved. Goldblum was solemn. He persisted in his refusal to testify and indicated he would follow his attorney's advice. Glaser told him that he would have to infer that the rumors were true if Goldblum would not deny them. Goldblum refused to talk about it any further. Goldblum then left the group and walked back down the hall to his own office with Glaser following behind. In Goldblum's office, Glaser begged him to disclose what he knew and sign an affidavit. Goldblum stalled for time, saying he would talk to somebody about it. He added that someday Glaser would find out he was innocent.

"That same afternoon, Loeb received a call from Bill Raff who, with other EFLIC employees investigating the fraud, had discovered 'hard evidence' of bogus insurance. Raff wanted to arrange a meeting with Loeb. Instead, Loeb arranged for Raff to meet that evening with representatives from Seidman & Seidman at the hotel where Milton Kroll was staying. The meeting lasted well into the morning hours. Raff's group revealed to the auditors not only evidence of fictitious insurance, but also the [forged documents] . . . operation [a few blocks away].

"On the morning of Friday, March 30, Larry Baker of the California Department of Insurance, who had by then learned of Raff's findings, went to the Los Angeles office of the SEC with Seidman & Seidman representatives to share with them the latest discoveries. Following that meeting, Baker met with a representative of the California Attorney General's office to decide what steps could be taken to prevent the destruction of records and the flight of persons possibly involved in the fraud. Earlier that day, Baker had learned of Levin's removal of the certificates of deposit from the Wells Fargo safe deposit box, and he feared that further assets would be taken and possibly spirited out of the country. The California examiners had also observed Collins and Symonds removing records from the . . . [forged documents] office and loading them in a truck. Something had to be done fast. The officials concluded that the situation was an appropriate one in which to exercise the summary seizure procedures provided for under Section 1013 of the California Insurance Code. While the seizure order was being drafted, a Department attorney called the branch manager of Wells Fargo Bank, informed him of the pending seizure and told him not to let any EFLIC assets go out. The seizure order was served on the bank a short while later.

"At 5:30 p.m., Baker and Ed Germann of the Department arrived at the Company offices and went immediately to the sixth floor, where EFLIC was headquartered. They served everyone they could find with copies of the order and asked all employees to leave the premises. The Company's auditors, Seidman & Seidman, had a very large crew on the premises implementing security at the request of the SEC. Baker informed the auditors of what was happening and went over the procedures that were to be put into effect. The locks on EFLIC's doors were changed and armed security guards were posted. Although the California

Insurance Department had jurisdiction only over EFLIC, and not EFCA, Baker decided that since he could not tell which operations were attributable to which entity, he would, for the time being, exercise control over all Company operations. During the rest of the evening, Baker took statements from any of the officers willing to talk about the Company's operations and what they knew of the fraud. At 4:00 a.m., Baker ended his eventful day and left the premises.

"At 7 a.m. the next morning, a Saturday, Baker returned. As he entered the parking garage at EFCA's offices, he noticed a Rolls Royce pulling into the space marked 'Fred Levin.' As Levin and his attorney got out of the car, Baker introduced himself and asked Levin to accompany him to the 28th floor. When they arrived at the executive suite, they encountered the California Insurance Commissioner talking with Goldblum. Levin and Goldblum were then formally served with a copy of the seizure order. Goldblum was hostile. He fumed that the seizure was a big mistake, and that the Department was interfering with the right of the Company's salesmen to earn a living. Baker cut Goldblum's speech off, and informed him and Levin of their Fifth Amendment rights. Having done so, Baker began to question the two concerning the whereabouts of EFLIC's assets. Levin's attorney intervened, however, and the conversation ended.

"That afternoon, various meetings were underway. A number of EFCA officers and directors were meeting with representatives of the SEC and Seidman & Seidman to discuss the crisis. Baker, at this point suspicious of everyone in EFCA's management, left that meeting after a short while. He next met with Raff and the other Company employees who had uncovered some aspects of the fraud at EFLIC. The group again outlined what they had learned. . . . Meanwhile, at the insistence of director Robert Bowie, Seidman & Seidman conducted a telephone survey of a sample of supposed EFLIC policyholders. Of 82 listed policyholders, only 6 of the 35 reached by telephone confirmed that they owned the policies attributed to them. The survey gave those concerned some idea of the magnitude of the fraud at EFLIC.

"On Sunday, April 1, a special meeting of the EFCA Board of

Directors commenced at 4:15 p.m. All the members of the board were in attendance, including Stanley Goldblum, Herbert Glaser, Fred Levin, Samuel Lowell, Judson Sayre, Gale Livingston, Nelson Loud, Robert Bowie and Yura Arkus-Duntov. The following individuals also attended: Rodney Loeb, Lawrence Williams, and John Schneider, all members of EFCA's legal department; Richards Barger; Stuart Buchalter and Jerry Nemer of the law firm of Buchalter, Nemer, Fields & Savitch, specialists in insolvency law who had been retained by Loeb; and Milton Kroll and Peter Panarites of Freedman, Levy, Kroll & Symonds.

"The meeting was called to order and presided over by Rodney Loeb. After relating the chronology of events which led up to the special board meeting, he repeated the allegations raised by Dirks and summarized some of the evidence thus far discovered which tended to show that EFLIC had manufactured life insurance policies and that these policies had been sold to a number of reinsurers. (As of this time, the funding and other frauds described in this report were still undiscovered.) Next, Stuart Buchalter summarized his discussions with the SEC, indicating that the SEC had concluded that an enormous number of false insurance policies were on EFLIC's books, and that a number of other purported assets were of questionable validity. Buchalter advised the directors that the SEC was demanding that Goldblum, Levin and Lowell resign as officers and directors, and that the Company terminate Smith, Arthur Lewis, Edens, Collins, Banks and Symonds. Before any more details of the SEC's fraud investigation were revealed, the directors requested that Lowell, Goldblum and Levin resign and leave the premises.

"Before leaving, however, the three officers insisted that their services were necessary to run the Company. They agreed they would resign, but said they were willing to act as consultants for a fee in order to help save the Company. This suggestion was immediately rebuffed by Bowie, who insisted that the Company was in no position to contract with these men, and that any such discussion should be deferred until later. The three then requested severance pay. Goldblum argued that, 'Even the lowest clerk gets severance pay. I've been with the company thirteen years.' Again, Bowie replied that this was not a subject for discussion.

"Goldblum and Levin then left the room. Lowell stayed behind to make a statement to the assembled group. He said that while he had 'played games with numbers' and capitalized certain expense items, he was not involved in the phony insurance operation. Bowie again cut off Lowell's speech, saying this was not the time for such a statement and asking Lowell to leave the room, so that the meeting could continue.

"Prior to the meeting, EFCA's legal department had prepared letters of resignation for the three officers. Goldblum signed his before leaving the premises, but Levin and Lowell indicated they would not sign before speaking with their lawyers. After the three exited, the meeting continued for four more hours and concluded after accountants from Seidman & Seidman reported their findings regarding bogus policies to the directors.

"Baker, meanwhile, spent Sunday reviewing Company files and speaking with two former EFLIC employees who had been involved in the fraud—Alan Green and Allan Venuziou. Green explained to Baker how the bogus policies were created and reinsured, and how the false policy numbers were scrambled on the computer. More importantly, he confirmed that a number of present EFLIC employees were involved in the conspiracy. . . .

". . . The California Department of Insurance, and later the Special Deputy, took immediate steps to determine the nature and extent of the fraud and to protect the interests of the EFLIC policyholders. Their attempt to ascertain the percentage of bogus policies was hindered by the sabotage of the data processing system which apparently occurred immediately prior to EFLIC's seizure. As a result of efforts to preserve the security of the computer tapes and programs, computer operations were shut down for a three week period.

"The data-processing system had been organized so that all policies could be easily retrieved by type. This was true as to the bogus policies which were coded as 'Class 99.' When discovery of the fraud was imminent, certain persons at EFLIC attempted to delay or to prevent discovery by mixing the bogus business with the real business. However, the authorities discovered how this

mixing had been accomplished, which permitted the investigators and Touche Ross & Co. [doing the post audit] to get an early
estimate that approximately two-thirds of EFLIC's policies were
manufactured. This estimate has proved to be substantially
correct.

"Employees at EFLIC were subsequently able to refine the
separation of good and bad policies by comparing the initial
computer runs against the cash receipts tape for 1972 since only
legitimate policyholders were shown as making payments. In
certain cases it was necessary to examine premium history cards
and policy record files by hand.

"On Monday April 2, the general public first learned of the
fraud when an article by William Blundell appeared that morning
on the front page of the Wall Street Journal. The article caused
an immediate panic among EFCA's employees, creditors and
stockholders, and among EFLIC's reinsurers and policyholders.
When EFCA's doors opened on Monday, the Company was in a
state of upheaval. Employees arriving that morning were greeted
by security guards who screened them on entry. The guards had
pictures of each of the known conspirators and orders not to let
them enter the premises unescorted. When . . . [they] arrived,
Baker told them to go up to Rodney Loeb's office. Loeb had been
authorized by the Board of Directors to terminate anyone
connected with the fraud. When the group arrived at Loeb's
office, they were fired at one time. Upon being terminated, Lewis
offered his consultant services for $200 a day. Loeb replied that if
the window were open, he would throw him out. Later that day,
Michael Sultan was also fired by Loeb, when the SEC informed
him that evidence of Sultan's complicity had been discovered.

"The special meeting of the Board of Directors was reconvened
that afternoon. Present were Bowie, Livingston, Sayre, Glaser,
Loud, Arkus-Duntov, Loeb, Williams, Buchalter and Brian Man-
ion, attorney for director Gale Livingston. Glaser presided over
the meeting, and the main topic for discussion was the complaint
to be filed the next day by the SEC charging EFCA with fraud and
violations of other federal securities laws. The Board had to
decide if it would consent to a permanent injunction drafted by
the SEC which enjoined EFCA from future fraudulent acts,

provided a plan of operation under which Glaser was to be interim manager, and appointed Touche Ross & Co. to audit the Company's financial statements.

"Earlier that day, Glaser and Williams spent several hours at the SEC discussing what provisions would be included in the injunction. At the Board meeting, some directors objected to the language of the SEC's complaint. They were told that unless they agreed, the SEC would move immediately to seek a receivership under which the management of the corporation would be turned over to the SEC and the courts. Following extensive discussion for several hours, the directors finally agreed to approve the proposed decree. After voting the approval, and almost as an afterthought, the directors took one final step. They authorized the filing of a petition under Chapter X of the Bankruptcy Act if it was later deemed to be appropriate by the SEC and the federal District Court. . . . The petition was filed and approved on April 5, 1973.

"The decade of fraud at EFCA had come to an end. . . .

"The most frequently asked question about the EFCA fraud probably is, 'Where did all the money go?' This question rests upon two assumptions: (1) that EFCA was a prosperous corporate giant with substantial real income and assets; and (2) that the fraud consisted of stealing huge amounts of those sums. Both assumptions appear to be incorrect.

"First, it is now known that EFCA never was a true corporate giant. When the fraud was discovered, EFCA proved to be a 'paper giant.' While several of its subsidiaries had value and were untainted by the fraud, as an overall matter the Company's reported statistics were mostly a fraud. Simply put, EFCA never had the assets it reported; never had the revenues; never had the sales; never had the net worth; and never made the profits. Thus, despite all of its acquisitions, the Company appears to have always been relatively small, devoid of equity, and totally unprofitable.

"It is now apparent that EFCA sustained operating losses for years in its home office, insurance and marketing operations, and probably in the financing of its funding business as well. On a consolidated basis, deficits from the Company's losing operations clearly exceeded total earnings from its few profitable subsidiaries. Moreover, the most profitable subsidiaries were but recently acquired: Bankers [National Life Insurance] in 1971 and Northern [Life Insurance] in 1972.

"Thus, it appears that the only way EFCA was able to report any net earnings at all was through the fraud. As the following table demonstrates, from 1964 to 1972 the Company reported net earnings of $76 million. During the same years, the fraud generated at least $143 million of bogus income, more than $114 million of which came from funding and insurance. Without this bogus income, EFCA undoubtedly would have reported a loss in every year of its operations and, for all years taken together, it would have reported aggregate net operating losses in the millions of dollars.

COMPARISON OF ESTIMATED BOGUS FUNDING AND INSURANCE INCOME TO REPORTED NET EARNINGS (1964–1972)

	Bogus Funding Income	Bogus Insurance Income	Minimum Gross Income From Fraud	Reported Consolidated Earnings
1964	$ 361,000	$ 0	$ 361,000	$ 389,467
1965	1,068,000	0	1,068,000	795,944
1966	3,155,000	0	3,155,000	1,177,355
1967	3,549,000	0	3,549,000	2,530,380
1968	5,152,000	0	5,152,000	7,825,857
1969	17,200,000	350,000	17,550,000	10,911,632
1970	15,600,000	4,000,000	19,600,000	11,715,625
1971	17,900,000	10,000,000	27,900,000	18,192,000
1972	21,000,000	14,667,000	35,667,000	22,617,000
TOTAL	$85,345,000	$29,017,000	$114,412,000	$76,155,260

[Totals are incorrect in the Bankruptcy Report.]

"It should be noted that this table shows only the estimated amounts of bogus income from funding and insurance. A sizeable amount of other bogus income was generated over the course of the fraud through a grab-bag of accounting 'dirty tricks' which have not been fully explained in this report [The Trustee's

Bankruptcy Report] because of their relative insignificance. . . .

"From the foregoing, it should be apparent that the first assumption underlying the myth of the looted giant is false: There was no real giant to loot. It also appears that the second assumption is false. Despite the fact that large amounts of cash did come in to EFCA through borrowings, no evidence has yet been found that the conspirators drained the Company's treasury. It is probable that substantially all of the cash left over after paying off loans and making acquisitions was exhausted by operating losses, although the amount of these losses cannot be determined because of the dismal state of the Company's records. With the exception of the three-quarters of a million dollars in embezzlements and peccadillos . . . it does not appear that there was significant looting. This is not to say that the conspirators were not enriched by the fraud. They received generous emoluments, and the ringleaders realized hundreds of thousands and, in two instances, millions of dollars in wrongful profits from stock sales. But they do not appear to have dipped directly into the till for large sums.

"This conclusion is supported by all of the available evidence. First, the Trustee's lawyers and accountants have scrutinized EFCA's books and records in painstaking detail over a year and a half. A large share of this enormous amount of time was spent on a balance sheet audit as of April 5, 1973, the results of which have already been reported by the Trustee. Equally large amounts of time have been spent studying available historical records maintained by the Company and its former auditors, and reviewing the hundreds of files maintained by the conspirators themselves.

"Throughout this intensive search, a special effort has been made to look for clues of looting. For example, sample tests of cash receipts and disbursements were made for selected periods of the Company's operations. In addition, some individual transactions have been analyzed for hints of theft. Although many questions are raised by the records, none appear to point in the direction of massive looting by the conspirators.

"Evidence taken from more than 100 witnesses—including many of the fraud participants themselves—also buttresses this conclusion. The Trustee's lawyers have taken or reviewed testimony from most of the key conspirators. In addition, dozens of other persons who might know of such looting if it in fact took place have been interviewed. None of this evidence indicates that any substantial sums of money were embezzled from the Company other than as described in this report. Of course, the possibility of substantial theft remains, especially in view of the unlikelihood that a conspirator guilty of looting would admit to it and the impossibility of determining the actual cash flow in and out of EFCA over the years. Consequently, the Trustee intends to pursue this possibility in the context of contemplated litigation and otherwise. Based upon presently available information, however, it does not appear that the EFCA fraud involved large-scale looting of the sort imagined by those who ask where all the money went.

"A great deal has been written about the EFCA fraud. Much of the literature seems to characterize the fraud as the brilliant brain-child of 'with-it' business and computer wizards. . . . First, EFCA appears never to have had people experienced in management at its top executive level. The four founders, for example, were all salesmen by background. Two of these men—Michael Riordan and Stanley Goldblum—dominated the management of EFCA as long as they were associated with it. Neither had any experience in business outside of sales before they started the Company. With a few exceptions, other 'top executives' tended to be either lower-level accountants or lawyers—none of whom had significant business experience prior to the time they were put in charge of EFCA. Thus, Jerome Evans had a variety of bookkeeping jobs prior to becoming the chief financial officer of the Company, but it is safe to say that he never managed more than a handful of people before he was put in charge of EFCA's operations. Samuel Lowell, while he worked at one time for a big-eight accounting firm, also seems to have had no prior management background. Fred Levin was a lawyer with the Illinois Insurance Department when he was hired by Presidential, and he too had little or no executive experience before assuming a major management role at EFCA. Furthermore, the top managers—who tended to be the top fraud participants—were primarily assisted in running both EFCA and the fraud by a growing corps of vice presidents in their 20's and early 30's most of whom also do not appear to have held any previous management positions. In short, the majority of EFCA's managers appear to have been inexperienced men, lacking in seasoned business judgment, who played at high finance—and failed miserably in the process.

"Not only did these men fail at running the Company; in fact, they did not run the fraud any better. As this report demonstrates, there simply was no 'grand scheme.' Every step of this fraud was jerry-built—one misstep requiring another more complicated misstep to conceal all that had gone before. It is true that the conspirators can sometimes be credited for a degree of inventiveness in extricating themselves from near hopeless situations. On the whole, however, their helter-skelter, hand-to-mouth efforts demonstrate a striking lack of analytical insight and forethought. Indeed, some of the devices used to further or conceal the fraud are totally devoid of economic sense and seem to be in almost open defiance of generally accepted accounting principles and auditing standards. For example, although the conspirators were creating bogus income both from the insurance operation and from funding, they never figured out how to effectively coordinate the steps of the fraud. This failure created growing imbalances in inter-company accounts which might have been eliminated by effective administration and a degree of farsightedness. Moreover, from the outset, no one appears ever to have given serious thought to a way out of the scheme.

"Oddly enough, the slipshod character of much of the fraud may be a reflection of the attitude of some conspirators who appear to have looked upon the fraud as a game. The curious flippancy of the conspirators is illustrated by a sheet of game instructions given to Samuel Lowell by Arthur Lewis which was found in a Lowell file entitled 'Kudos.' This document explains how to play 'Sam-O-Wits.' The 'player' is instructed to reply to questions concerning EFCA's financial statements by saying, 'That was caused by a . . . ,' followed by his choice of one word from each of three columns on the sheet. The 'player' is admonished to 'emphasize the third word' and, if asked to explain in greater detail, he is told to 'comment that the subject is so complex and technical that it took two years to understand it.' The three columns are as follows:

Column 1	Column 2	Column 3
Complicated	Phase III	Adjustment
Complex	Commission	Reinstatement
Preliminary	Persistency	Provision
Convoluted	Morbidity	Experience
Favorable	Recapture	Retrocession
Mature	Actuarial	Fluctuation
Consolidated	Non-Refund	Ruling

". . . Probably because they were discovered first, the insurance aspects of the EFCA fraud have received the most publicity, and the scandal has frequently been characterized as an insurance fraud. However, as this [Bankruptcy] report has shown, the insurance activity was merely one particular phase of a much larger stock fraud that began at or before the time of EFCA's first public offering in 1964. The fraud was designed to pump up the value of the Company's stock by systematically inflating EFCA's reported earnings through every means available to the conspirators.

"The funding and insurance devices contributed the most bogus income to EFCA's reported earnings, and thus had the biggest impact upon the Company's earnings. Although this report has focused upon these revenue-inflation devices, many others were used as well to keep EFCA's stock flying high. For example, in 1968—in addition to the estimated $5.5 million of bogus funding income recorded—approximately $3 million of bogus revenue was generated by recording as income in that year the difference between market value and cost of various securities, even though these securities were still held by the Company and had not been sold. Another oft-used trick involved the 'sale' of future income from some aspect of EFCA's business for a promissory note which was to be paid-off out of that income as it was received. In several instances, although the 'sale' amounted to a mere financing arrangement, the full amount of the note was improperly recorded as income in the year of the transaction.

Another ploy involved overstating the percentage of completion on real estate projects in order to recognize a greater amount of income than was proper. Still another device involved improperly recognizing more than $1 million of income earned by a recently acquired subsidiary, despite the fact that the acquisition was rescinded during the year the income was recognized.

"The list of bogus income creating devices is a long one, and all the examples may not yet be known. The point is that all of these devices had as their goal the fraudulent inflation of the market price of EFCA's common stock. Hence, as this [bankruptcy] report has tried to demonstrate, the primary impact of the fraud was upon holders of EFCA securities and others who were misled by the Company's fraudulent financial statements. There was no impact upon its insurance policyholders—and relatively little impact upon EFLIC's reinsurers. Thus, insurance was merely the last phase of what should now be seen as a classic stock fraud. . . .

"If the EFCA fraud was truly as haphazard and disconnected as it has been portrayed in this report, then it is legitimate to ask how it persisted for a decade without detection. Obviously a number of factors contributed to the longevity of the conspiracy. Foremost, of course, were the lies, audacity and luck of the ringleaders. Of almost equal importance was the surprising ability of the originators of the fraud to recruit new participants over the years. Closely related was the moral blindness of those participants, including several who helped execute the scheme and then left the Company, but remained silent. It is noteworthy that in the end, the fraud was undone by the spite of a former conspirator who had been terminated, not by anyone's conscience pangs.

"The foregoing factors explain how the conspiracy was sustained for so long from within the Company. Responsibility for failing to detect the fraud [according to the Trustee] rests primarily with the accounting firms retained to certify the financial condition of EFCA and its subsidiaries. As this report makes clear, the fraud took place 'on paper'—in the books and records of the Company and some of its subsidiaries. Aside from the perpetrators themselves, only the auditors, as part of their annual examinations, had regular opportunities to review these books and records. In the Trustee's judgment, had the auditors properly discharged their obligations, the fraud would have been caught years ago. . . .

"From 1961 to 1970, EFCA and most of its subsidiaries were audited by Wolfson Weiner. There is strong evidence that several of the accountants in charge of these audits were aware of or suspected the fraud and cooperated in its concealment. Such a conclusion seems irresistible to the Trustee if only because Wolfson Weiner's performance was so manifestly incompetent for so many years as to be inexplicable on any other basis.

"First, EFCA's books and records were a literal mess over the entire life of the fraud, and it seems reasonably clear that the Company never had adequate internal controls in many areas, including its funding operations. Thus, it is difficult to see how Wolfson Weiner performed any audits at all. Had the auditors done their job by requiring management to maintain orderly records and to develop adequate control procedures as a condition of annual certification, it would have been impossible to get the funding fraud off the ground.

"Equally important, Wolfson Weiner failed in numerous respects to conduct its examinations in accordance with generally accepted auditing standards. The omissions and errors were legion, and many examples are recounted in the body of this report. Four prominent instances will serve to illustrate this essential point: Evans' first bogus commission entry in 1964; Templeton's problems with funded loans receivable in 1968; the treatment of the net trail commissions in 1969; and the patently inadequate support for funded loans at year end 1972. Substantial income was booked or justified in each instance virtually without supporting detail and on the strength of inherently unacceptable explanations. Reasonable tests of EFCA's accounting records and other auditing procedures necessary in the circumstances should have exposed the impropriety of these and many other improper entries and thereby exposed the fraud.

"After Seidman & Seidman combined practices with the Los Angeles office of Wolfson Weiner, the audits for EFCA and most of its subsidiaries in 1971 and 1972 were performed by that firm. But the change was in name only. After the combination of practices the same people were left in control of the EFCA audit and apparently no Seidman representative reviewed their performance. Hence, the imprimatur of Seidman & Seidman on EFCA's financial statements did not signify any notable change in underlying procedures. It is not surprising, therefore, that the 1971 and 1972 EFCA audits were also conducted incompetently.

"The 1972 audit by Seidman was especially deficient because only on that occasion did a single accounting firm audit each aspect of the funding operation. As has been explained elsewhere in this report, the funding operation consisted of four basic activities: sale of programs, financing, purchase of mutual fund shares and issuance of insurance. These activities were conducted in three entities: EFC-Cal, EFSC and EFLIC. The various accounting aspects of the funding fraud at these three companies were not integrated with each other. A single bogus transaction could not be traced through the books and records of the respective entities involved, because no effort was made by the conspirators to develop mutually consistent documentary support. Thus, for example, on the books of EFLIC, journal entries were made to record fictitious insurance premium income in an inter-company account as a receivable due from EFC-Cal, and bogus files were developed at EFLIC as needed to support this fictitious income. On EFC-Cal's books, however, no corresponding entries were made to show premiums payable to EFLIC.

"Through 1971, Wolfson Weiner (later Seidman & Seidman) examined the books of EFC-Cal and EFSC, while Haskins & Sells examined the books of EFLIC. Numerous improper entries should have been discerned by a careful auditor from the books of EFC-Cal and EFSC alone. When in 1972 Seidman & Seidman audited EFLIC, as well as EFC-Cal and EFSC, the funding fraud ought to have been nearly self-revealing, because of the obvious inconsistencies between the books and records of the three companies. Evidently, however, the accountants from Seidman & Seidman who examined EFLIC's books did not coordinate their work with personnel who audited the parent and other subsidiaries (who were mostly former Wolfson Weiner accountants). In any event, the discrepancies were either not discovered or ignored. . . .

"It is by now obvious that the fraud was not merely an

insurance scandal. However, the fact remains that a massive fraud was perpetrated on the books of EFLIC, the Company's primary insurance subsidiary. More than $2 billion in face amount of bogus policies were reinsured by EFLIC, and almost $30 million of fictitious premium and other income was reported by that company. For a number of reasons it appears to the Trustee that Haskins & Sells should have detected sufficient evidence of this aspect of the fraud to have prompted its discovery.

"For one thing, Haskins & Sells did not adequately check the procedures by which information was generated through EFLIC's data processing system. Very heavy reliance for information about EFLIC's operations was placed on print-outs and similar data produced by the Company's computers. Nevertheless, Haskins & Sells failed to review the internal controls of the computer installation. These controls were in fact weak or non-existent, a condition which made it possible for special print-outs which merged legitimate and bogus information to be prepared for the auditors.

"In the Trustee's judgment, this failure was a serious omission. However, the most fundamental shortcoming in Haskins & Sells' performance was its nearly complete dependence upon information from internal EFLIC sources. It failed to obtain verification of this information either from the books and records of affiliated companies or from third parties.

"Normally accountants auditing an insurance company have primary source records readily available from which to correlate reported data concerning premiums, insurance in-force and commissions paid. In a proper audit, tests are made to determine that all this information ties together and is internally consistent. Haskins & Sells did not have primary source records from which to perform such tests at EFLIC because records of both premiums earned and commissions paid to agents were kept by EFC-Cal, a separate entity. In these circumstances, EFLIC was not auditable apart from some reasonable verification of the premium and commission information furnished by its affiliate. Haskins & Sells should have tested EFC-Cal's records showing premium receipts, or the generation of premiums through funding, and commission payments to EFC-Cal salesmen. Had the auditors done so, they would have found glaring discrepancies which should have prompted discovery of the fraud.

"Nor did Haskins & Sells confirm insurance in-force directly with purported policyholders. Such confirmations were called for in EFLIC's case. Under principles of statutory accounting, policies are carried on the balance sheet of an underwriting company as a reserve liability. There would be limited, if any, reason for such a company to inflate the amount of in-force policies on its books since that would increase its liabilities. Under such circumstances, it might be argued there is no need to confirm the amount of insurance in-force.

"However, where a company reinsures a substantial portion of its business, the situation is materially different. The ceding company generates income from such business, while the reinsurer assumes the reserve liability. Hence, even a statutory reporting company has an incentive to overstate the amount of its in-force insurance when it reinsures much of its business. Where such a company converts from statutory accounting to generally accepted accounting principles ('GAAP'), the incentive is all the greater. This is so because GAAP accounting results in the accrual of income from policies at the same time reserves are set up. EFLIC began large-scale reinsurance in 1969 and converted to GAAP accounting in 1971. Thus, for both these reasons Haskins & Sells should have confirmed the amount of insurance the company claimed to be in-force. Such confirmation was even more vital in EFLIC's case in view of the absence of any testing by the auditors of primary source documents for EFLIC's principal income and expense items.

"[As a final postscript it should be noted that] literally hundreds of persons and firms had business relations with EFCA during the life of the fraud. To a varying degree, they all had some opportunity to observe the real workings of the Company. Others, including government regulators and investment analysts, had an ongoing professional interest in the Company's performance and presumably had regular occasion to review EFCA's financial statements. All these individuals and entities had at least a chance to spot clues of the scandal. Without intending to prejudge questions of legal duty, the Trustee does not find it surprising that no one did so.

"Although it is now evident that there were some discrepancies in EFCA's financial statements over the years, only someone examining the statements thoroughly, regularly and with a critical eye would have found them. And only someone with an exceedingly skeptical bent of mind would have then inferred massive fraud. Such an inference would have been hostile to the presumption of good faith and honest-dealing which customarily prevails in American business practice. To the Trustee, that presumption, though sometimes grievously abused, is probably indispensable to a vigorous and productive economy.

"When the scandal broke, lawsuits were filed all over the country naming as defendants nearly every person and company or institution that appeared to have had any significant contact with EFCA or its subsidiaries. Most of these lawsuits were filed when few of the facts were known and are evidently premised upon the assumption that these parties either knew or should have known about the fraud. Based upon the available evidence, this reaction seems to the Trustee unjustified. It appears rather that the banks, underwriters, reinsurers and others named in many of these lawsuits probably could only have discovered the fraud at EFCA by blind luck.

"The same probably can be said of most of EFCA's Board of Directors. During the better part of the fraud years, EFCA's outside directors included a Harvard professor, a senior partner of a New York investment banking firm, and two experienced business executives—all of whom appear to have played active roles as directors of the Company. Based upon present information, however, there is nothing to indicate that any of these outside directors knew about the fraud. And, of course, they clearly had nothing to do with its discovery. Whether these men should have discovered the fraud depends upon one's view of the role directors should or realistically can be expected to play in the affairs of a large, publicly held corporation engaged in complex business activity, as was EFCA.

"To the Trustee it seems unrealistic to expect directors to exercise the detailed oversight necessary to discover frauds perpetrated by determined and unprincipled executives. First, outside directors normally cannot make the major time commitment which such oversight would require. They are active in other pursuits and, indeed, are retained as directors because of the experience and judgment gained by reason of their principal activities. Moreover, outside directors rarely have substantial experience with the business of the company upon whose board they have been asked to sit, since active outsiders with such experience are often precluded from serving as directors by antitrust considerations or conflicts of interest. As a practical matter, even inside directors have scant opportunity to discover an accounting fraud conducted outside of their area of responsibility.

"The principal effect of imposing a duty to discover such frauds would probably be to discourage membership on corporate boards. An observation on this question fifty years ago by Judge Learned Hand seems no less apt today:

It seems to me too much to say that he [the director] must read the circulars sent out to prospective purchasers and test them against the facts. That was a matter he might properly leave to the officers charged with that duty. He might assume that those who prepared them would not make them fraudulent. To hold otherwise is practically to charge him with detailed supervision of the business, which, consistently carried out, would have taken most of his time. If a director must go so far as that, there will be no directors. (*Barnes* v. *Andrews,* 298 Fed. 614, 620 [S.D.N.Y. 1924].)

At a time when many corporations are seeking to diversify their boards of directors with members having a public interest orientation, it seems especially inappropriate to depart from the notion that directors, like investors and others, are entitled to presume that the top management of a public corporation is essentially honest and that its auditors competently perform their duties."

Thus, the Trustee's Bankruptcy Report ends.

Cleaning up the mess and determining the exact extent of the fraud are tremendous undertakings which are still going on.

The Illinois and California Insurance Commissions, the SEC, the Trustee's staff, and Touche Ross, the CPA firm assigned to perform the post audit, all converged on the MIS center because that was where a major part of the data was. The computer room resembled the gold weighing room at Fort Knox. Entry required signing in and wearing color-coded badges. Guards with guns stood around watching the computer and magnetic tapes and disks, having no idea what it was they were watching. The MIS staff went from 80 down to 40 people. The SEC examiners walked into the computer room and found a computer operator performing the standard process of erasing scratch tapes (tapes used for temporary storage of data during processing). The alarm was sounded. The entire data processing staff was ordered to go home, and the computer operation was shut down for three weeks. This was disastrous since there was still an insurance business to run and many of the almost 100 other subsidiaries were dependent upon the MIS computer center.

The magnetic tapes had been kept in another room on a completely uncontrolled basis. They were soon moved into the same room as the computer and watched. No programmers had access directly to any tape from then on, and no tapes were being scratched—the data on all used tapes were saved. This required introducing about 100 new tapes per day at a cost of $15 to $20 per reel. The auditors locked up all the master file tapes and made copies of them finally for the MIS staff to use in continuing the data processing function.

Touche Ross made extensive use of their computer program, Strata, for extracting data from the master files and producing the necessary reports revealing the detail and extent of the fraud. Ninety-nine percent of the bogus policies were found in this fashion. New methods had to be devised to use the computer in searching for that last 1 percent.

Warren White, an experienced management consultant familiar with data processing, was called in to assist Loeffler. White ran the computer center for several months until it was turned over to a facilities management company to operate. Shortly afterwards, it was completely disbanded, and Equity Funding, including all of its subsidiaries, found other service bureau sources to perform the computer processing needed to continue the operation of the company.

We are still left with the question, Was the Equity Funding case a computer fraud or more generally a computer abuse? This can be easily answered by applying the definitions of computer abuse stated earlier in this book and by identifying the roles played by the computer, thus determining who was right: Loeffler who claimed it was not a computer fraud, or Payne who claimed that it was.

A computer abuse is defined as any incident involving an intentional act where a victim suffered or could have suffered a loss, and a perpetrator made or could have made gain and is associated with computers. Certainly, the Equity Funding case involved an intentional act. Twenty-two persons have been convicted so far. The victim, or in this case victims, suffered loss; 7,000 stockholders were left holding worthless stock. The re-insurers and creditors of Equity Funding certainly lost large amounts of money, at least as indicated by more than 50 law suits currently in the courts.

The involvement of the computers is evident from Loeffler's Bankruptcy Report, which is riddled with descriptions of the roles played by computers. Loeffler identified three stages of the fraud: the inflated earnings phase, the foreign phase, and the insurance phase. Documentation makes it clear that computers were not involved in the first two phases. The role of the computer can therefore only be considered in the insurance phase of the fraud.

Computers have been identified as playing more than one role when involved in computer abuse. The computer (1) is the object, or the data in the computer are the objects, of the act; (2) creates a unique environment or unique form of assets; (3) is the instrument or tool of the act; or (4) represents a symbol used for intimidation or deception. The computers were not the objects of any kind of attacks. The data certainly were objects of attack when the master files of insurance policies on several occasions were manipulated. Reports of policies in force were printed with the two leading digits of the identification numbers left off. Alan Green added thousands of fake insurance policies to the master files by making copies of existing policy records and then modifying them to create the new bogus policies.

The second role of computers is also applicable in this case where, because of the nature of computerized files of data, the data stored on magnetic tapes were easily hidden and moved from the System 3 in the Actuary Department into the data center. Data stored in computer systems and computer media are not directly observable to the human eye. If all of the insurance had been stored on paper in a manual system, the fraud activities would have been quite different; but that would have made the fraud impossible to perpetrate since the volume of 64,000 bogus insurance policies precluded the use of manual methods.

The use of the computer as an instrument in the fraud is quite evident but not particularly sophisticated. Keeping an account of the bogus policies was a basic activity performed using the computer. It was also used to some degree in creating believable policy activity, such as premium payments, commission payments, mortality rates, and policy lapses. In this respect the computer was probably no more identifiable or important in the fraud than the office adding machines, as Loeffler stated.

Finally, the computer had another important role as a symbol used to deceive and intimidate the auditors. Payne's comment that "all of the industry assumed computers were always accurate" demonstrates the problem. It is too often assumed that if a report comes out of the computer, it must by definition be correct. The frequently heard adage, "Garbage in—garbage out," is not fully understood by some segments of business management and auditors. An even less acknowledged truth is that good data put in can easily be made into garbage when they come out the other end simply by the manipulation of the programs that process the data. Also, to stress the fact once again, the EDP role was to lend an air of authenticity to otherwise bogus data. Highly suspect data can be fed into a computer, massaged, and printed out on impressive, large sheets of paper in precise, ordered columns and can look quite authoritative, accurate, and impressive.

It is abundantly clear, based on the definitions of computer abuse, that the Equity Funding Corporation fraud was a major computer abuse. At the same time, Robert Loeffler in his concept of the fraud as a securities fraud is correct, based at least on what must be his definition of computer fraud, in saying that it was not a brilliantly conceived computer fraud. This is evident considering the ringleaders and brains of the fraud had little or no understanding of computer technology and certainly did not sit down together in a conference room and decide among themselves that they were going to make Equity Funding a brilliant success through the manipulation of computers. They probably had little or no knowledge of the actual roles played by the computers. As a securities fraud, computers played a minor and indirect role. However, in the insurance fraud aspect, the one receiving Insurance Commissioner Payne's attention, computers played a significant role that warrants describing the entire fraud as a case of computer abuse.

Much has been learned about how to make computers safer through the study of the EFCA fraud. A company the size of EFCA should never be allowed by its board of directors to function without a competent internal auditor. A company the size of EFCA with its degree of reliance on electronic data processing should never be allowed to function without an auditor who has extensive EDP auditing capabilities. Data processing should never be allowed to operate on an open shop basis where employees not having direct data processing responsibilities are allowed access to the master files of the accounting data of the organization. The insurance industry no longer needs to function with the same degree of reliance only on trust between insurance companies. The advent of data processing makes it highly cost effective to exchange large volumes of detailed accounting records between their computers.

State governments can also be faulted for the ineffectiveness of the state insurance commissions. The California and Illinois State Insurance Commissions having jurisdiction over Equity Funding fell far short of their responsibility. The U. S. Senate Subcommittee on Anti-trust and Monopoly knew of this situation as far back as 1960, when on August 4 of that year the following report was produced:

"The questionnaire disclosed that insurance department examiners as a whole are not only poorly paid but, in 19 States, are paid directly by the insurance company being examined. This practice raises serious questions of conflict of interest. The company under surveillance is allowed to compensate directly those people conducting the examination. It is reasonable to conclude that certain abuses could creep into this system. In addition, there are wide variations among the several States as to the per diem allowance paid examiners. Because of the wide range in the per diem allowance, in some States the amount is grossly inadequate, and in other States it is excessive.

"The fact that examiners are generally poorly compensated also suggests that they may not be completely qualified for their positions in the structure of State regulation. The economic alternatives available to a good examining staff member are sufficiently attractive to leave many insurance departments saddled with employees who are not fully competent to discharge the responsibilities placed upon them.

"The subcommittee feels that laxity of examinations is a serious problem in State regulation. Efficient State supervision requires far greater reliance upon frequent and thorough examinations of insurance companies and organizations than heretofore shown by many departments. . . .

"The subcommittee believes that the examination system, either by the individual States or of the convention type, should be a primary focus of the activities of regulation, especially in a more competitive environment to prevent insolvencies. Therefore, efforts should be directed at recruiting and retaining higher paid, better qualified examiners, free of company influence.

"The budgets of insurance departments are generally inadequate for the responsibilities placed on them. Budget figures reveal that approximately 4.27 percent of the total revenue collected by way of premium taxes is spent in insurance regulatory activities. In other words, 95.73 percent of the revenue collected is shifted to the general treasury of the State involved."

This situation outlined by the Senate Subcommittee in 1960 has not changed much in the intervening years according to the *United States Investor* magazine for April 21, 1973. It states that in 1970 slightly less than 5 percent of the revenue collected was allotted to the State Insurance Departments to meet their operating expenses. The Equity Funding case should certainly have an impact and result in much improved state insurance commissions. The California State Insurance Commission has been conducting an intensive data processing training program among its staff since it got caught with its pants down in the EFCA fraud.

As a postscript to this story, some of the sentences meted out to certain principal perpetrators in the EFCA fraud are interesting. Federal indictments were brought against 19 people by a federal grand jury on November 1, 1973, on 105 criminal counts. After all of the accused, plus at a later date three auditors, pleaded guilty, they were sentenced in court hearings, starting in April 1975 and extending through June of that year. Stanley Goldblum at forty-six years of age received a prison sentence of eight years, to be served at McNeil Island Federal Penitentiary in the state of Washington. He was fined $20,000. Fred Levin, age thirty-seven years, received a seven-year prison sentence; Samuel Lowell, five years; Michael Sulton, two years; David Capo, two years; Lawrence Collins, two years; William Mercado, six months and three years probation; Donald McClellan, six months and three years probation; Lester Keller, three months and three years probation; Alan Green, three months and three years probation; Jerome Evans, two years probation and a $5,000 fine; William Symonds, three years probation and a $1,000 fine; Mark Lewis, three years probation; Gary Beckerman, three years probation and a $1,000 fine. The three external auditors, Julian Weiner, Solomon Block, and Marvin Lichtig, were convicted in a separate trial and were to be sentenced in July 1975 for making false statements filed with the U.S. government and for securities fraud. All convicted criminals and several other people are still awaiting trial in the state of Illinois where they could be convicted and receive additional penalties.

Warren White, Loeffler's management and EDP consultant, was intensely devoted to the idea that the perpetrators of the fraud should get maximum sentences. He came to this position after seeing a sample of the hundreds of letters written to the Trustee telling of many families' financial ruin as a result of the devaluation of EFCA stock. The villains of this fraud perpetrated monstrous, horrible financial ruin on large numbers of trusting stockholders. Questioned as to the ethics of their activities, the perpetrators probably have their own rationalizations for their actions. They could easily claim that they were doing everything in their power to make Equity Funding a success, to maintain the financial stability needed to save all of those people through a strong securities position and price. In this respect they could conceive of themselves as defeated heroes rather than monstrous villains, and they might argue that if everyone had left them alone, they could have recovered from their problem, repurchased the bogus insurance policies, and Equity Funding would today be a successful, reputable insurance conglomerate with a record of great integrity and dedication to its policy holders and stockholders.

14 | PROGRAMMING A BANK COMPUTER TO STEAL

The victim in this case is a medium-sized bank with several local branches in a small city. An IBM 360/30 computer with on-line, IBM teller terminals is used, with a savings accounting package licensed by a software supplier. The terminals produce printed paper tape journal output of all activity, and the tape is archived for one year. The terminals can be locked with metal keys, but it was the bank's practice not to use them. However, the bank does maintain locked doors on the computer room. The computer operator functions independently of the programmer, although the programmer has access to live data in the computer files. The computer operator is not a programmer and is not familiar with programming.

There was no internal auditor during the period when the act occurred. Only three people had programming capability: the manager of data processing, his assistant serving as the systems analyst, and the perpetrator serving as the programmer.

The perpetrator had worked at the bank for a year and a half. He attended a trade school course in programming and learned assembly language coding (language understood by the computer) and RPG, but he was hired by the bank before completing the course and never learned COBOL (RPG and COBOL are higher level languages nearer to English that must be translated into computer language). He scored above 95 percent in all his classwork in the trade school. He was twenty years old at the time of the incident; his wife, who participated in the act, was nineteen years old. The perpetrator had a misdemeanor conviction for marijuana possession while attending high school; otherwise he had no police record. He is short, of slight physical build, and handsome. He comes from a broken home, got married at the age of seventeen, was divorced, and then married his present wife. He has been in financial difficulty since he was seventeen years old. He bought heavily on credit to lead a life significantly beyond his means, showing no concept of financial responsibility. His debts mounted, and he indicated that he constantly worried about them but that he did not know how to get proper help. He claims that before the incident he became distraught and decided to solve his problem once and for all one way or another.

In my interview with him in prison after his criminal hearing he said that his sentencing severity would depend on the degree of criminality of his acts; therefore, there were some things he could not tell me, such as the amount of planning involved. He tried to impress me with the impulsive nature of his acts, the small amount stolen in an environment where he could have stolen more, and the fact that he knew how to steal in a more clever fashion than he did to avoid detection. When asked why he did not use the more clever method, he said that he did not care if he was caught because it could be a successful solution to his problems as well as successful stealing of the money.

His work consisted of using a report generator program to produce special reports for management and to modify and maintain the savings accounting system. He wore his hair long and affected the style of a hippie, but was very meticulous in his work and ordered the tasks he was to perform by reasonable priorities. He liked his programming job very much but did not mix with the people he worked with. He had a completely different life-style—he knew he would never fit in or be successful in this kind of environment, because it was foreign to him. He said his associates would have been shocked at his kind of life-style (this probably refers to his occasional use of marijuana and high living). He said he did not dislike the people he worked with, but he was sure that they generally disliked him. His only friendly contact in the bank was the executive vice president, who occasionally worked late and during the same periods of time as the perpetrator. They became acquainted through casual conversations, and he said the perpetrator was an almost invisible worker but did his job exceedingly well.

The perpetrator lived in a nearby exclusive suburb in a very expensive apartment. He had thousands of dollars' worth of hi-fi equipment and drove an expensive automobile. He indicated that he had no friends. He was fired from his previous job as a cook in a hotel because he was caught using marijuana on the job. The perpetrator said that he was an honest person and would never think of stealing money from another person. When asked about the losses suffered by the account holders, he said he believed that they would not have lost anything because the insurance would have covered the losses. He concluded that the insurer and the government could afford financial loss, thereby justifying his act. He attempted to make me believe that his act was merely an unauthorized loan of $4,100 to pay off his current creditors. He said he intended to pay the money back over a period of time.

He claims he could have taken more elaborate precautions to avoid detection. For example, he could have taken the money from the certificate of deposit accounts where much less activity is experienced and quarterly reports are not made. He knew that quarterly reports would be produced on the first of the next month, and his act would be discovered at least at that time. However, he said that until that time he intended to hide the evidence of his act by further manipulation of accounts. In fact, he put the data identifying the accounts and amounts taken onto a magnetic tape so that he could keep track of these accounts in the process of returning the money and of further manipulating the accounts to avoid detection. He said that the method he used was one chosen almost at random—he could have used many different methods if he had wanted to. It was his practice to work in the evenings and early morning. So his presence in the office after hours, and in particular before working hours, did not arouse suspicion.

Interviews with other people indicated considerable discrepancies in the perpetrator's statements. He told the police at the time of his arrest that the idea for his act and advice on how to do it had come from an unidentified person. He told a very different story to the FBI and later the police concerning his motivation and plans. His story in the interview about deciding on his action gave the impression that it was compulsive and unplanned. However, the evidence and his testimony to the arresting officers and the FBI indicated that the action was in fact well planned and had the purpose of testing his chosen method of perpetrating the theft with a view to continuing it over a long period of time in order to take large amounts of money. He indicated to them that he did not want to wait until he was forty to fifty years old to obtain financial security; he wanted security now. He also indicated at one point that he was going to use the money from cashier's checks that he stole (and later forged after the computer-related incident) to go into the drug selling business.

He watched from a telephone booth as the police arrested his wife and told the police that, if he had had his rifle with the telescopic sight with him, he would have shot the arresting policemen and FBI agent. He had a 25-caliber pistol with him that he threw into a vacant lot just before he turned himself in to the men who were arresting his wife. On his subsequent arrest on the forgery charges, he was found carrying a 45-caliber pistol and a 25-caliber pistol. He claimed that he was going to use the larger pistol on the arresting officers and shoot himself with the smaller pistol.

The perpetrator's wife was employed. She is very attractive and dresses smartly. Between the two, they earned $1,100 per month. On May 23 the perpetrator's wife opened an account by mail with $20 in cash. She used a fictitious name and gave her address as General Delivery. On May 24, the perpetrator went through the computer listings of savings accounts looking at accounts in people's names beginning with A through D. He selected 41 accounts with large balances ($108,000 to $153,000) but normal activity levels. These accounts were from the same branch as his wife's account and within the same range of account numbers as his wife's account, thereby staying within the range of accounts that are included in the same control total figure produced by the computer.

On May 25, a Friday, he came to work at 7:45 A.M. before the other bank employees arrived at 8:30 A.M. His stories of what followed are conflicting. He told the police that he started the computer and wrote a program through an on-line terminal which caused a transfer of $100 from each of the 41 accounts into his wife's account. In the interview with me he denied using a program and said that he punched 41 transaction cards, started up the computer, and read the cards into the system to cause the transfers of funds. The bank controller thinks that the perpetrator started the computer and typed in transfer of fund commands one account at a time from the administrative terminal.

The controller indicated that there were only two ways in which the transfers could have taken place—by the terminal entry method he described, or by writing a special program that would read input cards and perform the transfer of funds. He thought that the perpetrator must have initialized the computer to begin a false day of operation. After concluding his act, the perpetrator would have had to remove and destroy all output indicating the fictitious day's transactions, including the exception reports, console log, and the paper tape log from the terminal (if, in fact, the terminal had been used). All these actions could have been done easily, leaving no trace that the computer had been run for a fictitious day. One hundred dollars was transferred as a no-book transfer entry from each of the 41 accounts, except that only $99.87 was transferred from one account. The perpetrator attributed this to an input typing error.

On four consecutive days the perpetrator's wife disguised herself in different wigs and used different rental cars on various occasions to withdraw a total of about $2,000 from her account at drive-in teller stations. Repeated withdrawals turned out to be necessary because of a limit of $500 on cash withdrawals.

On the following Tuesday a friend of the controller came in to transact business; when his pass book was put in the terminal, a report of the no-book transfer of $100 was issued. The teller asked the account holder if he was aware of the transfer. He indicated that he was not. This was overheard by the controller, who then looked at the report, listened to his friend's denial, and immediately concluded that a fraud or error could have occurred. By the next day, several other accounts were found to have $100 missing and transferred into a single account. The controller became convinced that fraud was involved. He deduced that it could have been done by one of four people. The act was discovered in full detail by performing a trial balance for the date identified in the first no-book transfer report. The exception report of the trial balance indicated line by line each no-book transfer of funds entry.

The police and the FBI were called in. They staked out the drive-in teller's window waiting for the appearance of the woman identified by the account number. At about noon on the next business day, the detective stakeout arrested the perpetrator's wife when she appeared at the drive-in teller's window. Her husband, who had been watching from a nearby telephone booth, came over to the police car after the arrest and turned himself in. The perpetrator was charged with theft, embezzlement, or misapplication over $500 by a bank employee. His wife was arrested for conspiracy. Both were released on bail under their own recognizance.

The perpetrator subsequently jumped bail and traveled to Nevada. He had stolen four cashier's checks, two of which he forged for $5,700 each, depositing the money in four different bank accounts. He kept in touch with his wife, gambled some of the money, bought a car, delivered it to his wife, who then resold the car as a means of obtaining some of the money. The police received information of his activities from his wife. A police detective, suspecting that the perpetrator was in Nevada, called the central credit service that supplies information about gamblers to the local gambling casinos. Within several hours, the perpetrator attempted to cash a personal check, and a credit check indicated he was a fugitive. He was immediately apprehended and was found to be carrying the two pistols mentioned earlier. He was charged with the additional count of check forgery and was returned and placed in the county jail where he nearly escaped by taking another prisoner's identity. He indicated in the interview that the reason for his attempt to escape was to get home, if only for several hours, before being captured again. After his escape attempt he was put into a state medical facility for 90 days of observation.

The total amount taken in the computer act before the two were apprehended was approximately $2,000. All but $800 was recovered. The wife of the perpetrator admitted her guilt, received a sentence of five years probation, and was directed to make restitution. The perpetrator received a sentence on the check forgery charge of nine months in the county jail (174 days credit), five years probation, requirement of restitution, and psychotherapy treatment. He received a sentence of three months (74 days credit) in jail consecutive with the nine months for his jail escape attempt. He had not yet been sentenced on the federal charges but probation was expected.

The perpetrator in this case fits the general profile of computer abuse perpetrators in several ways. He demonstrated the Robin Hood syndrome of believing that stealing from individuals is highly immoral but that stealing from an organization and in particular through a computer somehow does not hurt anyone and solves his problem. He is young, highly motivated, quite egotistical, and very bright. However, he differs from the perpetrator's profile in that he stated he did not consider his act as a game but a deadly serious attempt at solving his financial problems. The action did not represent a challenge to him, since he said it was so easy to perpetrate and since he made little attempt at hiding it. He also did not indicate a tendency toward the differential association syndrome in that his act was not condoned or would not have been accepted by his fellow workers. In fact, this case was the antithesis of the differential association theory, since he completely disassociated himself from the people he worked with. There may have been other associations outside his work with people who might have encouraged or accepted such action, but none was identified. This was a typical case of collusion, requiring a person with the skills, knowledge, and access to perform the technical part of the act and another person (in this case, his wife) to convert the act into financial gain.

In summary, there are three basic reasons why a fraud like this could have occurred. First, no particular screening of new employees was done. Second, programmers were allowed access to live data and the computer after hours, and there was limited separation of responsibility. Third, in the absence of an auditor, the controls in the system were not monitored, nor were the exception reports examined.

Since the incident, the terminals have been kept locked and elaborate control of the keys has been maintained. A new programmer was recently hired. She is the wife of an army man and is considered a short-term employee. She was hired because of her availability and her experience, which was urgently needed. There is no indication that increased attention is being paid to the screening of new employees. In fact, the controller expressed considerable concern that current public attitudes, litigation, and legislation are making it more difficult to carry out a thorough screening of potential employees.

15 | GANGING UP ON A BANK'S COMPUTER

The bank victim in this case is small, with about $150 million in assets. At the time of the incident, a small computer system was in use, with a staff of about eight programmers and eight computer operators. During the last quarter of the year, a conversion process was being conducted to convert to a larger system.

The bank is located in a medium-sized city. Its auditing function had no EDP capability at the time of the incident. The EDP staff was working on an overtime basis on the conversion process. During this period, the existing system had deteriorated significantly, since primary attention was being given to preparing for the new one. The conversion process was not completed until the next year because of considerable delays in development. The data processing operation was headed by the vice president for programming development and consisted of three parts: operations, customer services, and programming.

The alleged ringleader worked at the bank for approximately five years and became vice president of programming development. He was well liked and active socially, and he participated in many local service organizations. He was president of a local management association and active in various businessmen's service clubs. He was forty years old and has a large family. He dressed in conspicuous and flashy style. He was very voluble and was frequently engaged in extra moneymaking schemes. He had severe financial problems and was overdrawn at the bank. He had a vast array of credit cards and was known as a big spender. Overloaded in his work assignments, he was finding it difficult to do a good job because of the weight of these responsibilities.

His alleged role in the crime was based on the testimony of four other conspirators; however, the only evidence against him was in the form of accusations made by the operations supervisor. He was the last one to be tried. At his jury trial, he was represented by a very effective attorney and gave a strong impression of an honest bank official whose word was being weighed against the testimony of the other conspirators, who were young, hippie-type people. According to the police investigator, a lie detector test indicated that he was probably not telling the truth, whereas lie detector tests for a conspirator indicated he was probably telling the truth when describing the vice president's participation.

The primary conspirator was supervisor of computer operations at the bank, earning approximately $13,000 per year. He was twenty-five years old, married, and the father of a baby daughter at the time of his arrest. He and the vice president had organized an independent business, consisting of janitorial services for gas stations, but their business soon folded. He always dressed extravagantly and had a strong profile compared to the other employees. He had gambling problems. He ran the football pool in the bank, making approximately $50 per week, and some of the bank officers were his customers in this operation. He was a very amicable person, friendly with everyone in the bank. He had a high school education and went to a trade school in 1965 to learn computer operation. Originally he was hired as a janitor in the bank, but he worked his way up into computer operations. He had known the vice president for about five years and had worked for the bank for about that period of time. He indicated that he performed the technical parts of the fraud, relying on the bank vice president for the banking knowledge required to perpetrate it. He was convicted and given a two-year suspended sentence for violation of a state law: Conspiracy and Embezzlement by Employee of a Bank.

The next conspirator was an electrical design draftsman, not a bank employee. He was twenty-five years old, married, with one child, making approximately $13,000 per year. He was self-employed at one time, but his business failed. He had several bad checks that still had not been made good. He indicated that he did not gamble, but he did spend money on girls when he was drunk. He was a high school friend of the operations supervisor and played baseball, golf, and bowled with the other conspirators. He was the original instigator of the crime when he kidded with the operations supervisor about the possibility of transferring money into his savings account.

Another conspirator was twenty-seven years old, with an eighth-grade education, making about $7,000 as a carpenter. He was also a partner in a clothing shop. He had been a friend of the other conspirators since high school, but was not a bank employee. He was married, with a child. He indicated that he spent his share of the money on drinking, eating, and horse races. He also repaid a debt to a girlfriend in Las Vegas with money from the fraud.

The last conspirator was twenty-eight years old, married, with two children. He is a senior computer operator at a large company where he is still employed. He too is a childhood friend of the other conspirators.

The FBI was called into this case originally, but declined to participate in the investigation since it appeared to be appropriate for state prosecution. A detective in the prosecutor's office and the county prosecutor were the primary investigators. Neither was familiar with data processing, and they relied on employees of the bank to help them in gathering evidence in the case.

In early January 1971, a savings account customer reported to the bank that his 1970 fourth-quarter savings account statement was in error. The fourth-quarter statement beginning balance of approximately $12,000 reflected $6,000 less than the recorded ending balance of $18,000 on his previous statement, for the third quarter of 1970. He claimed he had made no withdrawals which could account for the $6,000 discrepancy. The validity of this complaint was established by examining the bank's record copies of the third- and fourth-quarter statements for his savings account. Examination of the bank's records, including the daily savings journals, daily savings trial balances, and savings input transactions, established that the balance in the account on November 2, 1970, had been reduced by $6,000. These records failed to reflect any recorded withdrawal transactions to account for this reduction. Further examination disclosed that the savings trial balances were in proof, indicating that other savings accounts would necessarily have to show a corresponding $6,000 total increase.

Continued review of records disclosed that on November 2, three main office savings accounts, subsequently closed during the fourth quarter of 1970, had increased balances, with no recorded deposit transactions supporting the increases. The three accounts with unsupported increases were in the names of the three nonemployee conspirators. A search of customer deposit and withdrawal slips for the period failed to disclose any documents pertaining to, or in support of, the unexplained decreases and increases in the accounts.

The savings accounts activities of the three conspirators were then reconstructed, using the bank's records. Efforts to locate the bank's record copy of withdrawal slips pertaining to the three accounts met with negative results. The absence of these documents indicated that they had been intentionally withdrawn from the files and probably destroyed. However, probably unknown to the perpetrators, microfilm of the deposit and withdrawal slips was available. Using the research procedures described above, a total of 25 savings accounts were discovered to have had unsupported decreases in balances, amounting to about $137,000, during the fourth quarter of 1970. Additional savings accounts in the names of the perpetrators were also found.

In addition to the total of six accounts found belonging to the perpetrators, ten additional savings accounts had unsupported increases, totaling $9,000, during the fourth quarter of 1970. However, none of the customers holding the ten additional accounts had withdrawn any of the funds represented by the unexplained increases. It was later concluded, and supported by the testimony of the perpetrators, that the purpose of these account changes was to confuse anyone checking for unexplained changes.

It was determined that the unsupported increases and decreases had been accomplished by unauthorized use of utility programs intended to change the content of any record stored in the system. Evidence of the use of these programs is recorded on the computer console log. An unsuccessful search for the console log indicated that it was probably destroyed.

The unauthorized access to the bank's computer apparently occurred on each of six weekends during the period. Available employee and security records showed that six people had access to the computer during those weekends, including the inside perpetrator.

A background investigation by the prosecutor indicated that the operations supervisor was a friend of the three outside conspirators. These four were arrested and admitted their guilt. They indicated that the withdrawals were later divided: two-thirds went to the operations supervisor, who was to share half this amount with his boss, the vice president; the remaining third went to the outside conspirators. The operations supervisor had told the outside conspirators that they had little to worry about, since he could successfully cover up any traces of the activities from within the bank. Two of the outside conspirators invested some of the proceeds with a stockbroker, one under joint account with the operations supervisor. They disposed of the remainder of the proceeds as described below.

The operations supervisor indicated that his boss had accompanied him several times to collect their share of the proceeds from the outside perpetrators. However, the others denied any knowledge of the identity of the alleged ringleader.

The operations supervisor stated that he put the majority of the money he received in his golf bag to hide it from his wife, but the golf bag was stolen from an unlocked automobile. Police files indicated that he had reported the theft of his golf bag on November 23, 1970. The golf bag has not been recovered.

On January 25, the vice president was arrested for his alleged complicity, after statements by the supervisor of operations had implicated him.

The operations supervisor described the beginning of the fraud by indicating that in August or September of 1970, while golfing with one of the outside perpetrators, they had joked about what could be done to perpetrate a fraud on the bank. He said he was called to his boss's office in September, when the vice president said that though they were working 50 to 70 hours per week, nobody in the bank seemed to care, and that in some way they should get even with the bank. The operations supervisor suggested the idea, based on his recent joking. Two weeks later, he said the vice president talked to him again and indicated how the fraud might be done using the utility program.

The bank proofed the accounts on a daily basis in each of the branches. The vice president is alleged to have used a copy of a trial balance of account numbers and balances to select several inactive, but not dormant, accounts. They decided to limit the activity to one fiscal quarter at a time. They needed to have a zero balance and close the outside conspirators' accounts by the end of the quarter, because the computer system dropped all records of accounts with zero balances at the end of each quarter. The savings application program installed with the new computer was known to be more thorough in the proofing of accounts. Therefore, the last withdrawal was made on December 21, prior to transfer to the new computer. With the destruction of the withdrawal slips on the closed accounts, they concluded that no records of the accounts would be left after the quarter. The only remaining evidence would be the reduced balances in the 25 accounts, and the mysterious increased balances in the remaining 10 accounts, with no other indication of where the proceeds from the reduced accounts went. Thus, the perpetrators badly underestimated the amount of residual information that would continue to be available to the bank after quarter-end.

The computer program being used was obsolete. It did not function very well at times, and it was common practice for the operations supervisor to be instructed by his superiors to change the content of files, using the utility program. The operations supervisor said that he planned to stop the whole operation after each person had gained $6,000, but he indicated that the other conspirators grew more greedy and wanted to keep going. The whole thing finally got out of hand, and it became obvious to him that the fraud was not going to work.

The operations supervisor felt the major reason for the partial success of the fraud was that the tellers had little dedication to their jobs; they rarely asked for identification and were not observant of customers' practices. Customers were simply given deposit and withdrawal slips, plus a quarterly statement. The operations supervisor had discovered that the bank was investigating a possible fraud when one of the programmers was called in by management to answer questions about the utility program, and on return to the computer room had joked to the operations supervisor in front of the staff that the supervisor was probably using the utility program to alter the accounts.

Only one of the three outside conspirators knew who the other outside participants were. One conspirator had already possessed two savings accounts in one of the branches. He had opened a third, with $10, at the instigation of the operations supervisor. He said that, while playing golf, he had joked with the operations supervisor suggesting that he transfer $2 million to his account and then skip town. The outside conspirators did not understand the process. They were told simply that a transfer of money from one account to another would occur through the computer. It was explained that this could be done for one quarter only, and that the savings accounts must be zeroed out before the end of the quarter. One of the outside conspirators also said he was told that the mailing of statements to the customers after the end of the quarter would be delayed, so that it would be too late for the bank to take action, and the bank would have to make up the losses. He related that the operations supervisor had said he would have to end the theft at the end of the quarter because they were changing to new computers, and he did not know how to use the new computers well enough to continue the fraud.

The director of security at the bank had been hired not long before the discovery of the fraud. He was detailed to carry out the investigation, with the assistance of the vice president, who was alleged to be involved in the fraud. The vice president insisted that he wanted to wait until conversion to the new computer occurred before conducting the investigation.

The security director indicated that although the bank had practically no screening practices for new employees, he could have detected the operations supervisor as a poor risk. In any case, the operations supervisor had been hired in a nontrust position that would not have required screening, but he should have been screened when elevated to a position of trust. The bank had no manuals on security. Policy was established by memos that were easily lost over a period of time; new employees had no access to the previous policy memos. There was an official attitude of complete trust in everyone in the bank. During the computer conversion period, most of the staff's attention was diverted to the conversion, and their regular jobs suffered, including any auditing or security precautions. As part of the investigation, a program was written to compare last quarter balances to current quarter balances, in order to trace all of the accounts that had been changed without supporting transactions.

In this case, as indicated, the bank was completing a conversion to a new computer system at the time of the fraud. The old system deteriorated as a result of lack of attention by the staff which was busy developing the new system. Rather than change the old program, management handled errors and special requirements by instructing the operations supervisor to make direct changes to the master file with a utility program, where the only record of change was made on the unmonitored operator's console log. The supervisor was in a position of trust. There was no dual control over the file changes he made. He could have easily rationalized that the changes he was making for the various executives constituted fraud, so he was doing nothing different in his fraud.

It is unlikely that screening of applicants would have stopped the hiring of either the supervisor or the vice president. The supervisor was a janitor in his first job and had shown his honesty for five years before being placed in one of the most sensitive positions of trust. Management probably did not understand EDP well enough to have much concern for the security of the bank in that environment. In spite of the security manager's indication that he would not have hired the vice president based on his known background, there was no real evidence that the information would have precluded the hiring. The vice president was a sophisticated, outgoing, and impressive man, as demonstrated by his high standing in the community. The jury could not believe he was guilty, in spite of the inferential evidence and the testimony of the other perpetrators.

The two employees involved had been working up to 60 hours per week, with no rewards or recognition, and probably were the targets of many complaints because the conversion effort was late. Considering their demonstrated desire to increase their income, it was possible they might perpetrate a fraud under the proper circumstances. Each could have reinforced the other in rationalizing and working themselves up to the fraudulent acts.

The operations supervisor and his three friends were convicted. The vice president was judged not guilty in a separate jury trial.

16 | A $1.4 MILLION EMBEZZLEMENT

A New York police detective was tailing his subject through the late afternoon traffic on Forty-second Street toward the Midtown Tunnel under the East River and out to the horse race track. He knew exactly where the balding, heavy, forty-one-year-old bank teller was headed because he had trailed him there several times before. He had never felt so sorry for a criminal suspect as this poor guy whose health was failing, confused to the point of driving right through red lights and stopping at green lights. It seemed like he was on his last legs, but the detective also knew the bank teller was carrying about $15,000 belonging to a lot of other people. He was going to do no more than enrich the race track. As usual at the race track, the detective recovered the torn-up betting tickets the bank teller discarded, indicating another losing day at $2,000 to $3,000 per race.

At the same time over in his home, a $275-per-month, two-bedroom garden apartment, a mother was greeting her daughters, home from school on this routine day, little realizing its importance in her family's life. And about halfway between home and the race track, in a building in Manhattan, 25 bank employees had been gathered together in a training room to be briefed by the auditors. They were to sift through three and one-half years of computer printouts, data input forms, deposit and withdrawal slips, and bank books in an attempt to reconstruct a $1.4 million embezzlement. The staff was warned of the need for secrecy and informed that they would have to work most of the night and all the next day.

The man at the focus of all this activity had never received so much attention in his entire life. He had worked for the bank for nine years, the last several years as a head teller with a current salary of $11,000. Everybody said he was a nice guy, well liked and very friendly. He lived a modest life in New Jersey and hadn't bought a new suit in three years, but he had other things to worry about than how he dressed. For this man is a "betaholic," hooked not on dope or alcohol but on gambling. As inflation ate away his salary and the years passed, he finally concluded that he was going to have to make it big now or not at all. He had been trying to increase his income by driving a taxi after work at the bank, but this had become a discouraging and dangerous job. He had been shot at twice while driving his taxi in the last three months.

He always believed he was smart enough to take money from the bank and not get caught. For years he said he had seen other tellers in other banks doing it, often making some stupid mistakes and getting caught, but a few did get away with it. They would usually steal small amounts by taking cash from depositors with Christmas Club accounts—tearing the coupons out of the books and destroying them. But this was pretty stupid because the errors ultimately had to show up.

Our supervisory teller was quite unhappy with his employer. Here he was at $11,000 a year and claiming that he was practically running the whole branch. He was also an expert at training new tellers. This made his job all the more difficult, as an almost continual stream of green tellers was processed through his branch. He had a supervisory computer terminal for administrative purposes, two cash boxes containing $10,000 to $50,000 each, and a key to the outside door of the vault.

He often ate lunch in the bank's main office cafeteria where he was quite friendly with the data processing personnel and the auditors who also ate there. However, he needed little help from them to know, from many years of experience, exactly how the bank operated even though most of the procedures had recently been converted to a computer system. He had one more piece of information, the combination to the inner door of the vault, which he easily obtained by observing the assistant manager opening the vault door. The vault room is accessible from the teller's area but is hidden from view when the door is partly closed. He said the vault contains three separate compartments; one holds the teller's locked cash boxes; the other two compartments are locked and require a combination to open them. One contains the reserve cash supply and the new bank books, and the other the savings bonds and traveler's checks supplies.

The big day for unleashing his fury at his frustration with his mundane life had arrived. He started by merely taking $5,000 from his cash box. He knew a sure thing at the race track, and his plan was to invest the $5,000, win a real financial stake in life, immediately return the $5,000 to the cash box, and be on his way to big gambling winnings. He lost $3,000 the first night and $2,000 the second night. He said the shortage in his cash box was handled routinely and never showed up as a problem for him.

He spent the next three and a half years trying to replace that $5,000. He took more cash, but finally the total became so large that he had to find another method. Enter the computer. "The computer didn't make it easier to steal but it sure did make it faster." In a short time he claims he had worked his way $68,000 into the hole, and in one short period had climbed back up to where he was only $28,000 short. But from there on it was all downhill, and he didn't even stop to notice where he was until over $1 million had been dropped.

Like many serious embezzlers, he used every means at his disposal to take money. He said he took it mostly in the form of cash from the vault. He was able to manipulate computer files by making unauthorized use of tellers' terminals to show that the bank had a specific level of assets but quite different from what the customers thought their level of assets to be in the bank. Apparently standing between the bank and the customers, he acted as a source of entropy as money flowed from customers into the bank and out to customers all through his hands and the hands of his green tellers. He created fictitious withdrawals from account records. He said he would also accept a valid deposit from a customer and correctly credit it to his account, but then through his terminal would make a deposit correction, reducing part or all of the transaction amount. Often a depositor whose account had been manipulated came to the bank to complain. The discrepancy in the balance was noted by the teller and reported to the supervisory teller, who explained the discrepancy to the teller and depositor by stating that it was caused by computer errors, and he would have them corrected in a few minutes. He said he would then make a fake telephone call to the data processing department to appease the teller and his irate depositor and use his supervisory teller terminal to make a correction, transferring money from another account and depositing it in the irate depositor's account. In some cases he claims he entered a special code into the computer for accounts he was manipulating, requiring that before a transaction was made the teller must obtain his approval. Mistakes seemed to happen quite frequently in his particular branch, but he said he was able to blame the green tellers for many of these.

He claims to have concentrated on accounts of $100,000 or more, with little activity except for depositors coming in four times a year to have interest entered into their pass books. Interest was a significant problem. Obviously the accounts from which he had taken money would not be credited with enough interest. Three methods were used to adjust interest. He prepared an item change form to have the interest amount corrected. In some cases these forms were signed by the manager or assistant manager, and in other cases the manager's name was probably forged. Another method was just to deposit the amount of the additional interest due so that the balance on the bank's records would be adjusted. When a depositor presented his bank book, he claims he would type in the interest figure and then post the adjusted balance through the teller terminal. He would sometimes make manual interest entries in customers' pass books to correct previous errors. In making these manual changes in front of the customers his hand would shake so much that customers occasionally commented on how nervous he was.

He explained to me another interesting method based on the fact that some of the accounts were day-of-deposit accounts which received interest on the last day of the quarter of the year. The time deposit accounts received interest two days after the last day of the quarter. Because of this difference in days on which interest was calculated, he was able to shift money into under-balanced accounts of one type in time to receive interest and then shift the money back into the other accounts when they were to receive interest.

In his later activities, if a customer opened a two-year certificate account, he said he would issue the necessary paper to the customer but would not enter the transaction on the machine. Thus the bank had no record of the customer having a two-year certificate deposit. He said this worked quite well for a while because he knew that he had two years generally before he had a problem. Later, however, he said the bank changed its procedures and posted interest on these accounts quarterly. This increased the amount of manipulation he had to do, and he started to worry that the number of corrections he was making might be noticed. Subsequently, he said he switched almost entirely to day-of-deposit accounts to supply his ever-increasing demand for cash.

He told me that manipulation in the opening of new accounts was easy. It required the use of two new pass books from the supply of blank, numbered pass books available in the vault. When an account was opened, he would enter the transaction under the account number of the second pass book but put the first pass book, which he was giving to the customer, into the machine. Therefore, the deposit would be recorded in a new account but with a different number than the customer thought he had with his shiny new pass book. Later, he would put through a correction on the terminal using the second account number. After cleaning out the account, he would then rip up the pass book, thus eliminating any current records of either of the accounts manipulated. Apparently no records were kept of the numbered new pass books awaiting use for new accounts.

He said the auditors gave him few problems. He was easily able to explain any discrepancies brought to him by the auditors, primarily by offering the excuse provided by his trainee tellers. He claims the auditors always gave him advance notice that they were coming to perform an audit. When they arrived, they went through exactly the same procedure every time. He could almost predict what each auditor was going to do moment by moment. However, he had many close calls. In one case he claims an auditor was counting his two cash boxes. He knew that the second box had a $20,000 shortage in it. Right before the auditor's eyes, using sleight-of-hand, he said he removed $20,000 from the box just counted and put it into the second box in time for the auditor to start counting again.

The only real discrepancies in this type of embezzlement are based on a bank thinking it has a specific asset value whereas the customers, treated as a whole, think they have a different asset value. The auditing method for discovering this is by executing confirmations, where the auditors send letters to customers quoting the account records and asking the customers to verify that these accounts are correct. He said there was no way for him to avoid this kind of discovery. However, the auditors apparently confirmed a small enough proportion of the total number of accounts that according to him the probability of confirming one of the 50 accounts he might currently be manipulating was very small. In three and a half years he said none of the accounts he was manipulating was ever confirmed.

Obviously he ultimately had to get caught. In the last several months of the embezzlement he was over $1 million in the hole. His accounting of the embezzlement was degenerating just as his health was degenerating, and he was making more mistakes. He kept records on little pieces of paper stuffed into his pockets, in his desk drawers, and other nooks and crannies. He knew he was going to be caught in a matter of time.

This takes us back to where the story started. The day before he placed his last bets he said he had taken $45,000 from his cash box. He had been betting up to $30,000 a day through a local bookie when he did not have time to get out to the race track. Even with this very large flow of money it took a quirk of fate finally to bring this embezzler to bay. The week before, the bookie joint had been raided by local and federal agents. In the raid they found the bookie's records, including the bank teller's name. They thought it was a little bit unusual for an $11,000-a-year bank teller to be making $30,000-a-day bets. This led to the surveillance and finally a notification to the bank of what had been happening.

On the fateful day the supervisory teller came to work as usual. This morning he said he found his office filled with more auditors than he had ever seen in his whole life. He assisted them without any indications on their part or his that the purpose of the audit was to discover where $1.4 million had gone. At noon he said the manager at the branch asked him to report to the main offices for the afternoon. He wandered around the main offices being shuttled from one secretary to another until finally in mid-afternoon he was called into a meeting with a New York City assistant district attorney. In a businesslike but friendly fashion the D.A. told the bank teller that he was being arrested for embezzlement. In a likewise friendly and at times joking manner, the supervisory teller with great relief told his entire story.

Later that afternoon he was locked up in the Tombs. A detective spent several hours explaining what had happened to the bank teller's wife. Since there is no specific law for embezzlement in New York, he was indicted by the grand jury on two counts of grand larceny in the second degree, one for $1 million and one for $45,000, and seven counts of forgery that identified seven individual change forms he had used. He was being held, pending $20,000 bail which he was unable to make. Subsequently bail was reduced to $5,000 and he was released, awaiting his trial.

The first charge simply stated that the defendant in the county of New York over a period of three years stole in excess of $1 million from the named bank. The defense attorney decisively argued that this count was fatally defective in that it failed to state the acts alleged to have been done by the defendant in the commission of the crime charged and that it failed to provide the defendant with adequate notice of the exact nature of the charges so that a proper defense could be raised. It also failed to protect the defendant from possible future charges by not properly describing and delineating the acts charged. To state simply that the defendant stole in excess of $1 million over a three-year period is totally insufficient to meet either the constitutional requirements or the requirements of the law. He also claimed that the forgery charges were not sufficient since the change form did not constitute a document subject to forgery and since the supervisory teller was authorized to use such documents, which were therefore not falsely made as defined in the law. This ploy didn't work, and ultimately the defendant pleaded guilty and was sentenced to two years in prison, to be served at the New York City Correctional Institution for Men at Rikers Island. The actual net sentence was 20 months.

Rikers Island Prison is a grim place to visit, let alone be locked up in, with the usual clanking steel bars, antiseptic hallways, and uniformed guards and prisoners. But for this embezzler, it was finally a great relief to be in prison. He said this was the best solution possible for his problem and felt he was overcoming his gambling weaknesses. He was serving as a clerk in the assistant warden's office and teaching high school mathematics, using computer-aided instruction terminals connected to a computer over telephone lines. He has a high school education and is well trained in banking; at one time the bank sent him to a management training course at New York University. He seemed to be very sorry for what he had done and accepts the fact that he is paying his debt to society. He hopes to start a new life with his wife and children when he leaves prison. Having to reveal his gambling weakness and embezzlement to his wife was the most difficult and unpleasant part of his whole experience. This is a common problem of white-collar criminals.

I asked him why he didn't give himself up to the bank management and accept whatever was coming to him after he had taken $1 million and realized that he was not going to recover. He said, "Man, I'm a gambler and the next day there was always that chance that I was going to hit it big, and some kind of miracle would happen to straighten out this whole mess."

I asked him how he felt about stealing money from all of his customers, including the nice little old ladies whose life savings were in the bank. He was quite offended by this and said that he never stole money from people. In fact, he said he was very careful in the beginning never to take more than $20,000 from any one account, knowing that the accounts were insured for up to $20,000. Later on, the $20,000 limit was raised and he never worried about it any more. He didn't steal money from people! He was just borrowing money from the insurance company and the bottomless pit of the federal government. He said he is an honest man and wouldn't steal money from people, but borrowing money from the bank was okay. For the first three years of his embezzlement he led a highly exciting life, engaged in a fascinating game with the bank and a challenging activity that made his work a satisfying experience. But that changed. The prosecuting attorney had great sympathy for this man because of the severe suffering of his family and what he had been through in trying to recover from his addiction to gambling.

This bank teller led a double life—in some ways similar to that of the ship captain in the movie *Captain's Paradise*, who lived the life of a complacent family man in his home port and in other ports that of a wild bachelor. In this case the embezzler lived the quiet family life at home and the exciting life of the big-time gambler in Manhattan.

This is the largest known embezzlement case for this particular type of bank. Although many banks have similar experiences, the size of the embezzlement, its association with computers, and its chance discovery caught the public's imagination, so that the case received great publicity. But the attention ended with the arrest of the suspect. Little becomes known of the subsequent fate of the perpetrator or the recovery of the victim. The audit investigation at the bank probably took many hundreds of man-hours to reconstruct the unauthorized activities and correct all of the changes that the embezzler alleges he had made. Just calculating the total loss for payment by the insurance company must have been a major undertaking. This modern and highly successful bank probably performed an excellent job of recovery, taking extensive corrective action to increase assurance that a similar act would not recur. Although recovery procedures in this case are not known, it is interesting to conjecture what might have been done based on the embezzler's and assistant district attorney's descriptions of the case.

First, the controls that were violated would have to be determined. These controls usually include dual control over cash ˜eserve supply and use of teller terminals. The supervisor said he had unquestioned access to and use of teller terminals, and the tellers accepted this mode of operation and did not report it to their superiors. He said unauthorized entries on tellers' daily proofs were either not questioned or not noticed by the tellers. There was unauthorized use of change forms to correct interest on manipulated accounts. And finally he claims the required vacation of two successive weeks was not enforced. Exceptions to the vacation rules in this case were apparently approved by an officer of the bank. The supervisory teller said that he was unable to take more than a few days' vacation at a time for fear of discovery.

Tellers should be instructed that they are not to allow anyone to use their teller terminals except for authorized personnel performing only a limited set of functions such as correcting teller errors, overriding certain conditions, and placing or removing stops or cautions on specific accounts. Tellers should also be instructed to question any attempt by anyone to use their teller terminals, even under the circumstances listed above. If they are not satisfied with the reasons given, they should report the incident to an officer. In any case, the journal tape that is produced as a copy of all actions taken on the teller terminals must be initialed by the person taking the action alongside the printed transaction data. Tellers should always compare bank book balances with teller terminal balances. In cases where the bank book balance does not agree with the teller terminal balance for that account, it must be reported immediately to an officer. These instances then must be recorded in a log and maintained by the manager. Any suspicious mispostings must also be reported to the auditor. Tellers should be advised that only they personally are allowed to make entries on their own proof sheets. Transactions between tellers must be cross-initialed in all cases. All transactions above a certain amount should require the authorization of an officer.

All keys and vault combinations would certainly require changing. All personnel should be periodically instructed on the safeguarding of keys and secret combinations. Combination locks should be used only when the dials are properly shielded from view. Stringent procedures for opening and closing accounts are needed. Officers must take turns completing the standard reports of supply cash and reserve cash. Supervisory tellers should not act as supply tellers and supply tellers should not assume supervisory teller responsibilities. Supply cash must be maintained at minimum levels. Officers should count all cash supplies on a surprise basis frequently.

Deposit and withdrawal tickets must be maintained in strict numerical sequence. Tellers' proof sheets must be checked frequently and all records kept to guard against theft, alteration, or destruction. New account deposits should be recorded on special deposit tickets. The teller terminal journal tapes should be collected each night and examined for completeness by verifying the log-in and log-out journaling.

The audit staff must follow strict procedures. Test data must be preselected from master records prior to an audit. Large samplings of withdrawals over a specified amount should be selected for signature verification. All tellers' deposit and withdrawal tickets should be listed and proven for preselected days. On the day of an audit, all checks received should be listed and balanced to the tellers' proof sheets for at least 50 percent of all tellers. Also on the day of an audit, all supply tellers' proofs, supervisors' reports, checks received, and prior day's deposit and withdrawal tickets should be immediately confiscated and maintained under audit control until the examination is finished. When the vault is initially opened on the morning of the audit, the tellers' cash boxes should be immediately removed and audit seals placed on all compartments within the vault containing cash and cash items.

A new account "welcome letter" to be mailed to all new depositors is a good practice. The primary purpose of this letter is to verify opening account balances and to verify the correct address of the depositor. Confirmation letters can be mailed to every account holder whenever a deposit or withdrawal correction over a specified amount is made. The confirmation letter should be returned to a special auditing department post office box. Every such correction should be initialed by an audit manager.

This appears to take care of the tellers. Now let's worry about the computers and computer programmers who make the computer terminals work, because bank embezzlement is not going to disappear, and computers will play increasingly important roles. In this case the computer system and its contents apparently were not violated or compromised. The computer was probably used the way it had been programmed. The crime involved manipulation of data going into or coming from the system. The question that often arises in such cases is, Could the computer have been programmed to detect the crime? One way would be to have the computer record and analyze the pattern of errors, omissions, and changes made by tellers and managers of bank operations. Reports of deviations from normal rates can be printed by employee name for examination by the auditors. The supervisory teller in this case said that the number of changes he made was explained by the problems with the new tellers he was training. However, the pattern of increasing change rates and large numbers of changes at interest calculation times might have been detected with a more advanced computer program.

For every dollar taken in armed robberies, embezzlers are taking several dollars. Myron McBryde, chairman of the Bank Administration Institutes Bank Security Commission, claims that embezzlement can occur at every bank—and does. "It is the ones that we don't know about that concern us, and probably there are some going on at every bank in the country. There is no fool-proof system of preventing embezzlement, because despite tight security procedures there are always individuals in the bank that are clever enough and desperate enough to devise systems to side step even the most comprehensive security measures."

17 | MAGNETS, LIGHTNING, NYLON PANTIES, AND RADAR

Computer abuse research has included attempts to track down the sources of horror stories that have been perpetuated throughout the data processing community. Some of these stories have resulted in unwarranted expenditures by data processing organizations in order to protect themselves from dangers that have been greatly exaggerated and sensationalized. In 1969 an article appeared on the front page of the *Wall Street Journal* depicting the problem of computer crime in a highly sensationalized fashion. Three cases were identified. The first was the 1966 case I had investigated in Minneapolis and so is a verified case. The other two were crimes that occurred in Wall Street brokerages. When I contacted the managements of these two firms, they were outraged that the journalist had distorted the cases so as to be almost unrecognizable. I was told that both cases had occurred several years earlier, before either of the firms had begun to use computers, and that both were strictly manual white-collar crimes involving a manipulation of securities that had nothing whatsoever to do with computers. Yet they had been depicted as new, high-technology computer crimes.

In the late 1960s, a number of horror stories were circulated about the erasing of data from magnetic tapes using small, hand-held magnets. These stories were circulated with considerable help from the manufacturers of magnetometers, devices that could be placed in doorways to detect the passage of magnets through them. I tracked down these tales as far as my resources would allow and was unable to prove that any of the incidents described had ever actually occurred. The closest I came was the Dow Chemical case in Midland, Michigan.

An antiwar group called "Beaver 55" attacked the Dow Chemical data processing facilities in February 1970 and destroyed equipment, punch cards, and magnetic tapes. The cost of reconstructing the data was reported in the *Wall Street Journal* to be $100,000. Several magnets were found among the rubble that was left. Some of the magnetic tapes that suffered minimal physical damage appeared to have had some of the data erased from them; therefore, there is some circumstantial evidence that magnets may have been used.

One of the stories circulated was about a disgruntled employee who wiped out thousands of magnetic tapes during one night. It was calculated that it would actually have taken that person several years working 40 hours per week without coffee breaks to erase that much data, using a relatively powerful hand-held magnet. Another story had a Boy Scout troop on tour through a data processing center where the scouts merely waved their little magnets around in the air and supposedly did extensive damage. Tests conducted at Stanford Research Institute and at the U.S. National Bureau of Standards indicate that this could not be done.

The erasure of data stored magnetically on tape requires the application of a relatively powerful magnetic force which can only be achieved by placing a magnet very close to the recording surface. Magnetic tape wound on a typical reel would limit the erasure to the first few wrappings. The tape would have to be unwound and the magnet placed on the recording surface to be sure of erasing the data. This would be a time-consuming job. There are many more effective ways of destroying data on magnetic tapes where the perpetrator can be sure that he has done significant damage. A cigarette lighter used to melt the tape, or a screwdriver, penknife, or can opener that could be used to score or otherwise physically damage the tape, would be far more effective tools and would not be caught by a magnetometer in a doorway. Most computer centers already have a most effective eraser for magnetic tapes present within the facilities. These devices are called degaussers. A degausser is an electrical appliance which creates a strong magnetic field—placing a reel of tape on it effectively erases the entire tape.

One case involving the use of a magnet was recently verified although the incident happened more than 10 years ago. A disgruntled employee erased the error checking code on several reels of tapes, using a small magnet. Older reels have large open sections on the flanges that expose the coiled tape. The code along the edge of the tape is used to check the correctness of the magnetic patterns that encode the data on the tape. This employee simply ran a small magnet up and down on the surface of the coil through the opening of the flange. By disconnecting the checking process, the data on the tapes were successfuly read in spite of the vandalism. This is the only verified case in the computer abuse study.

In my visits to computer centers I occasionally observe an installed magnetometer. I always ask the security manager if he has caught any magnets lately. This usually embarrasses him, and he reports that it is no longer actively used, or that it just came with the whole security system as a package and therefore was installed without much thought.

Soon after I was quoted in the press as revealing the lack of threat from the use of magnets, I received a telephone call from the president of a small firm which had just finished a three-year development program to produce a low-cost magnet detector. This company was just starting a national marketing program to sell these devices to catch all those bad guys running around with magnets. He insisted that the myths and apocryphal stories being circulated about the dangers of magnets were all true, and that he was ready to make his fortune. I assured him that to the degree that we had carried out our research, none of the stories appeared to be true and there was no particular danger from the use of magnets. It turned out that his device also extends to the detection of any kind of metal. Fortunately for him, the skyjacking activities were then at their height; as far as I know, he went on to make a fortune selling his devices as metal detectors in airports.

There is some danger of storing magnetic tapes in areas where strong magnetic fields are produced, for example, in the vicinity of some large electric motors, electric generators, and even some other electrical devices. Robert Courtney, manager of Computer Security and Privacy for IBM, reported that there is a spot on the floor of some subway trains where a reel of magnetic tape may be laid that will cause partial erasure. Tests in which magnetic tapes were put in strong radar beams indicate that radar has no direct effect on magnetic tapes. Lightning, on the other hand, can have a disastrous effect. An unverified case reported by the Associated Press in 1973 stated that in a civil suit conducted by the California Department of Corporations against a brokerage firm, a witness was called to provide data to support a claim by the state that the firm should be barred from selling commodity options. The witness claimed that lightning struck the computing center in Los Angeles. The lightning passed through the metal shelving holding the entire tape library containing the master files of the organization. This much electricity surging through the metal caused a sufficiently large magnetic field to erase the entire library of tapes. The witness reported that this caused millions of dollars' worth of data loss. This experience is another indication of the unique problems associated with introducing computer technology into sensitive and important business functions.

Many buildings housing computers are quite adequately protected from known levels of lightning activity. For example, the Sears Tower in Chicago and the General Electric Computer Services Business Division in Rockville, Maryland, both have elaborate sets of lightning rods at the tops of the buildings that are grounded to the steel structure of the building itself. Any lightning that might strike the building would automatically be grounded through the structure rather than through any of its contents. It is more likely that the smaller computer centers in small buildings not designed to house computers may suffer from lightning attacks.

Another form of electricity can be equally damaging to a

computer center. It is in the form of electrostatic electricity—the kind that we collect in walking across carpeting in dry weather. There have been a number of reports circulated as apocryphal stories about female computer operators wearing nylon under-clothing. Body movement can cause significant levels of electro-static electricity. When one of these operators gets charged up and moves close enough to computer circuitry or operator consoles on computer equipment, she can cause considerable, but usually temporary, harm to a computer. A surge of such electricity can cause what is known as "stuck junctions" in transistors, which paralyzes them so that they can no longer amplify. If the energy is high enough, it can actually attack the base emitter of transistors and fuse the junctions, requiring the replacement of large numbers of transistors and microcircuits.

Several years ago it became a fad to introduce nylon carpeting in computer centers. This wreaked all kinds of havoc until special carpeting was developed with grounded copper wires woven into the material to ground continuously any build-up of static charges on people around computers. Most modern computers and peripheral equipment have significant amounts of grounding and shielding to prevent these kinds of problems. Hewlett Packard computers are particularly good in this respect since the techniques for protecting their instruments have been carried over into their computer designs. Hewlett Packard instruments had to be well shielded because they were often used in electri-cally hostile environments.

Still another form of energy can come from radar. Several years ago, a computer installation near Baltimore's Friendship International Airport suffered when a new, high-powered radar system was installed at the airport. Every time the radar dish circled around, it gave the computer center a shot of high-frequency radio signals that was enough to cause thousands of stuck junctions in transistors. It took a considerable amount of detection work to discover the cause of this problem, which was solved simply by building a grounded conductive shield around one side of the computer.

Finally, another less likely but severe problem could develop from a massive electromagnetic pulse (EMP) emanating from an atomic bomb explosion. A computer center could be built in a fortress to protect it against concussion, but the EMP could put it out of commission for good. It is not known what levels of EMP can seriously affect electronic equipment, including computers. A study is currently being conducted at Stanford Research Institute to determine this.

Fires are among the most dangerous disasters in computer centers, which contain large amounts of PVC (polyvinyl chloride). PVC is the basis for many plastics used for computer cabinetry, parts, and insulation for wiring; but it burns easily and produces clouds of black, noxious smoke. With slightly more heat than is produced by its burning, it produces nascent chlorine—molecularly free chlorine which will combine chemically with many things with which it comes into contact. In particular, if it comes into contact with water, which is commonly used to extinguish fires, it immediately produces very strong hydrochloric acid in droplets that can devastate most metal surfaces, including connectors and wires in a computer system. Currently, there is considerable interest in finding ways to reduce or eliminate this problem.

Ironically, one of the dangers to computer systems stems from the actions taken to solve security problems. These are the secondary effects, such as spraying water from sprinkler systems onto computers before the power is cut off. In one incredible instance told by Robert Courtney of IBM, a new security officer was assigned to a computer center. He immediately proceeded to install an elaborate carbon dioxide release system that would fill the entire computer center with carbon dioxide automatically upon detection of sufficient heat or smoke. But when carbon dioxide levels are sufficient to extinguish a fire, they will also extinguish human life since the oxygen is replaced in the air. After being told of this, the security officer removed the automatic detection equipment and replaced it with a 6-foot brass lever and knob above the computer console so that the carbon dioxide could be discharged manually by the computer operator after he was sure that everyone else was out of the room. But there were parts of the room that the operator could not observe from his console. The security officer attempted to solve this problem by installing gas masks in the areas that could not be seen. He was stopped when it was explained to him that gas masks are of absolutely no use because they merely filter gases; they do not replace the oxygen that the CO_2 has replaced. At about the time he was starting to place 20-millimeter cannons at the front entrance of the computer center, across the street from a university where students sometimes rioted, he was replaced.

In one computer center I visited, a CO_2 fire extinguishing system had been installed under the raised flooring in the computer center, because of the high danger of electrical wiring fires in the cables connecting the equipment. Unfortunately, the system had never been tested. One day, when it went off accidentally, the room was cleared of people to protect them from asphyxiation. However, since CO_2 is heavier than air, it filtered down through conduit holes in the base floor under the computer system and seeped down into the rooms on the floor beneath the computer system where it almost killed several people working there. The solution to a problem can sometimes be worse than the problem itself. Great care and common sense must be used in designing any kind of security.

18 | GASOLINE AND COMPUTERS DON'T MIX

This was one of the most spectacular arson cases ever in the little city of Corners.* Jim Worth, the arson specialist for the fire department, was roused out of bed at 6:00 A.M. on a Sunday morning, June 23. Jim's whole career was with the fire department; he had no formal training in arson. His experience had been picked up along the way in working with other men in the arson investigation activity. He hurried over to the CS 2 Company, which occupies a building in an industrial section of Corners.

CS 2 is a small data processing service company which provides all kinds of computerized services to local business, using an IBM 360/40 medium-sized computer system. The building CS 2 occupies has the typical southern formal lawn, junipers, and palm tree gardens in front. It is much too large for CS 2's modest operation, but it had served them well until 5:05 A.M. on that Sunday morning in June.

* All names of persons, companies, and places in this case study have been changed.

1 | BUILDING WALL BLOWN OUT

2 | VIEW OF HALLWAY WITH LEANING DOOR

3 | VIEW OF HALLWAY WITH BENT WALL SECTIONS

4 | MATCH ON CARPETED FLOORING

5 | GASOLINE CANS

6 | OVERVIEW OF COMPUTER ROOM

7 | PERIPHERAL EQUIPMENT AND DISK PACKS

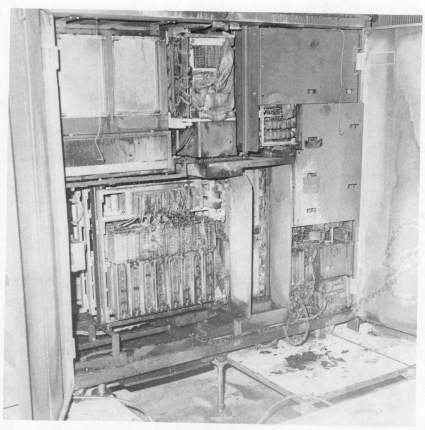

8 | CENTRAL PROCESSOR

9 | TELEX TAPE DRIVE

10 | GLOVE IN THE BEDROOM

11 | SHIRT AND SOCKS UNDER A MATTRESS

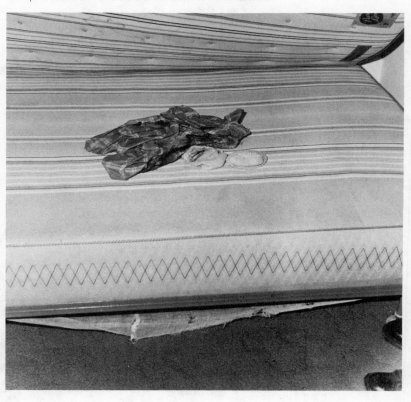

When Jim arrived, the firemen were completing their job of extinguishing a fire, the result of an explosion that blew out a major section of the rear wall of the one-story building. A large gash in the metal frame of the front door was clear evidence that someone had used something like a crowbar to force entry. A front office area was untouched. The computer had been housed on raised flooring to allow cables connecting the machines to be placed without causing interference to the operation staff. The computer area was surrounded on all four sides by thin, floor-to-ceiling partition walls, which left a 6-foot passageway entirely around the building walls. All four sides of the partition walls had been blown down by what must have been a terrific explosion. A large section of the back wall of the building looked as though it had been peeled back by a can opener (see Figure 1), but smaller objects had been untouched. Paper, pens, telephones sitting on desks, chairs, stacks of mail, books, and other common office fixtures were still in place and hadn't been moved.

Jim walked down the hallway, or what used to be a hallway, with the partition walls leaning against the building walls (see Figures 2 and 3). He stooped and picked up a match at the base of a doorway after carefully photographing it (see Figure 4). A few feet farther on he came upon two empty 5-gallon gasoline cans, red and white striped, with their lids firmly in place (see Figure 5). A singed right-hand cotton glove lay by the cans. More pictures were taken. This must have been where the arsonist stood when he lit his match. The smell of gasoline was still in the air. It looked like the arsonist had not counted on an explosion but had probably taken enough time in distributing the gasoline and screwing the lids back on his gas cans so that fumes developed to cause a terrific explosion. The arsonist could not have avoided being severely hurt when the explosion and flash of flame engulfed him.

Jim stepped up on the raised flooring where the partition wall had once stood (see Figure 6). The computer, peripheral equipment, and supplies occupied only one end of the large room. The drop-down acoustic ceiling was black above the computer, and sections of it were missing. Three long strings of fluorescent lights lay in disarray on the floor. Heavy 2-foot by 2-foot aluminum panels of flooring had been blown up in the air by the explosion from the gasoline fumes that found their way down underneath the floor. Stacks of paper for the two printers were burned around the edges. One of the printer covers was in the "up" position, one in the "down." The panel doors had been blown off on one side of the central processor—a large box 3 feet by 8 feet wide and standing almost 7 feet high. The insides of the processor had been heavily drenched with gasoline, and the equipment was charred almost beyond recognition (see Figure 8). All but one of the thermal circuit breakers were open.

The firemen insist that when they arrived they found the console panel of the central processor with its lights on, presumably in operation. They also found other peripheral equipment—a key punch, tape drives, and disk pack drives—all with their lights on, ready to work amid the crackling flames of the fire still burning from the remains of the gasoline; and it was starting to burn the plastic covers of the disk packs (see Figure 7). The sprinkler valves protruding from the ceiling had started working just as they were supposed to, mingling water and steam with the flames, but the computer presumably kept operating until the end. One of the firemen quipped, "This looks like the first gasoline-driven computer."

Disk packs were lined up on shelves, their covers blackened by fire. One of the Telex tape drive units was seriously damaged (see Figure 9). The front windows on these units automatically open and close for gaining access to the reels of magnetic tape mounted on the drive. These windows are normally either in an up position or fully down. Figure 9 shows the window in a half-opened position. Only a combination of unusual circumstances would account for this situation.

Dick Roy, manager of CS 2, indicated that his staff went home at midnight after completely shutting down all power on the computer and peripheral equipment in the computer room. The guard had just finished his rounds at 4:45 A.M., according to the guard post at the front door of the building. He reported that none of the equipment was on at that time. Probably the arsonist had been hiding in the dense shrubbery in front of the building until the guard had finished his round. He then pried open the front door and carried two 5-gallon cans of gasoline into the computer room. Presumably he turned on the computer and peripheral equipment, poured gasoline over much of the equipment, supplies, and disk packs, carried the cans out into the hallway, lit a match intending to start a fire, and blew the computer center and himself almost to smithereens. The gasoline fumes must have caused a terrific blast. One pint of gasoline in vapor form in an enclosed area is equivalent to two sticks of dynamite. The cans could have contained up to 80 pints. If most of it had evaporated, there was the equivalent of 160 sticks of dynamite in that building.

Some major questions needed answering. Why did he "power up" the equipment? Why did he leave one glove and the two incriminating cans? And what was the motive for such a crime? None of the reels of magnetic tape that contained all of CS 2's customers' data had been destroyed. If someone was bent on doing great harm to CS 2, he certainly would have made sure that the racks of magnetic tapes were destroyed in his attack.

On Monday, June 24, Jim Worth continued his investigation by calling on Dick Roy, manager of CS 2. He asked if there were any indications of disgruntled employees. He asked about the ownership of the building and the computers, which were leased from a third-party leasing company rather than directly from the manufacturers of the equipment. He asked about the amount of insurance and who would be the beneficiaries of that insurance. Roy's responses gave Jim little reason to suspect an inside job. He then asked the right question. Does CS 2 have any enemies? Roy responded by saying he didn't know of any, unless it might be the CS 1 Company from whom CS 2 had just lured a very prestigious customer. CS 1, located in the neighboring town of Apple, is in hot competition with CS 2.

Worth's next move was obvious; go talk to the CS 1 people. So he called on Brad Wolf, the president of CS 1. CS 2 is one of a dozen computer centers that form a subsidiary of a large manufacturing company. CS 1, on the other hand, is a privately owned local computer service company. Thirty-year-old Brad Wolf gave the impression of a highly successful, dynamic young businessman. Under questioning by Worth, Wolf said there were no bad feelings between the two firms, and he could think of no reason or motive for anyone to attack CS 2. He suggested that it must have been an inside job at CS 2 to collect on insurance.

Worth was not satisfied and asked if there were any employees at CS 1 who had not arrived for work that Monday following the fire, or if there were any employees who were just starting vacations or extended leaves of absence. The computer operations manager at CS 1 admitted that one of the computer operators, Wayne Garcia, had just taken an emergency leave of absence. Worth now had a hot suspect. He had a name, an address, and was looking for someone who most likely had suffered concussion, wounds, and serious burns.

He went to Garcia's residence and found that the twenty-four-year-old computer operator lived alone. His neighbor indicated that he had disappeared and no one had any idea where he had gone. After obtaining a search warrant, Jim searched Garcia's bedroom and found what he was looking for. Lying on the floor was the left-hand glove matching the one found at CS 2 (see Figure 10). Hidden under the mattress they found a charred and bloody sport shirt and a pair of socks (see Figure 11). Now Jim was almost sure he had his arsonist identified; but where was he?

The residence was staked out for three weeks, and a search of hospitals in the local area started. The arson investigator watching the house noticed a woman coming to the home every few days and taking mail away with her. The mystery woman was none other than Jill Wolf, wife of Brad Wolf, the president of CS 1. Jill was collecting Garcia's mail and paying his bills. Garcia had previously lived with the Wolfs for a long time. He was uneducated and was an extremely inhibited and introverted young man. Brad Wolf had taken him on as a protégé in an attempt to make something of his life. He hired him as a computer operator.

An interview with Garcia's sister then indicated that something even more unusual had occurred. Jill Wolf had written a check to a hospital at a resort area 400 miles north of Corners, for $1,400, and forged the name of Garcia's sister. Unfortunately, she had used the sister's maiden name because she had forgotten that the sister had recently married. This caused some consternation at the bank, but Mrs. Wolf deposited $1,400 in the sister's account to cover the check.

Now the action shifted to the resort area. There the investigators discovered that Garcia had been a patient at the hospital and was to remain at least 40 days to recover from serious burns he said he had suffered in a gasoline lawn mower accident. He later claimed it was a camping accident. Garcia may have been tipped off because he left just a few hours before the police arrived, and again, no one knew where he had gone. Jim Worth discovered that Garcia's mother lived in Dallas, Texas, and thought that might be a likely area to look. He sent a request to the Dallas arson investigators to check the hospitals for a burn patient answering Garcia's description. They were not much help until finally a $1 million arrest warrant was issued for Garcia. This forced them into action. Unknown to Garcia's mother he had gained admittance as a patient at a Dallas hospital where he was recovering from burns and a serious staph infection. On July 23 Garcia was arrested and returned to Corners, just one month after the explosion and fire. He pleaded not guilty to one count of arson and one count of burglary.

Worth was still not satisfied. He was convinced that there was more to it than one lone computer operator running off to blow up another computer business. And what about Garcia's close relationship with the Wolfs, and especially Mrs. Wolf's paying Garcia's hospital bill? Surely, there was at least a case for conspiracy against Mrs. Wolf. Worth looked into Garcia's past to see if he could come up with a motive. Garcia was totally dependent on the Wolfs. When he lived with them he did many of the chores around the house, and Wolf put him to work in his first paying job. Employees at CS 1 indicated that Garcia was very quiet, withdrawn, but nice. He spent most of his free time watching television and going to movies. A diary belonging to Garcia was found. It told of a life of discouragement, where nothing seemed to go right. The gasoline cans Garcia used were traced to Brad Wolf's garage where they had been filled with ethyl gasoline for use in Wolf's sports car.

Worth took a team of law enforcement officers to CS 1 and

proceeded simultaneously but separately to interview all possible suspects in the conspiracy. He did not plan to interview Wolf's secretary, Cheryl Bailey, but had a policeman watch over her during the other interviews. Brad Wolf, Jill Wolf, Robert Finch— the vice president of CS 1—and Jim Trench—the operations manager who was a part owner of CS 1—were questioned. Wolf and Trench had the same alibis, indicating that they were at Wolf's cabin at the resort area at the time of the fire. They claimed they had been gambling and fishing, but Jill Wolf said she had been with her husband at the cabin and that the Wolfs, including their daughter, had driven home after the brief holiday.

After the interviews, Worth was again not satisfied. As he started to leave the building, he remembered the secretary, Cheryl Bailey. Just on a hunch he sat down to ask her some questions. She immediately acted in a highly defensive manner, and Worth called in an investigator from the district attorney's office who was an expert in interviewing witnesses. He caught her telling one small lie and she finally revealed the whole story.

Wolf and Trench had in fact been at the cabin on Sunday, June 23, the day of the explosion. Jill Wolf was planning to drive up that day to join them. Garcia had phoned her indicating that he had gotten into some trouble and would like to ride up to the resort area with her. She later admitted that she drove him up there in his car but was unaware of the severe burns covering 15 percent of his body. Garcia checked into the hospital. At this point, Jill and Brad Wolf must have been aware of what Garcia had done and from then on attempted to hide him and pay his bills.

Worth now had enough evidence to go for a grand jury indictment of the Wolfs and possibly Jim Trench, the operations manager. But then another unexpected turn of events occurred. Trench completely disappeared. His car was found abandoned at the local airport. The day before the interviews at CS 1, Wolf had sent his secretary by air to the resort area to remove Trench's automobile and clothes from his cabin. That was the only purpose of the trip and did not seem logical because Wolf, two days later, returned with his family to the cabin.

The day before the grand jury met, Worth again became suspicious of the Wolfs and their unexplained activities. He had the police check with the Wolfs' travel agency and found that Jill Wolf had left town and gone to Mississippi. A quick check indicated that Brad Wolf had just purchased two one-way airline tickets to New Orleans and then on to Jamaica. The police rushed out to the Wolfs' home and caught Brad as he was walking from his house to his car. They found $5,000 in cash, the airline tickets in his pockets, and suitcases ready to go. He claimed that he and his wife had had this trip planned for some time, that he often carried as much as $5,000 in cash with him, and that his secretary had unsuccessfully tried to change the departure date at the travel agency so that he could stay in town until after the grand jury met.

The grand jury indicted the Wolfs and Jim Trench. Jill Wolf was apprehended in Mississippi and returned to Corners. The Wolfs were released under a bond large enough to keep them around home for a while. As the trial date approached, Garcia changed his plea from not guilty to not guilty by reason of insanity. Jim Trench, the operations manager, could still not be found. All three were charged with conspiracy and aiding and abetting. It was never proven that Brad Wolf had ever actually instructed Garcia to perform the arson.

At the trial, Garcia finally changed his plea to guilty. He stated that he had set the fire because he was afraid that he would lose his job, his only grip on life, because CS 2 had taken the large customer away from CS 1. He said he had planned the act for two weeks, calling CS 2 frequently to gain information about the scheduling of guards and general activity.

The Wolfs continued to claim their innocence. Cheryl Bailey, Wolf's secretary, attempted to change her testimony at the trial, but she was unsuccessful because the district attorney's investigator had taped her earlier testimony.

When the district attorney presented his summation to the jury at the criminal trial, the evidence was overwhelming against the Wolfs and Garcia and they were convicted. Brad Wolf was fined $4,000, sentenced to 60 days in jail, and put on three years probation. Jill Wolf was fined $1,000 and put on three years probation. Garcia was sentenced to two to twenty years in the state prison.

Eight months after the trial, the Corners police were still after Jim Trench to bring him back for trial. They got a tip that he was living in the East and that he had grown a beard as a disguise. As a routine investigation, they went to a retail credit reporting company and found that Trench was still using his credit cards. A hold was placed on these, and within a few days he walked into a store to make a purchase, using a credit card. While he was being waited on, the clerk checked the validity of the card. A red light came on at the console of the credit check device, and Trench immediately suspected that he had been discovered. He left the purchase and his credit card sitting on the counter, ran from the store right into the arms of the police, and was brought back to Corners to stand trial.

Several mysteries linger in this case. Why did Garcia power up the computer system before he poured gasoline on it to set it on fire? Was he attempting to put the blame for the arson onto someone else? Is it possible Garcia was attempting to frame a CS 2 employee, possibly by leaving one glove at the scene of the crime and putting the other in the employee's possession? Did Garcia have enough intelligence and motivation to plan and perpetrate this arson? Or did Wolf provide him with at least some of the motive by implying that Garcia might lose his job and the whole business might fail because of the loss of their customer to CS 2? Wolf had been complaining to CS 2 about the alleged theft of business from his firm; he had sent a letter to CS 2's attorneys about the matter.

Brad Wolf is now appealing the verdict against him and his wife. His appeal is based on the situation that there were eight overt acts presented to the jury, and the jury voted only on some of them. His claim is that for conviction, the jury must have had to vote on all eight overt acts. When I attempted to contact him for an interview, he refused to take my calls. Jim Worth told me that he wasn't surprised Wolf would not talk with me since the arson investigators had used so many covert activities and undercover people with aliases. Wolf would just suspect that I was another investigator.

The most interesting technical aspect in this case has to do with the recovery of CS 2 after the explosion and fire. The computer leasing company took back the damaged equipment and, it is presumed, received insurance claim money for the equipment. IBM conducted a post mortem on the IBM 360/40 processor, but the results of that are unknown except that the greatest damage done seemed to come from the water used in extinguishing the flames while the power was still on. Since CS 2 has a maintenance contract with IBM, IBM took most of the equipment away, repaired and refurbished it, and returned it to CS 2 in a few days at nominal charge. On Monday, June 24, the day after the explosion, CS 2 started using an IBM 370/135 computer system at a nearby company. Their customers would not even have known from a service point of view that the fire had occurred. Fortunately, all of the customers' data were stored on the magnetic tapes that were undamaged in the fire. If the magnetic tapes had been destroyed, there would still have been very little loss of data since CS 2 has a practice of copying all the customers' data on the tapes on a daily basis and storing a complete set of customers' data on tapes off site on a weekly basis. In fact, the off-site location for storing tapes is at one of the employees' homes.

CS 2 had a new 360/40 central processor shipped by airplane from their parent company headquarters. They were back in business again with their own equipment at 3:00 P.M. on the following Friday, June 28. The only equipment totally lost was the central processor and one tape drive. Twenty disk packs were lost in the fire, but they were used only for temporary storage of data. The losses sustained on the building, and the cost of refurbishing the building, were handled by the owner who leased it to CS 2. CS 2 had no financial problems in this regard.

Finally, CS 2 now has a different form of guard service. In the past, the guard service was hired to have guards roam through the building at unscheduled times. Now, the interior of the building is protected with motion detectors, and guards from a guard service merely check that the exterior perimeter of the building is secure.

19 | THE FASTEST TOES IN THE WEST

If it's conceivable, someone has tried it.

The problem with this case is that it is not a computer abuse but has serious implications for future abuse. The perpetrator and the victims both made gains and suffered losses. The victims offered a public challenge, "Try to beat us." The perpetrator accepted that challenge and did beat the victims at their own game, but in a surprising and unanticipated way.

It had to happen sooner or later, and Keith Taft was just the man to do it. Keith is a forty-one-year-old expert electronic engineer who consults for the exotic, solid state electronics companies in Silicon Valley—most famous for its prunes before the age of solid state electronics. He lives in Sunnyvale, a town between San Jose and San Francisco, just a four-hour drive from the California-Nevada border. He and his wife went to Reno one weekend in October 1969, and Keith fell in love with a game commonly known as Blackjack or Twenty-One.

He discovered that Blackjack is the only gambling game in the Nevada casinos where optimal play can result in a small advantage of the player over the House. He read the right books, *Beat*

228

the Dealer by Edward O. Thorpe and *The Casino Gambler's Guide* by Allan Wilson. Thorpe developed a method for playing Blackjack based on the remaining unplayed cards in the deck. Wilson corrected some errors in Thorpe's book and improved on the techniques. Keith used these counting techniques to play the game successfully on a small scale for over two years and was asked to leave casinos three times for winning too much. He repeated Thorpe's and Wilson's calculations using a large-scale computer and determined that on a practical basis in the long run a person could win about $10 per hour by making bets at the rate of $10 per hand.

The problem is that counting requires intense concentration and development of a superb memory. Keith's lifelong ambition is to eliminate through computer technology the mechanical processes that are involved in human labor and thought. Why should a person sit there concentrating, trying to remember the remaining cards, when a computer could do the job so much more efficiently and accurately? He calculated what a person could win on a practical basis in the long run if he had a computer to do the remembering and the calculations for him. He found that by making $10 bets he could increase a person's earnings to $20 per hour. However, Keith assumed that the casinos would resist the idea of his carrying in a computer if he proved that he could consistently beat them. There is no law in Nevada that makes it illegal for a gambler to use any methods he wishes in playing the games except for cheating by physically changing the odds in the games. However, gambling casinos in Nevada have the right to refuse to let anybody gamble in their facilities for any reason whatsoever.

Keith's profession provided the expertise needed to solve the problem of getting a computer into a casino and making it work. The standard mini-computers in 1972 were not fast enough. He needed 10 times the speed of one of these small computers—one that would operate at 400,000 calculations per second—to do all of the computation and keep up with the cards as they were played. He spent 1,000 hours studying the problem, and he spent another 1,000 hours designing and building a special purpose computer that would do the job. The 16-bit-word computer was made from solid state electronic components. It runs at 150

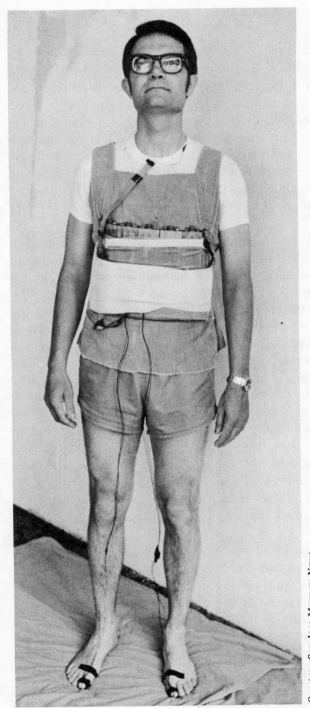

Courtesy San Jose Mercury News

Courtesy San Jose *Mercury News*

Courtesy San Jose *Mercury News*

nanoseconds per cycle (the time it takes to find a word in memory and execute a basic instruction). It has 1,000 8-bit words of read-only memory (ROM) to store the program. This was a tight squeeze for the extensive calculations that have to be performed, and great effort went into designing the program. A 64-word read/write memory (RAM) is used for the storing of data. The data would be the face values of all the cards that hadn't been played, plus the probabilities of dealer and player having card value scores of less-than-17, 17, 18, 19, 20, 21, and over 21 (bust) for each option: hitting, standing, doubling down, or splitting. The program ROM, memory control and RAM, central processor, and input/output circuits were housed in four compact brass boxes each a little larger than cigarette packages. He was able to strap the computer around his stomach, topped off with a row of batteries providing him with the necessary 6-volt supply of operating current for about 90 minutes of play. Taft is shown in the photographs wearing his computer.

The final, most tricky part of the problem then had to be solved—how to put the data into the computer secretly and get the results out. He needed a means of inputting the face values of the cards as they were played in such a way that it would go undetected by the dealer and anyone around him. This was solved by taping tiny switches to the bottoms and tops of his two big toes as shown. The switches are small gold-plated disks that snap from one position to another, the type that are used in Texas Instruments pocket calculators. He wired the switches up through his shoes and trousers to the computer, resulting in a 4-bit input mechanism for his purposes. Next he had to figure out how to get the playing instructions out of the computer in a form that he could use, again without being detected. He did this by installing a row of seven miniature light-emitting diodes (LEDs) on the upper inside of his right eyeglasses frame, as shown. A problem developed because they were so close to his eyes that all he could see was an overlapping array of balloons of light. He solved this by using different colors for the different positions in his miniature output register.

Now he was all set to go except for one last thing. He didn't know how to operate the computer effectively, especially the toe switches. It took him about 200 hours of intensive practice to learn how to input card values at the needed rate of two cards per second, or 10,000 toe movements in eight hours of play. He practiced doing this while driving his car and playing license plate Blackjack, inputting numbers that he read from license plates on cars ahead of him.

Finally, with his $50,000 mini-computer strapped to his stomach, he went off to Reno and Las Vegas to try his technologically enhanced luck. He had changed the odds to about 51 percent for him and 49 percent for the House. He would only play for about an hour in any one casino, because he had to return to his camper in the parking lot to exchange his depleted batteries for recharged ones. Taft found the main advantage over his earlier manual counting methods of playing Blackjack was the elimination of labor and the need for high concentration. He was able to carry on normal conversations with the dealer and other players while playing, and so deceive the dealer into believing that he was just another lucky player and was not using the counting technique. During the several weeks that he spent 200 hours on weekends playing Blackjack, he was only asked to leave the casinos two times because of his winning and what he thought was some suspicion on the part of the dealer of his shifty eyes as he read the output from his computer.

His problem then changed from technological to economic. He had promised his wife that he would limit himself to a bankroll of $4,000. This made him greatly undercapitalized. Because of the small difference in odds, he could lose large amounts of money very quickly, and he would only be assured of winning over the long run. At his best, he won $1,300 in 90 minutes; at his worst, he lost $4,400 in 30 hours. In fact, he lost heavily for three weekends in a row. He calculated the odds of that string of losses on a large-scale computer and concluded that the odds were at least one in a billion that he would have experienced such a loss run.

Now it is important to know a little more about Keith Taft to appreciate and understand what happened next. Keith, his wife, and four children lead a closely knit family life in Sunnyvale. They are devout Baptists. Keith was running off to spend all his weekends away from home and church in the Reno and Las Vegas gambling dens of iniquity. His family and his pastor helped convince him that this was not a particularly Christian life. He also felt that God was telling him something through his run of losses—losses that could not have occurred without a force, God's force, larger than technology and human reason or understanding. He thought about his goals and decided there must be something more to life than spending the rest of it in dark, smoke-filled, unfriendly gambling casinos. On top of this the casinos hate winners, and with only a few exceptions, he was treated in a highly unfriendly manner. By the end of 1973 he had proved with great satisfaction that he could beat the casinos with a computer; so he gave up his gambling career.

There were some significant issues to consider seriously as a result of this remarkable technological caper. The Nevada state attorney general concluded that Taft was not breaking the law in what he was doing; however, a man was recently arrested in Las Vegas when found using an electronic device in his pocket in a gambling casino. His device was confiscated, and he is currently being charged with gambling cheating, a serious offense in Nevada. This should be a valuable case to test the legal definition of cheating. Taft's activities do not even seem to be unethical since the gambling casinos have encouraged the use of counting methods to attract attention and publicity even though they throw the counters out when they start winning too much. Keith concludes that he would have been thrown out and possibly had his computer confiscated if the casinos had discovered the wires under his long hair leading into his eyeglasses.

Another technological method using a mini-computer is currently being tried to beat the game of Roulette. The method is being kept secret but involves calculating the rotational velocity and position of the wheel and the ball. This technique would work only in Nevada where bets are allowed after the wheel and ball have been set into motion. It would not work in Europe where betting is not allowed after the wheel has started. No conclusive results of this method have been reported yet.

Taft concluded that the time, expense, hard work, and long hours in an unfriendly and unpleasant atmosphere for a person talented enough to do far more valuable things in life weighed heavily against making technical beating of the casinos a fruitful endeavor. Besides, a gambling casino is a business making a profit and would not let him consistently win large amounts of money. He would simply not be allowed to play, or the rules would be changed to shift the odds back in favor of the House again.

The commercial value of his hidden mini-computer seems limited. Chess and poker do not appear amenable to computer methods since these are games more of strategy and psychology than of memory where the computer has its strength. Computers might be useful in tournament bridge but would certainly be disallowed if discovered. The gambling computer would probably also not be attractive to the international jet set gamblers. They would not have the patience necessary for learning the toes-input technique.

But Keith Taft has ended up a winner anyway. He recently told his story to the public. Over 100 newspaper articles have been published describing his feat, along with the pictures that are in the figures accompanying this chapter. He has appeared on television and is starting negotiations to assist television and motion picture scriptwriters. So today he is leading quite an exciting life, as well as continuing his professional electronic engineering career and interest in robotics—the technology of relieving people from performing mechanical, mind-numbing work. This surely is more worthwhile and satisfying than winning at Blackjack.

This case study illustrates a new potential for computer abuse in the form of covert, real-time use of computers to gain unfair advantage. For example, a debate raged briefly over student use of pocket calculators in classes because some students could not afford them. Since the cost has been considerably reduced, pocket calculators are now considered common replacements for slide rules. The problem arises again when preprogrammed pocket computers are available which perform functions that students are currently expected to learn and be tested on. This situation can be extrapolated to the larger issue of fairness in the advantage of a covertly electronically enhanced person over another person in business and other competitive relationships. Of course, it would certainly be fair if he was dealing with a computer instead of another person. The one with the most expensive or advanced computer and software will win. Will we eventually need firearm-type laws, where carrying concealed computers is a crime and permits are required?

20 | PRIVACY AND CONFIDENTIALITY

Privacy is a human right. It is not a technological issue but a social, legal, and political one that is properly addressed by such people as Alan F. Westin—a professor of law at Columbia University and an expert on constitutional law—and former Senator Sam Ervin. However, the impact of technology on society is becoming so diverse and deep that the social and technological issues are now intertwined. We find sociologists and law researchers attempting to address the technological issues, and technologists attempting to address the social and legal issues. Few of these people are capable of being professionally competent in both areas. Technologists incorrectly use the term "privacy" in referring to the privacy of computer systems. Sociologists, lawyers, and politicians confuse the roles of data files, software, and hardware.

Some definitions may help keep us on the right track. Privacy is a human right and, in the United States of America, a constitutional right. Supreme Court Justice Louis Brandeis stated: "It is the right to be left alone—the right most valued by civilized men." (Today, he might have had to say "the right most valued by civilized persons.") The most thorough modern treatment of the right of privacy can be found in Alan Westin's book, *Privacy and Freedom.* The issue concerns what personal information is going to be collected about people, who has access to it, and what is going to be done with it.

"Confidentiality" is a term of concern for both experts on privacy and computer technologists. It concerns the policies and rules for the disclosure of personal information and control of that disclosure. The more confidential information is, the more restrictive the policies, rules, and controls must be. The technologists and privacy experts must come together to determine the policies, rules, and controls for confidentiality to be imposed on private information within the practical limits set by technology.

Security is purely a technological and operational issue. It is the means by which the confidentiality policies and rules may be correctly and effectively carried out. In summary, security preserves the confidentiality of personal information to satisfy the rights of privacy and to protect from malicious damage.

Personal information has been collected and stored since the recording of information began. Originally, it was probably on stone tablets, then on papyrus, and more recently on paper stored in manila folders in filing cabinets. Some of it is now stored on punch cards and magnetic tape, and a little has lately been stored electronically, magnetically, and optically in computer systems. The term "databank" has been used to mean a collection of information about individuals assembled in one place for easy access by a number of users. Here it is important to distinguish between information and data. A databank as a collection of information may sound confusing. Information is data put into humanly usable form. For example, data are the numbers on an accounting sheet, and information is data formatted on an accounting sheet with the headings titled so that the data have meaning. Data stored in manual files are often information because the data can be directly read and have meaning for man; therefore, the manual file should really be called an information bank. A databank would describe what is stored in a computer system. The data does not become information until computer programs are executed by the computer system to convert the data into readable and directly meaningful form on paper, microfilm, or in spoken words.

Legislative efforts have been going on since the mid-1960s in efforts to preserve the right of privacy. At that time, Congressman Cornelius Gallagher from New Jersey was the champion of privacy in the new era of computers—that is, until he was sent off to prison at the Allenwood Prison Camp in Pennsylvania for a variety of crimes including income tax evasion and conspiracy. He was alleged to have been involved with organized crime, which was probably at least part of his motivation for worrying about the privacy of people and the growing use of databanks.

Almost everything that could be said about the right of privacy and the role computers play had been said by about 1968; but it wasn't until 1973 and 1974 that we finally had some explicit privacy laws. This is probably because it took that long to get up enough momentum and attention to pass legislation. Over the past several years there has been a continual backlog of over 50 bills regarding privacy awaiting action in Congress, and probably more than that among the state legislatures. William Bagley was a champion for privacy in the early 1970s in the State of California Assembly. He held numerous hearings throughout California on the issue. A legislative aid told me that when Assemblyman Bagley put out a press release on tax reform, it appeared on page 42 of the newspapers. When he put out a press release on privacy, it appeared on page 2 with his picture. He and other legislators getting this kind of exposure were not about to hurry the legislation through. This is possibly another reason why legislation moves so slowly on this issue. Also, the privacy issue does not have deadlines associated with it as do other issues such as taxes, budgets, and welfare programs requiring great financial outlays.

The abuse of privacy of individuals comes about from unrestricted collection of data about people, from storing inaccurate or incomplete data, from its unauthorized disclosure, and from incorrect or otherwise harmful conclusions drawn from it. It is argued that if fewer data are stored, then all of those other bad things won't happen. That may be true, but storing more data is necessary for maintaining increased levels of living standards and, unfortunately, bigger government.

The growth of government services to citizens is rapidly leading to a welfare state in America. Casper Weinberger, the former head of the Department of Health, Education and Welfare, stated in 1975 that "above all, we must recognize that personal freedoms diminish as the welfare state grows. The price of more and more public programs is less and less freedom."

Most people are willing to give up incrementally small amounts of data about themselves for even the smallest of conveniences and services in return. In the pre-computer age, the increment of data was used for its intended purpose and discarded or saved in a relatively inaccessible way for other uses. Fortunately it was expensive to save and use information. It has been said that government bureaucracy is inefficient enough to make most governments tolerable to live with. At the same time, society was also less safe in some ways—for example, government regulatory and law enforcement agencies were not nearly as effective because they were not able to collect, store, and retrieve data very well.

Many people believe that good guys don't have to worry about violation of their privacy since they have nothing about them that they are not proud of or willing to have other people know. People who have good credit ratings should be quite willing to have credit data about them stored in computerized credit reporting systems. Wherever they go their credit rating is easily accessible, making purchases on credit easy for them. The danger to these people may not be the storage of personal data but the storage of incorrect or incomplete data. For example, I recently underwent a medical examination to determine the cause of heart palpitations. My doctor wrote, "Suspected heart palpitations" in his notes. Further investigation revealed an upset stomach condition caused by coffee. Stopping the coffee stopped the heart palpitations, but I keep thinking about those words, "Suspected heart palpitations," where they will be recorded and what databank they may end up in that could affect my eligibility for life insurance, for example.

There is great continuing concern over computerized law

enforcement databanks, primarily because arrest records are stored in them, but often disposition data indicating conviction or exoneration does not get into the system. There are numerous cases reported of individuals who have been turned down for employment because of arrest records alone. One solution to this suggested by a public defender in Oakland, California, was that since an arrest is a public action entered onto public records in police stations and sometimes reported in newspapers, arrest records should be maintained as public information freely available to anybody and treated strictly as only suspected wrongdoing, but by law no discriminatory actions based on arrest records alone should be permitted. This may not stigmatize a person in Oakland, but the resulting discrimination in rural and midwestern America is still strong. The battles and issues rage on in the attempt to balance public good and social needs with personal privacy in the storage of such data.

In the computer age communications and computer technology have facilitated the efficient storing, processing, and transmission of small amounts of data about large numbers of people. Note that the technology may not economically support the efficient storing of large amounts of data about small numbers of people. The problems in privacy are the increased exposure of automated data and the rapid advancement of technology, without sufficient advances in the supportive functions that render that technology safe while allowing accuracy, completeness, and authorized disclosure.

The role and the focus of computer technology in the privacy issue has been most clearly identified in a project done for the Computer Science and Engineering Board of the National Academy of Sciences and funded by the Russell Sage Foundation. The results of this study were presented by Alan F. Westin and Michael A. Baker in their book, *Databanks in a Free Society*. Fifty-five site investigations of advanced record-keeping organizations were carried out and 14 of these were presented as case studies in the book.

An indication of the increasing numbers of records is shown most vividly in the first table in the accompanying figures from Westin and Baker's book. In parallel with the increasing number

INCREASES IN THE VOLUME OF ANNUAL TRANSACTIONS
AFFECTING ORGANIZATIONAL DATA PROCESSING

TYPE OF TRANSACTION	PRECOMPUTER ERA			COMPUTER ERA		OVERALL INCREASE
	1940	1955	Increase 1940–55, Percent	1970	Increase 1955–70, Percent	1940–70, Percent
Checks written[a]	1.2 billion	2.1 billion	75	7.2 billion	243	600
Telephones in use[b]	19.3 million	56.2 million	191	120.2 million	114	522
Individual social security payments[c]	222,000	8 million	3,504	26.2 million	228	11,702
Individual federal tax returns[d]	14.6 million	58.3 million	299	77 million	32	427
Public welfare recipients[e]	4.6 million	5.6 million	22	13.3 million	137	189
Airline passengers[f]	Originating 3 million	Originating 42 million	1,300	Enplaning 171 million	307	5,600
Persons entering hospitals for treatment[g]	10.1 million	21.1 million	109	31.7 million	50	213

a *Checks Written:* These figures are the result of an estimate prepared for the project by the American Bankers Association. They represent a very rough estimate based on Federal Reserve Board statistics. Both personal and commercial checking transactions are included.

b *Telephones in Use:* These figures include both personal and business phones in A T & T companies, in its subsidiaries, and in independent phone companies in the U.S. They are taken from *Statistics of Communications Common Carriers,* a publication of the Federal Communications Commission.

c *Individual Social Security Payments:* This estimate was prepared for the project from the records of the Social Security Administration.

d *Individual Federal Tax Returns:* These figures represent nonbusiness returns filed by individuals (including joint returns) for the years indicated. They are taken from *Statistics of Income, Individual Income Tax Returns,* an annual publication of the Internal Revenue Service.

e *Public Welfare Recipients:* Recipients under five different kinds of programs are included: Old Age Assistance, Aid to Families with Dependent Children, Aid to the Blind, Aid to the Permanently and Totally Disabled, and General Assistance. The figure for 1940 does not include APTD recipients, as that program had not yet been established. Sources include *Historical Statistics of the United States: Colonial Times to 1957* and *Statistical Abstract of the United States, 1971.* Both are U.S. Department of Commerce, Bureau of the Census publications.

f *Airline Passengers:* These figures represent an estimate prepared for the project by the U.S. Air Transport Association on the basis of Civil Aeronautics Board statistics. The percentage increases between 1955 and 1970 and 1940 and 1970 are exaggerated to some extent by the following change in recording definitions: for 1940 and 1955, the figures refer to *originating* passengers; if, in the course of a trip, a passenger took more than one plane, he would only be counted once. The figures for 1970, however, refer to *enplaning* passengers; if a passenger took three different planes to reach his destination, he would be counted three times. This difference in recording definitions has the effect of *exaggerating* the percentage differences from 1940 and 1955 to 1970.

g *Persons Entering Hospitals for Treatment:* Figures for 1955 and 1970 are from *Hospitals, Guide Issue,* an annual publication of the American Hospital Association. The 1940 figure was taken from *Historical Statistics of the United States: Colonial Times to 1957, op. cit.* All three figures include multiple admissions of the same individual in a given year.

TYPE OF TRANSACTION	PRECOMPUTER ERA			COMPUTER ERA		OVERALL INCREASE
	1940	1955	Increase 1940–55, Percent	1970	Increase 1955–70, Percent	1940–70, Percent
Persons covered by private hospitalization insurance[h]	12 million	107.7 million	797	181.5 million	69	1,513
Motor-vehicle registrations[i]	32.5 million	62.7 million	93	108.4 million	73	230
Passports issued[j]	26,000 (new and renewals)	528,000 (new and renewals)	1,931	(New only) 2.2 million	317	8,362
Students enrolled in colleges and universities[k]	1.5 million	2.6 million	73	(1969) 6.9 million	165	360
Applications received for federal employment[l]	1 million	1.7 million	70	2.9 million	71	190
New York Stock Exchange transactions[m]	282.7 million	820.5 million	190	3.2 billion	290	1,032
Pieces of mail handled, U.S. Post Office (all classes)[n]	27.8 billion	55.3 billion	99	84.9 billion	52	205

h Persons Covered by Private Hospital Insurance: All data for this entry are from Source Book of Health Insurance Data, an annual publication of the Health Insurance Institute, New York City.

i Motor-vehicle Registrations: All data for this entry are from Historical Statistics of the United States: Colonial Times to 1957, op. cit.

j Passports Issued: Figures for this entry are from Summary of Passport Statistics, an annual report of the U.S. Bureau of Customs.

k Students Enrolled in Colleges and Universities: Data for this entry are from Statistical Abstract, op. cit. and Historical Statistics of

l Applications Received for Federal Employment: Figures for this entry are the result of an estimate prepared for the project by the U.S. Civil Service Commission.

m New York Stock Exchange Transactions: This entry is the result of an estimate prepared for the project by the Research Department of the New York Stock Exchange.

n Pieces of Mail Handled, U.S. Post Office: Figures for this entry were taken from Statistical Abstract of the United States, 1971, op. cit. and Historical Statistics of the United States: Colonial Times to 1957, op. cit.

of records, the number of computers in the United States has risen from 70,000 in 1961, to 90,000 in 1972, 150,000 in 1975, and an anticipated 500,000 (including small mini-computers) by 1980. By 1972, computerization had become a necessity for survival. There was no choice, and the process was now irreversible. However, at that time there were relatively few shared databanks of personal information. The authors conclude and I agree that the public media sensationalized the privacy issue and made it appear that far more was being done. This was encouraged by EDP technologists publicly announcing extensive plans for huge shared databanks, few of which ever achieved the claimed degree of performance.

Westin and Baker stated: "The organizations we visited have not extended the scope of their information collection of individuals as a direct result of computerization. . . . Content of computerized records about individuals has not been increased in scope compared to what was collected in their manual counterpart during the pre-computer era (1940 to 1955) . . . increased collection of personal information occurred for other reasons such as new laws and more services to people that required more data." They went on to say that they found a reduced volume of data when computerization took place. Because of the expense and distrust of unproven computers, computer records tended to contain cryptic facts and to be less sensitive. Computerization did not change the amount of coded information; it just perpetuated this information from what was being done in the manual systems. There was no change in the "Forgive and forget" policies concerning personal information. "The first fifteen years of automation haven't altered relationships between people, data and organizations." The book sums up the effects of computerization on record keeping: "(1) Data became more up to date. (2) More effective use was made of data. (3) Faster handling of inquiries resulted. (4) New inter-organizational exchange of activities resulted. (5) More large record systems appeared. (6) More accurate records with fewer but different and more serious kinds of errors have occurred. (7) Greater security was more possible than in manual based systems, but little is done in this regard other than providing physical security. The potential for security, however, is far greater in computerized systems."

The authors conclude, probably too simplistically, that technology has no bearing on the privacy issue. The issue is, Should a piece of information be collected and stored? Computer technology has not created revolutionary new powers of data surveillance, but it brings increased efficiencies. The policies are not changed from the previous manual systems. "Man is still in charge of the machines." Thus ends this report on the status of the issues in 1972.

Another milestone was reached in 1974 with the publication of the U.S. Department of Health, Education and Welfare report on Records, Computers and the Rights of Citizens. This project was headed by Dr. Willis Ware, senior scientist at the Rand Corporation in Santa Monica, California. The executive secretary of the project was David Martin, an attorney with DHEW. The report formed the basis for the development of federal and state legislation in 1974. Unfortunately, the first few pages of the report were used for writing new legislation without taking into account the unanswered questions and implications stated in the remainder of the report.

Senator Ervin and his U.S. Senate Committee on Government Operations produced a privacy bill. Congressmen Edward Koch and Barry Goldwater, Jr., strange political bedfellows from the liberal and conservative sides of the House, also produced a bill. Compromises in both Houses ended up with legislation signed into law by President Ford on December 31, 1974, called the Privacy Act of 1974, Public Law No. 90-579. Besides imposing strict controls on databanks in federal agencies, it established a Privacy Protection Study Commission with a budget of $1.5 million over two years to study the impact of the new law, changes, and possible extensions into the private sector. The commission is chaired by David F. Linowes, a CPA in New York City. The vice chairman is Dr. Willis Ware of the Rand Corporation. Koch and Goldwater represent Congress on the commission. The other members are William B. Dickinson, a retired newspaper editor from Philadelphia; William O. Bailey, an insurance company executive from Hartford; and Robert J. Tennessen, a Minnesota legislator. Carole Parsons, former assistant executive director of the President's Domestic Council Committee on Privacy, is the executive director of this important commission.

The safe use of computers is embodied in just one word in the Privacy Act of 1974. The National Bureau of Standards, the Office of Management and Budget, and a number of other government agencies have spent considerable time and resources considering that word. It appears in Section E, Agency Requirements, Subsection 10:
"Establish

                appropriate

                            administrative, technical and physical safeguards to ensure the security and confidentiality of records and to protect against any anticipated threats or hazards. . . ." The meaning of "appropriate" could be determined by referring to a few words in the text following, where it is stated, "Against any anticipated threats or hazards." That is what computer abuse research and this book are all about: how to decide on appropriate safeguards by considering actual experience so that we can determine the anticipated threats and hazards.

In considering the overall problem of computer abuse, we find the violation of privacy to be only one of many threats and hazards in the use of computers. There is great danger of attempting to make computers safer by concentrating only on the privacy issue. The problem must be attacked on a broader front. Databanks almost all reside in computer systems in which all kinds of other sensitive data are also present. Compromises of computer systems, for whatever purpose and against whatever targets, endanger databanks of personal data as well as the other sensitive data. Protection of the databank must at the same time include protection of all data in the system and the system itself if the optimum expenditure of resources in making computers safer is to be achieved.

When we look at the current privacy legislation from the viewpoint of the general problem of computer abuse, based on actual experience, several weaknesses appear. The current legislation provides no instrumentation to monitor violations or determine the performance of databank custodians in complying with the law. A precedent for this may be seen in banking law where banks are required, in keeping their customers' money safe, to report any fraud or embezzlement to the FBI and

Treasury Department, which maintain and report statistics on this kind of activity. Similarly, laws that keep people's data safe in databanks should also require the custodians of the databanks to report any anomalies in their computer systems for whatever reason that might have compromised the personal data stored there. Many of the cases of computer abuse, including some described in this book, provide examples where compromises of computer systems for various reasons (not necessarily including invasion of privacy) could have resulted in privacy invasion; or possibly the private data may no longer be under the exclusive control of the custodians.

Current legislation also fails to require safeguards or certain actions or sanctions when a computer system containing a databank of private data is compromised for whatever targets, accidentally or intentionally. In such situations the individuals whose data are stored in the computer systems can no longer be assured of confidentiality. This can occur even when the system is compromised for some purpose such as embezzlement, financial theft, or malicious mischief not related to the personal data at all. It is suggested that when such a situation occurs, the custodian of the databank should be required to inform all individuals whose data may have been compromised that the incident occurred. This would give added incentive to the custodian to show extra concern for the security of the entire computer system, knowing that the additional penalty of the cost of informing many individuals could result from such a violation of security.

This oversight in the current legislation is partly the result of confidentiality compromises based only on theory rather than on information empirically derived from actual experience in the overall problem of computer security. The computer abuse study at Stanford Research Institute, funded by grants from the National Science Foundation and other sources, has been the only significant attempt to approach the problem empirically.

Twenty-five cases of alleged violation of privacy are found among the 374 reported cases of computer abuse. Several are taken from trade publications and newspapers. The *Computerworld* trade newspaper reported on September 30, 1970, that the

U.S. Department of Defense was a victim and a Department of Defense Public Relations employee and a Pentagon EDP employee were suspects. It was claimed that the Public Relations man bribed the Pentagon EDP employee to make a computer run in order to compile the results of 1,000 attendee questionnaires for a Canadian National Exposition in Toronto for the express purpose of selling the information.

Computerworld reported in January 1972 that a Chicago policeman is alleged to have obtained an FBI National Crime Information Center (NCIC) dossier concerning a businessman and gave it to his brother-in-law, a lawyer, who was considering accepting the businessman as a client. A federal grand jury indictment in Chicago resulted from this act. Again, on September 27, 1972, *Computerworld* reported that civil charges had been filed against the Iowa State Commissioner of Public Safety by Freeland Walker and the Iowa Civil Liberties Union, claiming that a criminal file pertaining to Walker was sent to the FBI NCIC stating that he was a known criminal; in fact he had seven arrests but no convictions.

The *San Francisco Examiner* on July 13, 1973, and February 24, 1974, reported that the Senate Watergate Committee was investigating secret ownership of a computer service owned by Herbert Kalmbach, President Nixon's personal attorney. This service firm was using a computer to perform mailing services for the California "McGovern for President" Committee. The service is alleged to have caused political mailings using computerized mailing lists to be lost or delayed, and in one case, completed the mailing so that the campaign literature arrived at voters' residences one day after the national election.

In another case a different computer service company in the same area used a computerized mailing list rented from the state of California for commercial purposes. However, the list was limited by law to political mailings. The state sued the firm and settled out of court for a $22,000 penalty.

The derived data problem is another technological issue not yet clearly understood nor treated in current legislation. The problem takes at least two forms: First, to what extent may data not identified with individuals be analytically or statistically associated with them? For example, there may be information in one file about an unidentified individual with a specified salary and other personal details, including the census tract in which he resides. Another file could have information about an identified individual stating his salary and place of residence. By matching the known information common to both of these files, the file of data about the unidentified individual can easily be identified from the name supplied in the other file. This kind of problem often occurs when data about individuals are unique or limited to small numbers of people.

The second kind of derived data problem is that there are types of personal data that may be represented programmatically rather than directly in the form of stored data. A file can contain names of individuals and limited amounts of data which can be processed by computer programs that contain generic data to produce significant additional information about the individual. Thus, this type of program must also be treated with the same sensitivity as the data that the program produces. Current legislation does not appear to take into account programmatically derived personal information.

The cost of privacy-motivated confidentiality, especially with advancing technology, is unknown; only a few specific databanks have been studied relative to the cost of confidentiality. This cost is associated with data accessibility control, maintaining accuracy and completeness, and otherwise providing for adequate security. The issue of cost was not so important in legislation that constrains only government agencies—the taxpayer could pay the bill. If the legislation is to be extended into the private sector, at issue could be the expense of controls amounting to many millions of dollars. Extension of the legislation into the private sector must be done, but very cautiously, and slowly enough to assure that efficiency of designing confidentiality into new systems can be accomplished without having to go to the far greater expense of retrofitting current systems.

The issue of universal identifiers for people is another part of the privacy debate. The Privacy Act of 1974 outlaws the use of the Social Security number among government agencies except where prescribed by law. Congressman Goldwater asked me for my opinion on the use of universal identifiers. I told him I had to answer that question two ways. First, as a professional in computer technology, I would have to support strongly the use of universal identifiers from the viewpoint of efficiency, accuracy, and completeness in maintaining databanks in computer systems and computer networks. On the other hand, as a citizen residing in Los Altos, California, I would have to oppose strongly the use of the Social Security number as a universal identifier because I conclude that technology has not advanced far enough that confidentiality could be maintained sufficiently in the greatly enlarged databanks and inexpensive collection of private information that could result from the use of universal identifiers. Part of our privacy today lies in the fact that dispersal of data and the inefficiency of combining files and matching names increase the cost of combining personal information about us in one easily accessible place.

Personal identification of people is rapidly being automated, making universal identification of people possible in other ways than by requiring a set of digits or alphabetical letters. Personal identification can basically be achieved in only three ways: according to what a person knows, what a person is, or what a person has. Automatic identification of people at bank-operated cash dispensers and automated teller terminals is based on what a person knows in the form of a secret four- or five-digit code which he memorizes and types into the terminal, and what he has in the form of a magnetic stripe plastic card containing identification data. Identifying people according to what they are is not yet particularly advanced on an automated basis. People can be identified by other people from memory according to what they look like or from photographs.

A number of attempts at automated identification are being experimentally tried and developed at the present time, such as a method of identification based on the unique length of people's fingers. An automatic finger length measuring terminal has recently become available from the Identimation Company in New Jersey, and the results are promising, at least for relatively small populations based on experience to date. The Calspan Company has recently marketed an automatic fingerprint reader using a laser light source.

A serious question not yet sufficiently addressed for these types of devices is the acceptance by the public of their use. For example, a terminal that requires large numbers of people to place their hands and fingers on the same surface as everyone else poses a sanitary, aesthetic, and ethnic problem. The surfaces will collect skin oil and dirt rapidly. I am not going to put my hand on that same surface where a person who just finished eating a peanut butter and jelly sandwich placed his. There are still some people of one race unwilling to touch anything previously touched by a person of another race. The fingerprint device presents another problem. People, especially citizens of the United Kingdom, associate fingerprinting with criminality and will resist the concept of being identified by their prints.

Another method was researched by a Japanese team which concluded that lip prints could be more easily recognized automatically than fingerprints. This would have resulted in people having to kiss their terminals to be properly identified. Another method proposed to IBM by a Canadian inventor consisted of using the unique shapes of people's skulls to identify them. A person would put his head inside a helmet-like device, and mechanical probes would determine the shape of his skull. If he was an imposter, then clamps could be applied to trap the person's head inside the helmet. A more reasonable approach might be identifying people by their brain wave patterns. However, at present this also requires that a person must place his head in some kind of a device to pick up the brain waves.

Research in identifying people by voice recognition has been going on at Stanford Research Institute and a number of other research organizations with little success. However, new successes with the most common manual method known is gaining support. Dr. Hewitt Crane at SRI has perfected a simple, inexpensive pen wired to an electronic device interfaced to a computer. The ball point of the pen gimbals on the pen shaft so that it is deflected away from the direction of the pen movement. This produces a time history of the path of the pen and its pressure on the paper. Other similar devices are being tested.

The obvious use of these devices is for handwritten character recognition for data input to a computer, and the SRI device has been licensed for this purpose by Xebec Corporation. But even more intriguing is that all the human dynamics of handwritten signatures can be captured in a computer. Thus, people could go right on using the traditional handwritten signature for identification, but now it can be automatically monitored. However, a significant amount of testing and prototype work for product development remains to be done.

With all these identification methods, two practical criteria of effectiveness must be considered. The false alarm rate (failure to identify an authorized person) and the impostor pass rate (acceptance of an impostor) must both be low. The criteria for acceptance that a person is who he says he is can be set high, resulting in a desirably low impostor pass rate but an unacceptably high false alarm rate. Conversely, the criteria for acceptance can be relaxed, resulting in a desirably low false alarm rate but an unacceptably high impostor pass rate.

In another aspect of privacy, electronic surveillance is becoming highly advanced, with the use of wiretapping and the recording of conversations by means of a vast array of miniature, hidden eavesdropping bugs. None of this has involved computers as surveillance tools. However, eavesdropping has become so inexpensive and presumably so common that large volumes of spoken words are recorded, but only small amounts of specific conversations on limited subjects are of interest to the surveillants.

The problem is how to separate the needed information from long recordings. Enter the computer. Speech recognition (identification of spoken words, not identification of the speaker) is developing rapidly. The electronic analog signals from voice recordings could be searched by computers for key spoken words by matching them with patterns of preselected spoken words. The computer automatically stores the location on the recording and copies that region of the recording, thus saving much human effort. Another great advantage is that in authorized surveillance the recording need not be heard except for the parts pertinent to an investigation, thus preserving some of the privacy of people surveilled except for what must officially be known.

Of course, all of this increased power to obtain personal

information, while increasing the effectiveness of the forces of good, also increases the effectiveness of the forces of evil. The net result is an increasing pressure on society to sort out the good from evil and to preclude the use of computer technology from the evildoers. Society, in the United States at least, is too late in controlling the antisocial use of handguns. Will it be too late for computer technology as well, a vastly more complex issue? What new technological and societal issues will rapidly evolve with the development of electronic fund transfer systems, vending machine banking, automatic voice recognition and understanding by computers, as well as the development of technological surveillance?

21 | THE BELMONT-PAWSEY PRIVACY CASE

The American Civil Liberties Union of Northern California went to bat for two psychiatric social workers in a little known privacy issue at law that is of historical value. The present California law could have resulted in a different court verdict today compared to the results in 1972. However, there are still many jurisdictions not as advanced in privacy matters where a similar situation and verdict could occur.

The case is vividly described, although obviously one-sided, in the Petitioners' Memorandum of Points and Authorities from which this case study is taken. It was written for an appeal on November 5, 1971, by Charles C. Marson and Paul N. Halvonik, ACLU attorneys for the petitioners.

Josephine Belmont and Glenda Pawsey were psychiatric social workers employed by the California State Department of Social Welfare in 1968. The department announced the advent of a centralized computer system for the storage and retrieval of the information collected by such employees in the course of their work with clients—the mentally and emotionally disturbed. The department demanded that its employees furnish data for its computer of the most sensitive possible nature: information concerning psychiatric assessments, the nature of any mental disability, legal and illegal alcohol and drug use, histories of criminal offenses and sex offenses, mental retardation, pregnancies out of wedlock—the whole gamut of intimate personal information that, were the clients being treated privately, never would escape a psychiatrist's locked files.

In spite of repeated protests by numerous members of its psychiatric staff, according to the Petitioners' Memorandum the department demanded that employees supply that information in the total absence of (1) any effort to ensure the confidentiality of the information when inserted in the system, (2) any definition of those persons "authorized" or "not authorized" to have access to the information, (3) any written rule or regulation governing access to the information, (4) any means of identifying those given access, (5) any means of informing the workers or their clients what use had been made of the data, or (6) any limitation on the potential use of the data. In addition, the department announced an intention to interface its system with similar systems possessed by unspecified other agencies of federal, state, and local government and to open its files for undescribed governmental and private "research." The department responded to criticism by hiring outside consultants to study the issues of privacy and security but, when the consultants made criticisms and recommendations for improvement, rejected the suggestions of its own consultants and pressed ahead substantially with its original plan.

The psychiatric social workers employed by the department are professionals who take seriously their obligations to their clients. In California a social worker has standing to assert the constitutional rights of his clients. An important precedent-setting case in this regard is *Parrish* v. *Civil Service Commission* 66 Cal.2d 260 (1967). In addition, the professional ethics by which the workers were bound specifically obligated them both to respect the privacy of their clients and to use responsibly the information gained in the course of professional relationships.

Not surprisingly, therefore, many psychiatric social workers balked at the department's plan and refused to supply the information demanded. After nearly a year of negotiations, meetings, consultations, and threats, the ranks of those refusing dwindled to two, Belmont and Pawsey.

On May 8, 1969, they were notified of disciplinary action—five days suspension without pay—as a consequence of their refusal. Various charges were named, including insubordination, but at the subsequent hearing it was stipulated by all parties that they would be charged with violating Government Code Section 19572(o) (willful disobedience). They filed appeals with the State Personnel Board. After a hearing, the board affirmed the department's action. The Petitioners' Memorandum was the basis for bringing that decision to the court for review.

During the course of the hearing before the State Personnel Board, Belmont and Pawsey offered to prove all of the allegations concerning the department's data processing system. The attorney general, representing the department, objected to the relevance of the Offer of Proof, and after pleadings were exchanged, the objection was sustained. The hearing officer expressed the opinion, later adopted by the board, that while the department's arrangements for the security and privacy of the data "may or may not be adequate," it was no business of the psychiatric social workers. The evidence was excluded and the punitive actions affirmed.

Thus in one sense the question before the court, on review of the decision of the State Personnel Board, was a very narrow one—whether the board properly or improperly excluded the evidence set forth in the Offer of Proof. This raised other questions, some of which are of enormous consequence and had never been answered by any court—questions such as the extent, if any, to which the federal and state constitutions and California statutory and tort law protect individuals from the state government centralized computer-based storage and dissemination of harmful confidential data concerning the most intimate aspects of their personal lives, with little or no provision for the security or confidentiality of the data.

The Petitioners' Memorandum went on to argue that this was a case of profound importance. The issues posed by the current technological explosion in data storage and retrieval were posed in this case for the first time as issues of constitutional, statutory, and common law.

It was Belmont's and Pawsey's view as represented by their attorneys that the state and federal constitutions and California's statutory and common law were big enough to fit this case; relevant enough and elastic enough to protect them and their clients from the bureaucratic mindlessness with which the State Department of Social Welfare proceeded here. To be sure, only analogies are available; there are no cases on point. But such was the novelty of the issues presented here that neither side had direct recourse to precedent. The court was told it would break new ground whatever it decides.

It was the attorneys' position that Belmont and Pawsey were entitled, by constitutional, statutory, and common law, to refuse the orders of their employers. This is an unusual position but not an impossible one. It has been successful before in other cases. If there is any room in the law for such refusal—any small universe of demands by a public employer so illegal and so outrageous, according to the attorneys, that a public employee may defy them—then they urged that the doctrine applies here.

They argued that the storage and dissemination of the data demanded of the psychiatric social workers in the manner announced by the department (1) would have constituted the common-law tort of invasion of the privacy of clients, (2) would have violated the state and federal constitutional right to privacy of clients, (3) would have exposed the workers and their employer to civil and criminal liability, and (4) would have constituted a violation of the workers' professional ethics. They also argued that Government Code Section 19572(o) (willful disobedience) did not apply to the circumstances of this case.

The Petitioners' Memorandum then stated five arguments.

1. Obedience to the department's orders would have exposed the workers to tort liability for the invasion of their clients' privacy. They were therefore entitled to refuse.

2. Obedience to the department's orders would have resulted in the wholesale violation of the state and federal constitutional right of privacy of clients. The workers cannot be punished for their disobedience.

3. Obedience to the department's orders would have exposed workers to both civil and criminal liability under federal statutes. Therefore they may not be punished for disobedience.

4. Obedience to the department's orders would have forced the workers to violate their professional ethics. They cannot therefore be punished for refusing.

5. A state employee does not violate Section 19572(o) if he has a valid reason for disobedience. Belmont and Pawsey, having a valid reason, did not violate the Section.

The support for these arguments then followed.

Most orders of a public employer must be obeyed by the employee, or the latter can be punished. Belmont and Pawsey recognized this, and would never support a general right of an employee to "veto" his employer's orders without suffering the consequences.

But there is a small area into which a public employer cannot order its employee to venture and punish him for refusing. The leading California case is *Parrish* v. *Civil Service Commission* (1967) in which a county social worker refused orders to participate in a massive pre-dawn "bed-check" raid on welfare clients. The court reversed his dismissal, holding that the order was in effect an order to violate the constitutional rights of the welfare recipients and therefore the employee could not be punished for disobeying it. Central to the employee's argument, and to the court's conclusion, was the notion that obedience to the order would have exposed the employee to civil liability. This conclusion is hardly remarkable, since no sane system of law would permit a government employee to be put to the Hobson's choice of civil liability or punishment for disobedience.

So putting aside for a moment the constitutional implications of the orders disobeyed, it is relevant to know whether the facts contained in the Offer of Proof would demonstrate that the workers, in obeying the orders, would have exposed themselves to civil liability. The attorneys submitted that they would.

Although the invasion of privacy was a relatively new tort, it was firmly embedded in California tort law. As the law of privacy has grown, it has developed into four distinct and separate kinds of invasions. Professor William Prosser has detailed these branches in perhaps the leading modern summary of the privacy tort. He calls the third branch (the one relevant to this case) "the public disclosure of private facts."

While the privacy law dealing with the public disclosure of private facts is only one branch of privacy, it was the one most firmly established in California. This is due to the fact that what Prosser calls the leading case in this branch of privacy law is also the first California case on the subject of privacy—*Melvin* v. *Reid* (1931).

In *Melvin* v. *Reid,* the plaintiff had for several years been a notorious prostitute and had been tried, though acquitted, for murder. After her acquittal she decided to reform, gave up her occupation, became rehabilitated, married, made friends, and took a respectable position in society. Some eight years later the defendants produced a movie titled *The Red Kimono*, which depicted true events in the plaintiff's earlier life as a prostitute. The film used the plaintiff's maiden name and was advertised as depicting her actual life story. This, of course, caused her great injury, and she brought suit for damages.

The court candidly recognized that no California case had yet established the right of privacy. Yet the court reversed the sustaining of a demurrer, holding that a cause of action was stated, and finding a right of privacy inherent in Article One, Section One, of the California Constitution, which protects the right of "pursuing and obtaining safety and happiness." The court assumed that the events depicted in the movie were true, but spoke of privacy as the right "to be let alone."

Thus the privacy tort was born in California in the context of the public disclosure of private facts, and its focus has remained there ever since. Other cases were quoted by the attorneys, and these cases illustrated the principle that, in privacy law generally and in California law particularly, the unwarranted disclosure of private or confidential facts concerning a person gives rise to tort liability. Belmont and Pawsey offered to prove, in effect, that this was exactly what their employers ordered them to do.

Certainly the facts that the workers were ordered to feed into the department's EDP system were sufficiently private and confidential—whether a client was mentally ill, an alcoholic, a sex offender, incarcerated in a mental institution, and the like.

And just as certainly the disclosure of those facts would have been unwarranted because they were to be disclosed to "authorized persons" whom the attorneys alleged no one could identify and no scrap of paper described. The department repeatedly refused to define "authorized persons"; they were selected by no ascertainable standard, had "little or no legitimate use" for the data, and seemingly had access to more data than necessary. According to the attorneys, although the department did not broadcast the facts to the general public, they came close to it. They announced an intent to accomplish the placing of the information in a computerized library to which a large but undefined group would have access and then refused to keep track of who used this library or to define who was eligible to use it. Surely this is the functional equivalent of publication. In addition, the information Belmont and Pawsey were commanded to disclose would not have been reasonably secure from unauthorized access nor was much of it necessary to the department's announced purposes. Finally, they argued that the future promised that the dissemination of the data would be multiplied widely and irresponsibly.

The genius of the common law is that its principles can grow to remain relevant to the advancing times. Admittedly, no case holds that persons in the precise position of Belmont and Pawsey would have been liable in tort, but novelty of factual application is nothing new to the common law. The disclosures they were ordered to make fit every requirement of the tort of invasion of privacy by the public disclosure of private facts, and they would have been liable under that theory if they had obeyed. They were thus entitled to refuse as stated in point one above.

If Belmont and Pawsey could have established that furnishing the information demanded would have been a violation of their clients' constitutional rights, then they couldn't be punished for disobeying. It had already been established that the tort of invasion of privacy by means of the public disclosure of private facts is a violation of Article One, Section One, of the California Constitution in the *Melvin* v. *Reid* case. It remained to be demonstrated that such an invasion was a violation of the United States Constitution as well.

According to the attorneys, the leading case from the United States Supreme Court is *Griswold* v. *Connecticut* (1965). There they said the Court established the right of privacy as of constitutional dimension, striking down a state law prohibiting the use of contraceptive devices or the giving of advice concerning them as a violation of the right of privacy of married couples. It is overoptimistic to read that case as establishing the constitutional status of the right of privacy generally, since the Court was concerned with an intrusion into a very sensitive and intimate sphere of human feelings and emotions. But even by that standard that case applies here, because the data Belmont and Pawsey were commanded to disclose could not have been more sensitive and intimate, and the impact of its disclosure could hardly be more brutalizing to human feelings and emotions.

The attorneys further argued that within that limitation courts have begun widely to recognize the Griswold privacy concept, even outside the sphere of marriage. For example, if the California Supreme Court in the Parrish case mentioned earlier had not been able to dispose of the case on Fourth Amendment grounds, indications were strong that it might have granted relief on a privacy theory based on the Griswold case.

Since the Griswold case, the constitutional right of privacy has spread rapidly in federal decisions. The attorneys referenced *Doe* v. *McMillan* (D.C. Cir. 1971), in which the Court of Appeals issued an injunction pending appeal restraining the publication of tests and disciplinary records of named students in the District of Columbia schools. The plaintiffs' sole claim was invasion of the constitutional right of privacy. In issuing the injunction pending appeal, the Court of Appeals called the contention "worthy of serious consideration on the merits." Other cases were also cited.

Most importantly, even though the notion that privacy is a constitutional right is relatively new, it has already been applied to the public-disclosure-of-private-facts category of privacy cases where state agencies have been involved. In one case in 1963 cited by the attorneys, the plaintiff went to a city police department to complain of an assault. Over her protests that no bruises would show, and without summoning an available policewoman, one of the defendant police officers inveigled the plaintiff into submitting to being repeatedly photographed in the nude by insisting that the pictures were "necessary" for his investigation. Then he and other defendants circulated the nude photographs among the personnel of the police department.

The plaintiff sued in the federal court, claiming an invasion of her constitutional right of privacy. Since she sued under 42 U.S.C., Sections 1979 and 1983, protecting only "rights . . . secured by the Constitution," the constitutional stature of the right invaded was essential to her claim. The court held that her complaint stated a cause of action for the invasion of a constitutional right of privacy found in the Due Process Clause of the Fourteenth Amendment.

And in another case in 1967, a case with obvious similarities to this one, a criminal indictment obtained due to a misunderstanding against an obviously innocent defendant had been dismissed. The police insisted on a right to retain the defendant's photograph and fingerprints in their rogue's gallery. But on application of the defendant the court ordered them expunged and destroyed, holding that their retention would violate the defendant's constitutional right of privacy.

Thus invasions of privacy involving the public disclosure of private facts have, when agencies of the state are at fault, achieved constitutional dimension. Finally, on argument two regarding constitutional right violation the attorneys argued it was sufficient to note that every legal requisite of such an invasion was met. Therefore Belmont and Pawsey could not, according to the Parrish case, be disciplined for their refusal to join in the wholesale violation of their clients' constitutional rights.

On argument three regarding disobedience of orders the attorneys stated that 42 U.S. Code, Section 1983, provides a civil cause of action to any person who suffers a deprivation of constitutional rights, under color of state law, custom, or usage, against the person who so deprives him. Public agencies are not sued under the section, which is premised on individual liability. Since it is demonstrated in point two that such a deprivation would have resulted if Belmont and Pawsey had obeyed the department's orders, and since in so doing they would clearly have been acting under color of state law, custom, or usage, they would have been liable.

The attorneys stated that in addition, 18 U.S. Code, Section 242, makes it a misdemeanor wilfully to participate in any state activity which infringes any right secured by United States Constitution and provides for a fine of not more than $1,000, imprisonment for not more than one year, or both. In obeying their orders Belmont and Pawsey would have been liable under this section as well because they knew all the facts. They could therefore decline to participate without incurring punishment.

On argument four the Code of Ethics by which Belmont and Pawsey in their profession are bound contains, among others, the following principles:

—I respect the privacy of the people I serve.

—I use in a responsible manner information gained in professional relationships.

—I accept responsibility to help protect the community against unethical practice by any individuals or organizations engaged in social welfare activities.

—I accept responsibility for working toward the creation and maintenance of conditions within agencies which enable social workers to conduct themselves in keeping with this code.

> from Code of Ethics, National Association of Social Workers. NASW Personnel Standards and Adjudication Procedures (1963) (in effect at the times relevant here).

Putting aside for a moment the intricacies of law, it was argued that if the facts set forth by Belmont and Pawsey are correct, they could not, in light of the principles quoted above, do anything but refuse to obey the orders in question. No intelligent state agency would put professional-level employees to such a choice, and no humane system of law would permit them to be put to a choice between punishment and violation of their professional ethics. This follows as a proposition of constitutional law from the Parrish case and should follow as a question of the statutory interpretation of Government Code, Section 19572(o).

THE BELMONT-PAWSEY PRIVACY CASE | 265

On the final argument the attorneys stated that there is very little law interpreting the phrase "willful disobedience" in Government Code Section 19572(o), but what law there is suggests that the term is not absolute. In a 1966 case the court, in reviewing a disciplinary action under Section 19572(o), said that the employee "had a right to disobey the orders of his superiors . . . only if there was in fact some valid reason which would excuse his disobedience." The employee had an excuse, and the court examined the excuse on the merits, but did not accept it. It found the disobedience "unwarranted" and therefore affirmed the discipline.

This means that if Belmont and Pawsey had a valid reason for disobeying orders, they did not violate Section 19572(o). Rather than restate the factual issues once again, the attorneys simply submitted that Belmont and Pawsey had a reasonable and good faith belief that obedience would invade their clients' right of privacy, violate their professional ethics, expose them to tort liability, and expose them to criminal liability. Any of those reasons should be treated as a "valid reason," and therefore they should have been entitled to prove that those reasons were present.

The attorneys concluded their Petitioners' Memorandum by saying that the power of the state to exact obedience from its employees is broad, but it is not limitless. Belmont and Pawsey have in good faith challenged that power, not in a trivial dispute but on an issue of tremendous significance. The attorneys thought that California law protects them, and that they were entitled to relief.

The appeal failed. The attorneys and the two psychiatric social workers decided not to pursue their case the last step to the U.S. Supreme Court.

This case clearly demonstrates the thrust of the privacy issue as a legal problem and the minor but catalytic and pervasive role of computers.

22 | CONSUMER AND RETAILER COMPUTER ABUSE

Computer abuses perpetrated by retailers against consumers are difficult to identify and classify because of the problem of determining intent. Intent is more clear-cut in computer abuses perpetrated by consumers against retailers. Intent is often fraud or retribution by the consumer to get even with a retailer for a wrong he thinks has been done to him. Here retailers include any organization dealing with the public as individual people, covering many kinds of government agencies as well as private sellers of goods and services.

Abusive acts by retailers involving computers can cause consumers anguish and loss of personal time and effort, along with financial losses. These acts, often termed "computer errors," are sometimes the result of management indifference, oversight, lack of understanding EDP, or just plain incompetence or greed. The systems analysts, computer programmers, and EDP operations staffs share the guilt for similar reasons but often don't comprehend or else avoid knowing the results of their work. In any case these are not "computer errors"; they are caused by people one way or another.

It must also be realized that computer-related incidents resulting in losses to consumers can be the result of conscious, ethical business decisions to limit the cost of implementing computer applications which are used to serve consumers. Management realizes that errors cannot be eliminated entirely, and the goal is to keep them to a tolerable level. However, the businesses making such decisions must also provide fair treatment for victims of errors. The lack of fair treatment in correcting errors is often more a source of abuse than the original error.

Good advice from consumer protection advocates is to write letters complaining of computer-related problems directly to the president of the company, or to legislators in the case of government agencies. Names and addresses can be obtained by telephoning the errant organization or from reference books in libraries. Don't fool around with letters "to the computer" or to lower-echelon people. Many responsible retailers and agencies are now putting instructions on bills and other correspondence to be followed in case of problems.

If statistics were collected and examined, it is likely they would show that the number of accounting and transaction errors in automated systems dealing with customers is far smaller today than in previous manual systems. It's just that the problems that do happen seem to be more perverse, nonsensical, maddening in their automated form, and seemingly difficult to overcome.

In one case a consumer—a computer programmer—struck back at his own profession. Every month his car insurance company mailed him a refund check for the same amount. He returned it each month with a letter stating he had already received his refund. His programming-trained mind told him that the computer had probably not been programmed to clear the account after the refund had been made. He became tired of this after a while and having checked with his lawyer took a more aggressive course of action. He cashed the next check and sent in a personal check for the same amount. His account was credited in the amount of the check, and he received a refund check the next month for double the original amount. By repeating this process he was doubling up every month. After several months the amount became so large that he got some attention. Finally his trip to fame and fortune ended when he received not a check, but a polite letter thanking him for bringing the error to the insurance company's attention. The program bug was promptly fixed.

It might be assumed that if retail and other businesses were abusing people before computers were in use, they are still doing it in the same ways and to the same degree today with computers. Westin and Baker indicate that this might be true concerning violation of privacy in their study of privacy and databanks. Some factors may alter this position; they are presented below.

The Association for Computing Machinery, one of the major professional societies in the computer field (30,000 members), has 46 members serving as volunteer ombudsmen throughout the United States to aid people having difficulties in transactions involving the use of computers. I sent a letter to these ombudsmen requesting that they report on consumer problems they have encountered. Eight ombudsmen replied, but in only two incidents was ombudsman activity reported: one involved investigation of vote-counting system failures in Detroit, the other involved assisting the state of Illinois attorney general in prosecuting a fraudulent computer dating service which was not, in fact, using a computer.

Annual reports for 1970, 1971, and 1972 of the State of New York attorney general's Bureau of Consumer Fraud and Detection indicated 20,400 to 22,700 investigations of consumer fraud per year completed. Five examples connected with computer use were cited, but there were no records indicating the total number of such cases. The examples given included computer dating bureaus that bilked customers, a computer programming school that failed to refund tuitions when it terminated classes, and public utility companies' failure to provide sufficient help to consumers in handling billing errors. Barnett Levy, assistant attorney general in charge, stated that most consumer frauds involve computers in some form simply because of their pervasive use throughout retail business.

Levy is looking for opportunities to attack excesses in personalized computer-produced letter advertising. He claims that making letters look as though they are individually typed, with personal information about each addressee imbedded in the text and signed by a fictitious person, is a fraudulent practice.

The New York state attorney general has been successful in preparing legislation to control excesses in computer dating services, trade schools, and billing practices. However, little of this legislation directly relates to the roles played by computers.

A number of cases are recorded of alleged abusive acts by businesses using computers to the detriment of consumers that resulted in law enforcement actions or litigation. However, many abuses identified only in newspaper accounts do not reach the formal complaint stage. Cases include problems with computer processing of insurance policies, fraudulent use of mailing lists, unfair and fraudulent billing practices, incomplete criminal records, and dating services and trade schools engaging in false advertising.

In one case a man and his wife were in a serious traffic accident at 12:10 A.M. on a Saturday morning. Later that same morning at 10:00 A.M. the man went to his auto insurance agent and asked if he could pay a premium which would reinstate a lapsed insurance policy that would then cover his accident loss. The agent said he didn't know if it would work but agreed to try it. He filled out a computer input form requesting reinstatement of the policy but left the time-of-day of reinstatement line blank. The computer was programmed to set the time at 12:01 A.M. of the day of reinstatement. The policy holder then submitted his accident report, the insurance company refused to pay off, and the policy holder sued the company. He won the suit, and the insurance company appealed on the basis that it never intended retroactively to reinstate lapsed insurance policies; an oversight resulted in the computer action. The appeal was lost when the judge concluded that a company's left hand is responsible for what its right hand does and must take responsibility for its computer actions. He should have more correctly pointed out that the computer actions were the results of conscious decisions by the systems analysts and programmers acting on behalf of the company.

The problems go on endlessly. In Arizona a programmer's error caused 400,000 motorists to be charged $6.00 too much for vehicle licenses. Another department of motor vehicles computer rejected a driver's license renewal application because the birth date stated was 2/3/72, making the applicant three years old. The birth date was correct as far as it went. The applicant was born in 1872 and was 103 years old!

A woman ordered vitamins by mail. Her money was accepted, but she never received the vitamins. The computer was programmed to accept only three-line addresses, and hers was four lines long. The last, most important line was dropped.

Computerworld reported two cases in which people very much alive were declared dead through errors in Social Security computerized payments systems. Mura Marshall in Walla Walla, Washington, was declared dead for three months because of a transposition of identifier digits. It took two more months and action by a congressman to resurrect her. Maria Puig of Miami, Florida, was declared dead twice in 1971. These cases could probably more easily have happened in manual systems than in computer systems, but they should be more preventable using computers. Here is one blamed on a computer that sounds rather far fetched. In Elk Grove Village, Everett Neal, a jobless auto salesman, filled out a job employment form at an agency and wrote at the bottom that he was tired of the auto business and wanted something more concrete. Presumably as the result of computerized selection, he was sent to the Sinmast Company where he got a job selling concrete.

All of these "computer errors" can easily be traced to people— whether it is the person preparing the input data or the programmer or a company policy. However, such problems can be reduced significantly as we get smarter in learning how to match the computer systems to the idiosyncrasies of people rather than forcing people to comply with the idiosyncrasies of computer systems.

Business fraud against consumers is typically one-to-many, one perpetrator with many victims. Computer abuse acts by consumers against retail businesses or government agencies may be just as frequent as abuses against consumers, but on an individual victim-perpetrator basis. The SRI case file contains 20 such cases against businesses. These cases include consumer vandalism against computers, computer input manipulation, counterfeiting to perpetrate fraud, and unauthorized use of computer time-sharing services. Consumers may be heavily influenced by their attitudes toward the intransigent computer, or consumer acts may be simply attributed to the criminal element in society now finding more opportunities associated with computers.

The American Federation of Information Processing Societies and *Time* magazine conducted 1,001 telephone interviews with a statistically drawn probability sample of the population of the United States in July and August 1971. The pertinent results are summarized below:

Computer Problems—34 percent of those surveyed reported that they have had a problem "because of a computer." Billing problems were most frequent, accounting for almost half of the difficulties reported. Others included problems with banks, paychecks, schools, computers at work, credit cards (only 2 percent) and, to a minor extent, with magazine subscriptions, purchase orders, credit, and taxes (1 percent each). About 75 percent of those surveyed reported they had never had problems in having an incorrect computerized bill corrected. Of the 24 percent who reported difficulties, 71 percent placed the blame on the personnel of the billing company while 12 percent felt the computer itself was at fault.

Computers and the Consumer—The public view of the use of computers in providing consumer benefits is generally positive. Approximately 89 percent felt computers will provide many kinds of information and services to us in our homes; 65 percent felt computers are helping to raise the standard of living; and 68 percent believe computers have helped increase the quality of products and services. However, on some topics, attitudes were less positive: 48 percent felt computers make it easier to get credit versus 31 percent who disagreed. Again, 48 percent felt the use of computers in teaching children in school should be increased, versus 25 percent who felt such use should be decreased.

Stories about the perverse nature of computer abuse, such as the well-circulated ones of persistent computer-produced dunning of consumers to pay $0.00 for a service or product, is a popular topic in newspapers. It is easy to see how these incidents can occur and just as easy to see how they will disappear with improved design of computer applications, growing business experience in using computers, and public tolerance of these types of problems. However, intentional, premeditated abuse by both sides—business and consumers—must be documented and investigated if it is to be finally controlled. The excesses of credit reporting services have already attracted controls in the form of the federal Fair Credit Reporting Act.

The following scenario depicts circumstances often leading to consumer problems. A business will go about automating a customer billing function by assigning a team of systems analysts and programmers, and may even include an accountant from the accounts receivable department familiar with the function but unfamiliar with computers. A budget and schedule are established. The specifications for the computer application are written according to what it is thought the manual procedures accomplish. These, in turn, are interpreted by the programmers who write the computer programs. In the end, the specifications are not complete or not correct, the programmers do not interpret them correctly, the programs are not complete and do not work correctly, and the budget and schedule have run out.

At this point anguish sets in. All the niceties, controls, and features to handle extraordinary and infrequent billing situations are dropped, and the programs are forced into production before the business is prepared to cope with a new and radical way of functioning. Most of the people who handled the unusual cases and complaints are given other assignments because it was assumed they would not be needed—that was one of the purposes of automating. The new billing system starts operation in a highly limited and rigid state. Customers are bombarded with wildly incorrect billings. Since the correction facilities of the programs were never fully completed, attempts at correction produce even more seriously incorrect results.

By this time, the viability of the business is affected and management becomes seriously concerned for the first time. The EDP staff is no longer trusted, consultants are called in, more money is now being spent than ever before on billing, but gradually the system is corrected and enhanced to full capability. Not as much money is being saved as hoped, but some is. Billing becomes more efficient, and customers grudgingly admit they now have fewer problems and are getting better service than before. Some of the people previously responsible for handling errors and complaints have been retrained in the new system and fulfill this function again. New and improved features are added to the system to handle unusual cases, to control fraud, and to produce improved performance reports. When everything is finally running smoothly, volume increases, and then, as volume increases and services expand, the system becomes overloaded and obsolete and a different computer is needed. Thus the entire conversion process is started all over again.

A technical problem in the automation process can often force rethinking of acceptable ethical business practices. This is best illustrated by an example that occurred in Washington, D.C. A bank there normally posted deposits and withdrawals in demand deposit accounts manually and in the order in which transactions occurred. A customer could make a deposit, then a withdrawal, and be assured they were posted in that order, thus avoiding overdraft situations. The process was then placed in the computer in a batch mode of operation. Each night all withdrawals were batched and posted to all accounts, and when overdraft conditions were found, penalties were automatically debited. Then deposits were batched and posted to all accounts. One of the bank's customers, a computer expert by chance, deposited a sum of money and then wrote a check the same day on part of the deposited sum. He was charged with an overdraft and complained to a bank officer who explained the way the computer system worked—the deposits and withdrawals are handled separately and not time-stamped, and there was nothing that could be done. Obviously unsatisfied with that, the customer finally found the manager of the computer operation and was shown exactly what the program directed the computer to do. The customer suggested this be changed and was told that it could be changed, but it was not standard banking procedure. He finally was able to convince the bank to send a notice to all customers explaining how the system functions and advising customers how to avoid overdrafts. Does this solve the problem?

These sad stories are common throughout business and are

often the cause of consumer problems. A similar history in government can be related in other applications such as welfare payments and vote counting by computer. Fortunately the art of putting applications on computers is improving; it is leaving the "cottage craft" stage and becoming an engineering-type discipline. Thus problems in automation are gradually being overcome.

23 | MAKING COMPUTERS SAFER

"When it comes to computer security, paranoia is not enough."
—RALPH JONES.

We have always needed security when valuable assets and sensitive resources must be safely and reliably stored, processed, and moved. Computer and data communications systems are used to store, process, and move growing amounts of those assets and resources. The means by which computers are made safe and reliable to use is called computer security. Many safeguards needed to make computers safe and reliable to use are carried over from the previous manual systems which the computers have replaced. However, because of the differences in the ways assets are stored, the different forms of assets, and the way they are processed, significant changes in the methods of security are needed.

The imposition of security in and around computer and data communications systems is motivated in two ways: first, by fear of losses, based on the publicized experience of victims of computer abuse. For example, the need for security got a big boost from the Equity Funding Insurance fraud. During periods when few computer crimes are publicized, interest in computer security drops off, but it always picks up with the next big crime. Unfortunately, sometimes paranoia sets in and overreaction results as it did with the scare we had in the late 1960s about magnets wiping out data on magnetic tapes.

The second motive for more security comes from being forced to provide security by law or government regulations. The Privacy Act of 1974 requires government agencies to establish adequate levels of safeguards when personal data must be protected. In some high-risk retail businesses there is a marketing motivation for security. This is the fiduciary responsibility that must be demonstrated, for example, by banks in order to reassure customers of the safety of their deposits.

Computer security consists of three groupings of safeguards. (1) Physical security is concerned with protection and access control of the computer environment, including the building housing the computer equipment, and the computing facilities, including data communications and air-conditioning equipment. (2) Operational and procedural security is concerned with putting constraints on employees in data processing organizations. (3) Internal computer security concerns the use of controls and protection mechanisms within the hardware, software, and data communications circuits of the computer system. Safeguards are needed for deterrence, prevention, detection, and recovery.

The best safeguards are those keeping bad things from happening in the first place through deterrence. If this doesn't work, then we must prevent loss when the bad thing happens; and if we suffer loss, we'd better detect it as soon as possible to optimize recovery.

In parallel with the development of an adequate security plan, insurance against EDP losses and EDP employee bonding should be obtained. Several large insurance companies now offer specialized data processing insurance, and more data processing organizations are now bonding their employees. Insuring and bonding is a tricky business because of the lack of experience in losses and the few precedents. A thorough understanding of the EDP insurance policies available and cooperative and close working relationships with insurance companies are necessary at this early stage to assure the effectiveness of EDP insurance programs.

The assets and sensitive resources to be protected must first be identified in planning for computer security to avoid the Fort Knox syndrome. There is often little need to build a huge fortress around a computer. The security must be matched to the size, form, and location of assets needing protection.

The next step is to identify the threats. Threats come from only two sources—forces and people. Forces include water, lightning, wind, fire, earthquake, and other acts of God. The potential population of people who can cause losses in computer systems are those who have the skills, knowledge, resources, and access. These people are motivated and attracted by personal gain, advancement, disgruntlement, incompetence, curiosity, convenience—and other reasons. The acts performed include errors, omissions, and all kinds of intentional activities. The objects or targets of these acts include computer hardware, software, data, paper forms, magnetic tapes, disks, other supplies, and other people. The locations of the objects are in and around computers, data communication networks, and on-line terminal areas. There are only three possible results of acts—disclosure, modification, and denial of use. A long list of types of losses can be generated, including monetary, denial of use or exclusive use of goods or services, denial of possession or exclusive possession of goods, loss of privacy, loss of personal health or well-being, and many others. This foregoing taxonomy of threats can be particularized to any computer installation under security review.

Once the assets to be protected are known and the threats have been identified, risk analysis can be conducted. Theoretically this involves calculating the frequency of a threat occurring expressed as a probability value per unit time multiplied by the loss in dollars that could result from the threat. This yields a rate of loss with respect to time, for example, in dollars per year. In practice, risk in dollars is not possible for a number of types of threats and losses, but the risk can still be evaluated on a comparative basis, at least by establishing a priority of risks.

The next step is to determine how much to spend for security based on the identified risks. It has been said that 100 percent security is attained if the safeguards increase the cost of the perpetrator's work factor higher than the possible gain to the perpetrator. The work factor is the effort in dollars and other resources to perpetrate an act. Unfortunately, this rule is not effective in practice because many perpetrators act irrationally and have not used the same formulas for gain and work factors as those developing the security. The best that can be done to determine how much to spend on security is based on the prudent person theory: If a data processing center were to suffer a loss, and a prudent person would conclude that there was adequate protection against that loss, then enough security has been provided. This assumes that perfect security is unobtainable; therefore, the risks can only be reduced to acceptable and reasonable levels.

Technologists tend to solve security problems using technical methods and devices, but developing computer security is first and foremost a "people" problem. The only purpose of a technical safeguard is to reduce the number of people who must be in positions of trust, and to reduce the amount of trust that must be placed in them. Beyond that, there will always be some nucleus of people in the most sensitive positions of trust. These are usually the computer systems and applications programmers, computer maintenance engineers, data preparation technicians, and computer operators. Computer security must start by assuring a reasonable level of integrity among these people in positions of trust. If the EDP personnel cannot be trusted, then forget all the technical methods of computer security—they will be worthless.

Computer security consists mostly of doing hundreds of common-sense things to protect the functioning of a computer system. Computer security consultants sometimes play one-upsmanship by reporting some new safeguard detail others have not thought of: "Aha! You must have a floor panel lifter tool beside each fire extinguisher because you must first gain access to put out a fire under the raised floor."

The traditional way of planning for security is to use the cookbook method based on functional checklists of safeguards. Almost every book on computer security has a functional checklist. Among the best books are James Martin's *Security, Accuracy and Privacy in Computer Systems* and AFIPS's *System Review Manual on Security*. The idea is that if all the safeguards described in the checklist are implemented, then adequate security has been provided. Unfortunately, this leads to the Maginot Line syndrome of building a formidable monolith of safeguards. The bad guy will "end run" these safeguards every time since he does not use the same checklist. He does not attack the strong points in the security—he looks for the weakest link. Therefore completeness and consistency are most important. The security planner must think like the enemy if he is going to protect the computer center effectively from him.

Checklists are useful tools, but they are not the answer to cost effective security. A new method called threat scenario analysis has been used with considerable success by Stanford Research Institute. This is a process of performing the assets, threat, and risk analysis described above, followed by the development of a set of scenarios that depict the various kinds of high-risk threats. These scenarios are then theoretically played out against the computer center, looking for weaknesses in the security. The ability to carry out a threat scenario analysis is considerably enhanced by having a thorough knowledge of actual experience of victims of computer abuse.

In addition, a set of security principles can be used to evaluate various alternative safeguards. Some of the more important principles are listed below:

1. Risk reduction. Each safeguard proposed must be evaluated on the basis of its effectiveness in reducing the risk of an identified threat.

2. Cost and degradation of performance. Each proposed safeguard must be evaluated on the basis of the cost that would be involved to implement, use, and maintain it. Also the degradation of performance of people or functions that are constrained by the safeguards must be considered.

3. Absence of reliance on design secrecy. A well-known principle in cryptography is to design a coding method assuming that the enemy knows as much about the method as the designer and putting all trust only in the keys to the code. The same holds true for any kind of security measure. However, this does not mean that the security methods must be unnecessarily exposed.

4. Least privilege. This principle is also known as the need-to-know. The idea is that the people who work in areas where safeguards are

installed should know only as much as is necessary about the safeguards and assets being protected to carry out their jobs effectively.

5.   Compartmentalization. Just as in the safe design of the hull of a ship, each safeguard in a computer center should be designed so that if it is compromised, the loss will be limited to the immediate area without weakening or compromising other areas or functions and thus exposing them to loss as well.

6.   Isolation. Good security requires the isolation of sensitive functions. For example, work areas should be laid out so that workers in one sensitive area do not have to walk through other sensitive areas to get to their work stations.

7.   Completeness, consistency, and reliability. A safeguard should be complete and consistent with respect to its specifications, and it should function reliably with a minimum of maintenance and human intervention or extraordinary control. The security in a computer center should be complete and consistent to avoid both weaknesses and excessive controls. Computer security is a chain as weak as its weakest link.

8.   Instrumentation and threat monitoring. Each safeguard should be instrumented so that attempts to violate it are recorded and brought to the attention of a responsible person.

9.   Personnel acceptance and tolerance. For assurance that a safeguard will function effectively, the people who are constrained by it and the people who make it work must accept the need for and purpose of the safeguard and tolerate the constraints it imposes.

10.   Sustainability. Safeguards must function effectively, not only when they are first installed but over the entire length of their periods of service. The worst weakness is the safeguard being trusted but no longer functioning.

11.   Auditability. Every safeguard must be testable so that an auditor can test it and ensure that it is functioning properly in compliance with specifications and standards.

12.   Legal and ethical considerations. Safeguards must comply with the law and must not impose unfair constraints on people. For example, management has a responsibility not to assign a position of trust that exceeds an employee's limit of temptation.

13.   Mutual suspicion. Each employee performing a sensitive task and each safeguard must assume he is in a hostile environment. The easiest way to compromise a computer system is to con an EDP employee into doing a favor.

In performing computer security surveys for clients of Stanford Research Institute, the first question we always ask is, Whose salary in the data processing organization depends on the quality of the security? In other words, who in line management is directly responsible for the security of the computer center? The second question is, Who is the independent auditor who determines that the line manager responsible for security is doing an adequate job and that security measures are in compliance with established standards? There must be periodic audits of computer security performed by a person independent from EDP line management.

Some of the safeguards found in well-run computer centers today include the following:

Physical security: Location of the computer center in a low crime area relatively free from sources of natural disasters such as flooding and fire, absence of signs indicating the location of the computer center, protected telephone and power lines, a protected air-conditioning system, positive access control of people entering and leaving sensitive areas, mandatory color-coded badges worn visibly by all employees, adequate smoke and fire detection equipment, fire suppression equipment, adequate water drains and equipment covers to protect from water damage, and backup electrical power.

Procedural and operational security: Separation of responsibility of people in sensitive jobs, dual control over sensitive functions where separation is not practical, periodic briefings and other methods to increase the sensitivity of personnel to the need for security, remote storage of backup supplies and copies of important data files and programs with their operating instructions, control and routine checking of operational logs and exception reports produced automatically by the computer, prohibiting computer programmers from entering the computer room except for emergencies, formal software development methods including independent quality assurance testing of all software, safe disposal of discarded computer output, effective magnetic tape and disk library controls, adequate documentation of security procedures including a disaster recovery plan.

Internal computer security: The operating system must have many characteristics for security and integrity, including adequate authorization for access to the system by users, isolation of user programs and data in the system, passwords used to identify users and their data files, cryptographic capabilities, adequate restart and recovery capability, a threat monitoring and exception reporting capability, and features that reduce the amount of real-time reliance on people.

These and many other safeguards are necessary today for the modern computer running in a sensitive environment.

There are significant limitations to safeguards. However, the primary reason for poor computer security today still lies with the inadequate sensitivity to security needs of people in data processing occupations. Perpetrators of computer abuse have told me time and time again, "Why go to all the trouble of technically compromising a computer center when all I have to do is con one of the trusted people into doing anything I want him to do?"

EDP management often resists efforts to increase the security of computer centers since top management is measuring them on the cost effective performance of the computer center, giving security a very low priority. Managers in data processing today are already managing such complex development and operation of computer systems that the idea of imposing a whole new level of complexity and constraints for security boggles their minds. Usually only the data processing manager victim who has just been blamed for not having enough security to prevent a major computer abuse is really sold on computer security.

The secondary effects of installing safeguards must also be carefully considered. Some security measures can be dangerous. For example, shooting large amounts of carbon dioxide into a room to suppress fires can be lethal to people in that room.

Commercially available computer systems today are not secure. The hardware and software were not designed nor implemented with security as a significant enough criterion. Applying Band-aids to an already insecure system to make it acceptably secure has been found to be unsuccessful and costly. The fault does not all lie with the computer manufacturers; the lion's share of blame is on the customers who purchase computer products. They have not demanded secure products with the willingness to pay for the added enhancements or to live with the reduced performance accompanying such safeguards. Dr. John Weil, former director of engineering for Honeywell Information Systems in Waltham, Massachusetts, told me that providing security in computer systems is like trying to push on a string. The customer at the other end has got to be pulling to make it work.

Some commercial computer products are better than others with respect to security. Burroughs computer systems have a degree of security included, although this is not because they were particularly designed with security as an important criterion. These computers and their operating systems restrict users to programming only in higher level languages and generally do not allow programming at the machine level where system compromises are much harder to control. They also have command languages that make the process of authorization and data file access safer and more straightforward in implementation.

Honeywell Information Systems offers a large time-sharing computer system called Multics (H6180) based on research at Massachusetts Institute of Technology (and earlier at Bell Telephone Laboratories). It is generally conceded by professional computer penetrators who test the security of computer systems that the hardware and software "ring structure" design of the Multics System is basically secure, and at the same time, offers great flexibility to users.

IBM offers a highly secure software operating system with their 370 line of computers called MVS (Multiple Virtual Systems). This operating system, like the Burroughs operating system, provides a virtual storage capability. This means simply that each user is provided storage for his data which looks as though it is completely independent of any other user's storage and is unlimited in size. The IBM System offers elaborate authorization and access control features, but less generality than Multics.

Computers like Multics and the 370 with MVS have a significant level of security that can be demonstrated in the pristine environment of the research laboratory. Once they have been duplicated on the production line, shipped by air or truck to customers' sites, and installed in the customers' own computer facilities where users and systems programmers then start changing the systems to meet their own needs and maintaining the systems themselves, all bets on security are off.

Computer scientists engaged in computer security research generally conclude that there is one massive unsolved problem in making computers adequately secure. That problem is that no one has been able to design and build a commercially available computer system that can be proven to be secure, and more importantly, that could be periodically proven to be secure on a practical basis over the lifetime of the system. It is generally agreed that it will be at least another five to eight years before there will be computer systems widely available that can be proven secure on a practical basis and maintained in that state for reasonable periods of time. In the meantime computer programming will have to mature from the present cottage craft into an engineering and business discipline. Programming disciplines and methodologies have already been sufficiently identified and are known by such terms as "structured programming" and "software engineering." However, it will take several years to see the programming profession accept and use these methodologies and have the opportunity to apply them to new generations of computer systems.

The computer manufacturers are progressing in the right direction, motivated more by the expected savings in programming efficiency and lower maintenance cost that accompany secure designs. However, as far as the security features are concerned, they are only able to produce what customers are willing to buy. The demand for secure computer systems is just starting to emerge. Legislation will probably be the largest incentive to force the need for secure computer systems. It must become clear to the business community, government, and finally the public that the safety of our economy and our society is growing increasingly dependent on the safe use of secure computers.

An ideal secure computer system including data communication capability would be one of proven design which could be run safe from compromise without human intervention. It would be served by computer operators who would be allowed only to perform tasks directed by and closely monitored by the computer. No maintenance by human beings would be allowed in its secure operational state. All failures short of being physically damaged from an external force would be failsafe, and a failure not automatically repairable or overcome would cause the system to shut down in an orderly, safe fashion and lock up all data files in a separate, secure storage.

It might take four trusted executives, including a special government inspector, simultaneously to insert and turn keys in the system console locks to change the mode of operation from "secure" to "open." Then human access to modify and repair the system would be allowed. Before returning the system to secure state again, a team of auditors would go through an elaborate process of reproving and testing the secure state. Once the system is again declared secure, another group of four executives would simultaneously turn their keys in the console locks to make the system again operable in secure state.

This idealized secure computer system would also monitor and control its physical environment. It would control as subsystems the air conditioning, fire detection and suppression equipment, personnel access control, and periphery intrusion alarms. For example, when a computer operator logs on at the start of his working shift, the computer will authorize the operator because his transit through the correct key-card-actuated access doors will have been monitored.

As business functions become more automated, there is no alternative but to automate the security for these activities. The automation of security is lagging behind the automation of business activities, because the expenditure for security is not directly or readily seen as contributing to the cost effectiveness of EDP. It is only when significant cases of computer abuse and computer reliability failures come along that there is an impetus to relate the need for safe use of reliable computers with business success and the profit motive.

Auditing is another function in business whose role in making computers safer has been neglected. Auditing in data processing can be considered in two historical eras: before the 1973 Equity Funding Insurance fraud and afterwards. Before the Equity Funding incident, the auditing profession was just awakening to the fact that its environment was rapidly changing as computers proliferated. Professional societies in the auditing field were starting to move, although very slowly, in developing standards to audit in EDP environments. But few auditors knew enough about computers, and to a great extent it was the blind leading the blind. The data processing community had only been distantly aware of the existence of auditors and their functions.

The concept of auditing "around" the computers was in vogue because it did not require that auditors know much about computer technology. They merely treated the computer as a black box—looking at what went into the box and what came out of it with no regard for what was happening inside. Some auditors felt that this approach was adequate. That may have been so with simple batch-operated computer systems and specialized data files. But while auditors were learning how to audit around these simple computer systems, computer technology was racing ahead with on-line, real-time, integrated-file networks of computer systems.

The Equity Funding Insurance fraud came along, and the cry went up, "Where were the auditors?" There were no internal auditors at Equity Funding; so they were not directly branded. However, the external certified public accounting firms took the brunt of the blame. After the Equity Funding fraud, many professional committees were formed to accelerate the development of EDP standards for auditing. Seminars and in-service training programs blossomed in an attempt to educate auditors in data processing.

A great debate arose over whether auditors should be trained to become EDP specialists or whether EDP specialists should be trained to become auditors. A new occupation sprang up almost overnight—that of EDP auditor. There aren't enough people available with the necessary skills to fill the EDP auditor needs, and the salaries of people with these skills are increasing faster than for other auditors. In the United States the American Institute of Certified Public Accountants is moving strongly to catch up by offering training programs and the development of auditing standards. The large CPA firms have been working just as hard developing their own capabilities, including significant computer audit tools. Software firms also started offering audit tools for sale. The Institute of Internal Auditors did not move quite fast enough, and a splinter group called the EDP Auditors Association already has several large chapters and a national organization. However, the Institute of Internal Auditors is now fully committed to carrying out significant research and educational projects in EDP.

The technical problem facing auditors is that they are required to perform independent audits based on documents of record. Computer programs have been written for auditors as stated above to extract data from files stored on magnetic tapes, disks, and in computer systems. Although the use of these audit programs has advanced auditors' capabilities, it does not solve the problem.

A typical auditor will keep his audit program on punch cards locked in a filing cabinet in his office. When he needs to extract data from files stored in the computer system, he personally carries his punch card deck containing the program into the computer room. He personally feeds the cards into a card reader, instructs the tape librarian to mount tapes onto the tape drives of the computer containing what he thinks are the correct data files, and instructs the computer operator to execute his program. The program runs and produces the required report on the line printer. The auditor removes his report, takes his punch cards, and returns to his office. He assumed that the program he was using was safe and had no Trojan horses in it, that the card reader correctly read the program into the memory of the computer, that the tape librarian actually mounted the correct tapes on the tape drives, that the computer operator pressed the right buttons in operating the computer, that the computer maintenance engineers had performed the maintenance of the computer correctly and had not introduced any hardware compromises, and that the computer system programmers had correctly maintained the computer-operating system.

None of these events or conditions need be true, and the auditor is not capable of determining that they are true without unreasonably large amounts of expert effort and an expenditure of resources that would be quite impractical. In the previous manual systems the auditor could walk into an accounting office, tell everyone to stop their work and leave the office. He could then lock the door and spend the rest of the day directly observing and working with source documents to carry out his independent audit. In today's computer technology all of these other people, the computer programmer, the tape librarian,

computer operator, computer engineer, and the system programmers, stand between the auditor and the source documents. He
must therefore implicitly trust all of these people, thus destroying
his independence as an auditor.

On top of this, many new accounting systems are being run in
computers in real-time as transactions occur through terminals
over telephone circuits. Therefore, the auditor cannot freeze the
processes and trace audit trails from products back to their
sources. All accounts are dynamic and in motion over wide
geographic areas. Auditors need controls and audit trails built
into computer systems, but data processing managers are suspicious of auditors and fearful that they will cause new levels of
complexity in a world already so complex that it challenges the
manager's capabilities to maintain control. The auditors must be
able to require that extensive controls be built into data processing systems if they are to do their job; but they don't know what
controls are needed, they don't understand the system analysts'
and programmers' jargon and methodologies, and they are
concerned that specifying the controls too rigorously will result
in compromises of independence between the line data processing functions and the staff audit functions.

One part of the solution is the development of a team approach
to auditing, where EDP specialists join the audit organization and
work side by side with auditors on these severe technical
problems. In addition, the computer systems designers and
developers must recognize the necessary role auditors play in
assuring that computers are maintained in secure states and
provide for them in new generations of computer products.

The use of computers is already resulting in increased safety
for business, government, and many other types of organizations.
However, there is a great untapped potential to protect sensitive
resources and assets in cost effective ways to a far wider extent
in computer and data communication systems. The problem is to
stimulate potential victims sufficiently that they will expend the
resources to take advantage of the opportunities. Legislators, law
enforcers, trade associations, professional societies, and the
computing equipment manufacturers and service companies will
meet the needs of computer users only when the users demand
safer computing systems and are willing to pay for them.

24 | THE FUTURE OF COMPUTER ABUSE

To err is human; to really foul things up requires a computer.

The pervasive penetration of computers and data communications into the functioning of society is enough to justify predictions of a growing level of abuse associated with use of information processing systems. As an extreme form of computer abuse, computer-related crime will occur just as crime has always occurred in social activities that provide great leverage for benefits to the perpetrator. This much is evident; but how will crime and other abuse manifest itself in an automated society? Will the incidence go up or down? Will losses from white-collar crime increase or decrease? Will the growth of automation cause a sufficient change in abusive methods to produce an actual change in types of crimes for which our laws might be inapplicable? The future of computer abuse can be depicted by extrapolating from what is known in view of our changing social and technical environments. However, these conclusions are based on my computer technology background and computer abuse research rather than on a broad range of behavioral science expertise.

Few wiretapping cases have been discovered, but telephonic communication of data is increasing rapidly, and the data being communicated include the actual transfer of assets. In one alleged case an oil company was reported to be engaged in highly competitive oil lease bidding in Alaska. A computer terminal in Alaska was connected to a computer in another state to simulate bidding and develop bidding strategies. The company started losing bids by small amounts and discovered the reason. An identical terminal in a shack three miles down line was tapped in. In a little different type of eavesdropping, computers were returned from Vietnam after the war, and small radio transmitters were found hidden in the central processors that had transmitted all data being processed to the enemy—whoever it may have been. These are the only known reported cases. The reason may be that data wiretapping is so successful, it is seldom caught. The more likely explanation is that there are too many easier ways to get the data to bother with wiretapping. However, as security increases around terminals and computers, data communications circuits may become the weakest link, resulting in an increase of reported wiretapping, but general use of encryption could solve this problem. Wiretapping is being anticipated in bank-operated cash-dispensing terminals connected to centrally located computers. Technological advancement for electronic funds transfer systems (EFTS) includes the networking of many computers through wire and microwave circuits.

IBM provides a sophisticated encryption feature in its EFTS products in anticipation of wiretapping attacks. The only sure way to protect data communication—short of continual human surveillance of data paths or prohibitive protective sheathing of lines—is encryption. Until recently small firms making data encryption devices were struggling to survive. Today they can't produce them fast enough to meet the demand. The U.S. National Bureau of Standards has offered an effective encryption method to agencies as a federal standard. It is based on a method offered to the government by IBM and can be implemented on an electronic microcircuit chip. The greatest fear about the crypto chip is not code breaking but that somebody might secretly replace them with counterfeit chips, making the coding ineffective. In any case, with increasing data communications encryption will become more common.

International data communications will result in the transfer of assets—such as computer programs, data files, writings, and funds—at increasing rates and for more varied purposes. This could lead to problems over tariffs, customs duties, and other government regulations. Swiss banks are making increasing use of time-sharing computer services in America over satellite telephone circuits. They use information in Switzerland derived from data residing in storage devices in the United States. A serious problem can be seen, because such data are immune from subpoena under Swiss law but are readily subpoenaed in the United States. The data may be accessed from terminals located anywhere in the world by knowing the passwords protecting them. Study of international computer and data communications applications and abuses, and study of known cases of international banking frauds to anticipate technological and legal means of control, are needed to prepare international agreements and laws to deter Equity Funding Insurance-type scandals at an international level.

The physical security and well-being of people are becoming increasingly dependent on the correct and reliable functioning of computers. Although only two cases of abuse have been reported that resulted in direct physical injury to people, neither involved computer-controlled activities. In one case a janitor associated with the Mafia was running embossing machines during the operators' lunch break to use blank credit cards and authentic names and account numbers; these produced duplicate cards that would avoid computerized rejections of false accounts when used for purchases. The perpetrator was caught but continued his activities to help authorities capture others in the organization. He was murdered on a street in New York City. In the second case a U.S. Army research center computer at the University of Wisconsin was bombed by political dissidents in 1970; $1.5 million damage was sustained, a 20-year collection of important data was lost, and a researcher was killed.

Computer-controlled applications are increasing, such as the scheduling of trains for the San Francisco Bay Area Rapid Transit (BART) system and the Seattle-Tacoma airport transit system; computer monitoring of patients in hospital intensive

292 CRIME BY COMPUTER

care wards; traffic lights controlled by computer; computer-assisted air traffic control; automated airliner landing; and computer-regulated electrical power and water distribution. Abuses, both intentional and through negligence, are likely to occur. A study of such dangers should be undertaken as a start toward developing safety principles and codes that might include proof of failsafe features and minimization of human intervention except in prescribed ways for override control.

Another aspect of personal safety is a growing concern: extortion and kidnaping represent increasingly popular types of crimes against banks and bank officials. This could extend to EDP occupations when perpetrators of more violent crime find less assets available by manual methods and, lacking the EDP skills and access, force people who have these skills and access to follow the criminals' bidding.

Only two recorded cases are known to have involved organized crime. One is the credit card case described above. The other occurred in the Midwest where the FBI made a simultaneous raid on several football pool betting establishments. In each one they found a computer output listing of the scheduled games and betting odds. The name of the paper company and page serial numbers were printed on each page. The FBI was able to trace the paper back to a specific computer center and even to the computer runs that produced the reports. The programmer who submitted the program for the computer runs was confronted with the evidence and admitted he was being paid to do the work. The payments and betting establishments were traced to organized crime activities.

Based on knowledge of several banks controlled by organized crime which have computers, and on the applicability of computers to such activities as loan sharking, gambling, and small business exploitation, circumstantial evidence indicates the likelihood of organized computer abuse. However, the lack of clear evidence suggests that for the first time in history, law enforcement may have the advantage in using a new technology first.

Continuing support of computer abuse research and the development of provably secure computer systems may result in control of computer abuse before it becomes a catastrophic problem. A reduction in all types of crime is possible where data related to vulnerable activities reach the computer for processing.

Consider the hypothesis that the incidence of all types of financial and informational crime will decrease, but that the losses per incident will increase as a direct result of the increasing use of computers and data communications. This is not saying that computer crime will decrease. It is expected to continue to rise merely from the proliferation of computers. The incidence expectations can be seen in the following diagram:

Figure 9 | THE HYPOTHETICAL FUTURE OF COMPUTER ABUSE

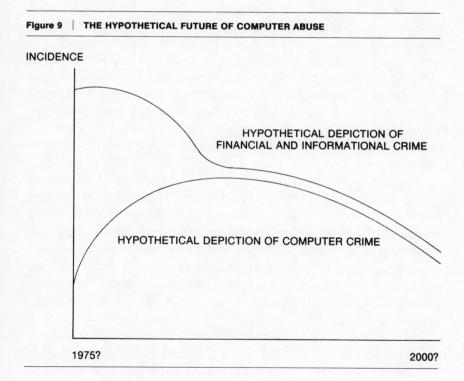

INCIDENCE

HYPOTHETICAL DEPICTION OF
FINANCIAL AND INFORMATIONAL CRIME

HYPOTHETICAL DEPICTION OF COMPUTER CRIME

1975?   2000?

A scale for incidence cannot be shown since there are no accurate data on numbers of crimes. Unfortunately, the arguments for and against this hypothesis are themselves still hypothetical although coming closer to being supported as more knowledge of experience is gained and subjected to deeper study.

First let us consider the arguments in opposition to this hypothesis. The FBI Uniform Crime Reports show a steady increase in the incidence of crime and associated losses. The 1967 Report of the President's Commission on Law Enforcement and Administration of Justice estimated the following annual losses:

Embezzlement	$ 200 million
Fraud	$1,350 million
Tax Fraud	$ 100 million
Forgery	$ 80 million

The annual white-collar crime losses in the United States were estimated in 1974 by the U.S. Chamber of Commerce to be not less than $40 billion, including only $0.1 billion ($100 million) loss from computer-related crime. By comparison, in 90 reported cases of computer abuse over an 11-year period, losses averaged only about $5 million per year and about $10 million averaged over the past 4 years. This is insignificant compared to all white-collar crime losses. However, this includes only reported cases. In addition, nonmonetary aspects may also be extremely damaging.

Computer technology has been increasing its impact on society for about 25 years. However, only 374 computer-related crimes have been reported since 1958. Is this enough to matter in comparison to the many other crimes and problems in our society? The incidence of crime is determined by social values, concentrations of populations, increasing complexity of life, restrictions of actions, increasing freedoms of choice, laws, law enforcement, effectiveness of organized crime, and advancing technology. EDP is just one part of that technology.

Even if EDP were to dominate those societal activities where financial and informational crime has its major impact, such technology does not appreciably change the number of potentially dishonest people and the opportunities for them to act. However, the concentration of data as a result of computer processing and mechanistic, inflexible rules of processing create new opportunities for dishonest people and organized crime. In fact, an "arms race" between organized crime and law enforcement agencies may be in the process of escalation, both sides using computers with unpredictable results. Increasing the security of computer systems will prove to be no different in effect from security associated with manual systems of the past. Finally, it could be argued that losses per incident will decrease as the use of mini-computers in small business grows, and incidence may rise because of lack of safeguards for small computers.

In contrast to the above argument and in support of the hypothesis that the incidence of all financial and informational crime will decrease and loss per incident will increase, first consider the impact of computers on business and government. There are about 150,000 computers in use in the United States, and by 1980 the total will be 500,000. In 1980, annual sales of computer hardware are expected to reach $18 billion and represent 14 percent of all equipment and machinery manufactured in the United States. Most of that equipment is to be used directly in the processing of the wealth and information of our society.

Stanford Research Institute estimates that 2,230,000 people were working directly with computers by 1975—about 3 percent of the 82 million work force. The AFIPS/Time report indicates that 7 percent of the work force in 1971 claimed they worked directly with computers. With opportunity to perpetrate financial and informational crimes, the fact that 3 to 7 percent of the work force is working directly with computers provides a strong but not conclusive argument that financial and informational crimes will tend to be associated with computer usage.

Computers are taking over the processes and environments where white-collar crimes have occurred in the past. Thus, if such crime is to occur, it will have to involve computers. Conclusions strongly supported by computer abuse research indicate that people with computer-related skills and access have the capability to perform computer-related crimes, and that there are far fewer of these people relative to opportunities for crime than the number engaged in previous manual processes replaced by computers. Therefore, the population of potential criminals may be growing smaller, at least relative to numbers of transactions subject to crime. The crimes will be more difficult to perpetrate because they will have to be performed in the structured, highly controllable computer environment that can be made more secure than previous manual systems.

Increased losses per incident of computer abuse are evident among cases being studied. One bank embezzlement study showed that losses associated with computers were larger by a factor of 10 than general bank embezzlement losses. The increasing complexity and skills needed and a greater protection of assets than was previously possible make the stakes in the game necessarily higher. Also consider that once access into a computer system has been created for theft or fraud, more assets become exposed and can be extracted per unit time because of their concentration and the speed of access.

These arguments strongly indicate that the incidence of all financial and informational crime could decrease, but the losses per incident could increase over the next few years. Further study may support this position.

Today business and government are more vulnerable to white-collar crime through use of computers than they ever were before or probably ever will be in the future. This is because of the lack of progress in recognizing the threat and taking protective action in a period of rapid transition from manual, paper-based business activities to the on-line, real-time, integrated-file, paperless systems of the future.

Progress in recognizing the threat and acting to control it has been slow in coming because of the natural tendency to delay expending resources on solving a problem until that problem manifests itself in sufficiently obvious and serious ways. One purpose of this book is to demonstrate that the problem could start to assume serious proportions.

There is significant evidence that steps to control the problem are being initiated. Many traditional security precautions in other areas are now being adapted and efficiently applied to EDP. For example, the moving of EDP facilities to more protectable areas in buildings and the limiting of physical access seems to be reducing vandalism from external threats. A new, emerging capability to audit financial activity in EDP systems, which started several years ago in banks, is now spreading rapidly to other industries and governments.

EDP auditing is becoming an important security function. Safety in using EDP will depend principally on this function for the next few years until more powerful technological solutions are achieved. EDP audit techniques and adaptions of traditional security practices can do no more than contain the problem today. They can't protect society from computer abuse perpetrated by the computer systems programmers, computer operators, and maintenance engineers. No practical way has been devised to audit the work of these people sufficiently because of the increasing complexity of computer systems and the lack of standards, discipline, and structured practices in their design and construction. A large computer system exceeds in complexity man's capability of demonstrating its integrity over periods of time—the assurance that it conforms to a complete, adequate, and consistent set of specifications, and contains no compromising parts beyond those required in the specifications. It is anticipated that this basic requirement will be achieved when the design, development, and construction methodologies mature from cottage crafts to technologically sound disciplines, and when security principles become an integral part of system design from the start. This will require another generation of computers after these steps become common practice. We can anticipate that these new systems and equally secure environments in which to put them will surface in the early 1980s, assuming that forthcoming technological advances in system types and use do not preclude the security concepts and methodologies now being developed.

It must be recognized that the time could come when new applications of computers and new computer system designs would be limited by the lack of safety in their use. It is essential to monitor and report on computer abuse in order to reduce the danger of applied technology advancing beyond this point without our knowing it.

REFERENCES

Page : line

13 : 10   Loeffler, Robert M. *Report of the Trustee of Equity Funding Corporation of America.* Equity Funding Corporation of America. February 22, October 31, 1974.

17 : 25   Sutherland, Edwin. *The Professional Thief.* University of Chicago Press. 1937.

17 : 31   Kevan, Q., et al. "The Role of Criminalistics in White Collar Crimes." *Journal of Criminal Law, Criminology and Police Science,* Vol. 62, No. 3. 1971. pp. 437–449.

23 : 14   Chamber of Commerce of the United States of America. *A Handbook on White Collar Crime.* 1974.

24 : 3   Parker, Donn B.; Nycum, Susan; and Oura, S. Stephen. *Computer Abuse.* Stanford Research Institute. December 1973.

24 : 21   Westin, Alan F., and Baker, Michael A. *Databanks in a Free Society.* Quadrangle Books. 1972.

24 : 22   McKnight, Gerald. *Computer Crime.* Michael Joseph, London. 1974.

Page : line

30 : 3   Chamber of Commerce of the United States of America. *A Handbook on White Collar Crime.* 1974.

44 : 21   Cressey, Donald R. *Other People's Money: A Study in the Social Psychology of Embezzlement.* Wadsworth. 1971. p. 120.

47 : 4   Sutherland, Edwin. *The Professional Thief.* University of Chicago Press. 1937.

49 : 21   Armer, Paul. *The Individual: His Privacy, Self-Image and Obsolescence.* Committee on Science and Aeronautics. U.S. House of Representatives. 1970.

81 : 14   Suzuki, Sudatoshi. "Computer Catches Kidnaper." *FBI Law Enforcement Bulletin.* June 1975.

119 : 3   Loeffler, Robert M. *Report of the Trustee of Equity Funding Corporation of America.* Equity Funding Corporation of America. February 22, October 31, 1974.

120 : 22 Soble, Ronald L., and Dallos, Robert E. *The Impossible Dream. The Equity Funding Story: The Fraud of the Century.* G. P. Putnam. 1975.

120 : 24 Dirks, Raymond L., and Gross, Leonard. *The Great Wall*
132 : 16 *Street Scandal.* McGraw-Hill. 1974.

133 : 31 Soble, Ronald L., and Dallos, Robert E. *The Impossible*
134 : 28 *Dream. The Equity Funding Story: The Fraud of the*
134 : 39 *Century.* G. P. Putnam. 1975.

138 : 31 Loeffler, Robert M. *Report of the Trustee of Equity Funding Corporation of America.* Equity Funding Corporation of America. February 22, October 31, 1974.

203 : 29 *Bank Systems and Equipment Magazine.* May 1973. p. 34.

205 : 26 Tiffany, Willard. "Are Computer Files Vulnerable to Magnets?" *The Office Magazine.* September 1972. p. 51.

205 : 28 Geller, S. B. *The Effects of Magnetic Storage Media Used in Computers.* U.S. Department of Commerce, National Bureau of Standards Technical Note 735. July 1972.

229 : 1   Thorpe, Edward O. *Beat the Dealer.* Random House. 1962.

229 : 2   Wilson, Alan. *The Casino Gambler's Guide.* Harper and Row. 1965.

238 : 4   Westin, Alan F. *Privacy and Freedom.* Atheneum. 1967.

Page : line

241 : 32   Westin, Alan F., and Baker, Michael A. *Databanks in a Free Society.* Quadrangle Books. 1972.

246 : 11   Ware, Willis. *Records, Computers and the Rights of Citizens. Report of the Secretary's Advisory Committee on Automated Personal Data Systems,* No. (OS) 73–94. U.S. Department of Health, Education and Welfare. July 1973.

249 : 36   Hoffman, L. J., and Miller, W. F. "How to Obtain a Personal Dossier from a Statistical Data Bank." *Datamation Magazine.* May 1970.

250 : 23   Goldstein, Robert C. *The Cost of Privacy.* Honeywell Information Systems. 1974.

259 : 36   Prosser, William. "Privacy." *California Law Review,* Vol. 48. 1960. p. 383.

268 : 9   Westin, Alan F., and Baker, Michael A. *Databanks in a Free Society.* Quadrangle Books. 1972.

268 : 23   Lefkowitz, Louis J. *Annual Reports.* State of New York Attorney General's Bureau of Consumer Fraud and Detection. 1970, 1971, 1972.

271 : 11   AFIPS, Time Magazine. *National Survey of Public Attitudes Toward Computers.* Time, Inc. 1971.

278 : 37   Martin, James. *Security, Accuracy and Privacy in Computer Systems.* Prentice-Hall. 1973.

278 : 38   Patrick, Robert L. *System Review Manual on Security.* American Federation of Information Processing Societies Press. 1974.

283 : 6   Smith, L. *Architecture for Secure Computing Systems.* Mitre Corp. 1975.

284 : 19   Neumann, P. G., et al. *A Provably Secure Operating System.* Stanford Research Institute. 1975.

289 : 13   Parker, Donn B. *The Nature of Computer-Related Crime.* Proc. ACM/IEEE International Conference on Computer Communications. 1972.

294 : 13   Chamber of Commerce of the United States of America. *A Handbook on White Collar Crime.* 1974.

295 : 22   AFIPS, Time Magazine. *National Survey of Public Attitudes Toward Computers.* Time, Inc. 1971.

INDEX